EARTH IS THE MOTHER
OF ALL DRAMA QUEENS

Unmasking the Truth behind our Life Stories

Library of Congress Control Number: 2004097220

ISBN: 0-9761495-1-6

Cover Design: David Handschuh

Author Photo: Eric Werner

Published by:
PhoeniX in Print
P.O. Box 81234
Chicago IL 60681-0234

Manufactured and Printed in the United States

10 9 8 7 6 5 4 3 2 1

To Maiysha and Ellen–
And all my angels
Who've showered me with love and direction,
On stage and from the wings.

I love you, heart and soul.

In loving memory of

VERNON D. JARRETT, Ph.D.

Award winning syndicated columnist, civil rights activist, TV talk show host, radio newsman, consummate historian and scholar, educator, mentor, motivator, humorist and dependable friend who lovingly demanded that we dedicate ourselves to excellence, and passionately seek and report the Whole Truth.

We miss seeing you on the stage, Vernon.
You are beyond our footlights,
but your commanding presence
and powerful legacy remain forever.

Prelude to Drama

All the world's a stage,
And all the men and women merely players;
They have their exits and their entrances,
And one man in his time plays many parts;
His acts being seven ages.

As You Like It, William Shakespeare

I remember the first big story I covered as a TV news reporter. A girl had vanished from her quiet Twin Cities neighborhood in the dead of winter. My cameraman Duane and I shadowed the police for more than a week as they searched for this child.

Duane, the kind of newshound who slept with police and fire radios blaring, wasn't optimistic that she'd be found alive. As the mother of a two-year-old, I was confident that this story would end happily ever after. For good measure, I prayed.

One evening after we had abandoned the search, the news director walked to his office door and announced to the newsroom that they had found the girl's body. One of her neighbors was in custody. He directed me to grab a cameraman and rush to the parents' home.

Huh? Was I really expected to impose myself on this child's family immediately after they'd received such heartbreaking news? Would I want a lawn full of reporters waiting for a sound bite if I had just gotten word that someone had snatched the life out of my baby's body? Would he?

i

"What am I supposed to say, 'Cry into my mike?'" I asked him. I refused to go.

Not quite sure that I'd ever learn to emotionally detach from the human pathos of news events, I began to rethink my new profession—my second, after teaching high school in inner city Chicago. In the classroom, caring not only mattered, it was required. I doubted that I was emotionally equipped for the news business.

That job went downhill from there, but I'm glad I didn't quit the business. For the next 20 years, my assignments gave me as many emotional highs as lows. I was among the press corps greeting Nelson Mandela when he arrived in the United States soon after his release from prison. I interviewed famous luminaries such as Alex Haley while he was writing *Roots*, First Ladies, governors, big city mayors, captains of commerce, Cabinet members, a sitting president, and presidential hopefuls. I also covered airline crashes, drive-by shootings, and serial killings—and I was as likely as the tragedies' survivors to scream, "How could God allow this to happen?"

I'm convinced that we ask that question because we don't understand the nature of God. But, of course, how could we? After all, we've been told that God expresses His displeasure with us through violence, pestilence, genocide, and even torture. Revered leaders portray us as filthy rags, unworthy in God's sight because we carry the stain of someone else's ancient sin. They warn that God has favorites, and most of us are not among them; we will be left behind. *Be afraid!*

Oddly enough, the same people tell us that God is Love. Is Love violent, unforgiving, and vengeful? Does Love forsake or kill? In time of inexplicable tragedy, we don't know what to think. Did God do it? Why didn't He prevent it? What's up?

What's real and what's drama? Were we created in God's image, or was God created in ours? Something urged me to investigate; but once again, I felt ill equipped to tackle the story. For five years, I stubbornly refused to do it.

One day, I was given the option of accepting this assignment, or losing the miracle of the quest. I got busy.

After poring through countless texts, web pages, transcripts, audio and videotapes, I noticed that some credible themes surfaced repeatedly. They came from unrelated sources such as the apostles James and Paul, scientists Galileo, Einstein, and Shakespeare the bard. In different ways, each said the same thing: Reality is not what we believe it is.

Hmmm. It occurred to me that our "reality" has shifted through the ages. At one time, Earth was believed to be the center of the Universe; the moon and sun revolved around it. The Bible writers depicted it as a flat planet covered by a dome through which God peered down on us.

Of course reality itself hasn't changed. Human understanding of it has changed, sometimes resentfully. Remember when Galileo Galilei's telescope affirmed Copernicus's heliocentric theory that Earth revolved around the Sun? The Church was outraged. They imprisoned the man for heresy, and didn't exonerate him for 350 years. Luckily, times had changed a bit when Einstein challenged "reality" with proof that solid matter is merely invisible energy.

It makes you wonder: what's real? Shakespeare poetically asserted that Earthlings are merely actors on an imaginary stage. The apostle James insisted that no matter what circumstances look like on the surface, we should regard it as a good thing.

Like Einstein and Galileo, did they know something we don't? Could Life be simpler than we realize? I guess it depends on how we define "Life". Science is not my beat; but it doesn't have to be for me to know that Life is not a breathing body. Life is *inside* the body; it's invisible.

Our five senses can detect things that have Life within them—but we can't see, smell, touch, taste or hear Life itself. Many of us think that anything we can't see or touch isn't real. Does that mean Life, as we currently understand it, isn't real?

What if Shakespeare's theater metaphor is valid, and Earth is simply a place to act out melodramas, murder mysteries, sci-fi adventures, tragedies, and love stories—and then move on?

Who knows? The buildings in which we are sitting right now could be merely elaborate props. The people who play major roles in our lives could have agreed a long time ago to share this stage with us right now to add some tension, lessons, comic relief, fear, romance, or even denouement to our daily dramas. Zooming to a tighter shot, this new "reality" portrayed a fascinating picture: physical bodies are merely costumes; our personalities are simply roles, characters we're playing right now. The real you and I are the souls inside the costumes. Interesting hypothesis, but could I prove it?

Journalists and other investigators rely on two principal resources: primary (original or first-hand) data and information collected by previous seekers. There was a wealth of scholarly and theological research that preceded my quest, but I sensed that this exercise was intended to be more practical than theoretical or scholarly.

And that brings me to one of the reasons I refused this assignment for so many years: the primary research. Along with some of my most hilarious real life dramas, I'd also have to bare some of my most humiliating. Having strangers laugh with me was OK, but laughing at me? *Why me, Lord?*

It wasn't until I neared the end of my task that I fully understood why I was such a perfect fit for this assignment. This was a story that only I could report; a story so spellbinding that an editor from a major publishing company suggested that it would make a great novel.

There was just one problem, that pesky disclaimer: "All of the characters and events are fictitious. Any resemblance to actual persons, living or dead, is purely coincidental."

The events and characters in this book are not fictitious. However, in the spirit of the theater, I took poetic license and changed the names and pertinent details to protect the identities of the souls who played villainous roles in some of my evolutionary dramas.

Although it reads like a novel, *EARTH Is the MOTHER of All Drama Queens* is technically classified as a memoir. What you'll discover, however, is that this really is not my life story; it's yours—viewed through my lens and performed on my stage. You also may find my research methodology to be a bit unconventional. However, this set of investigative tools was quite effective in unmasking the Truth I was assigned to find.

It took 20 years; but now that I've gathered the pertinent data, confirmed and analyzed the details, I can boldly report these findings:

1. Life is *always* fair.

2. God is *never* far.

3. Death is not THE END.

4. Absolutely *nothing* is unforgivable.

These "realities" may be difficult for you to accept; the good news is that you don't have to. I've been a journalist long enough to know that a dozen reporters could be dispatched to a scene, and each might return with a different interpretation. To quote Nobel Prize winning biochemist Albert Szent-Gyorgi, "Discovery consists in seeing what everyone else has seen and thinking what no one else has thought."

Consider this as merely my personal discovery, unmasked

during my spiritual sleuthing expeditions and studies. Examining these same data, your conclusions might be quite different; that's OK. I'm not trying to convince you that my interpretation is the only one, or even the correct one.

My desire is not to mold opinion, frighten, or manipulate you into accepting a different reality. However, as you sit in the audience of my life dramas and witness the revelations that unfold during the various scenes, you may finally be able to understand why some of us don't seem to get what we deserve or deserve what we get; why prayers and affirmations don't always give us the results we want; and why, despite it all, we should "count it all joy!" as the Bible suggests.

What can be seen is temporary,
But what cannot be seen is eternal.

2 Corinthians 4:18

1. Oh, So Moving

I would have to say that the curtain rises on most of my real life dramas with the same scene:

> *Setting: Chicago. Tastefully furnished living room with comfortable seating. Contemporary artwork covers every wall. Room is warmly lit. In front of a large bookcase, a tall, slender woman is crouched over an open box.*

I'm moving. Again. What's up with that? I must have been a nomad in a previous life. Or maybe I spent years in solitary confinement, and now I can't stand to be in one place too long. I haven't figured it out. What I do know is that by the time I was 30, I had lived in 18 places. No joke, 18! And those are the homes that I can remember.

When I look back at what seems to be a very unsettled life, it's very clear to me that, starting with Home 19, someone (or something) else hand-picked my new home and sent me there for a very specific purpose. In fact, I'm so convinced of it that when I get the signal that it's time to move—and believe me, the signs are very clear—I simply wait to be led to my next place.

I've begun to trust that. After a while, it's always revealed why the new home was selected for me. When that purpose has been fulfilled, the curtain rises on another moving drama.

Talk about drama! The move to Home #19 was laced with it.

I had a dispute with my landlord, and he threatened me with a five-day notice. *Bully me? I'll teach him!* I cleared out of his place in four days!

The only thing that bugged me was that I had lived in that lovely Hyde Park townhouse only five months. That's the record for the shortest time I've lived anywhere.

My hasty decision to move was risky; but a newspaper listing, describing an even more beautiful place in South Shore, pulled my butt out of the fire.

Another move! Thank God, my daughter, Angel, was visiting my ex-husband for the summer. I don't think a five-year old— even one as mature and precocious as my little Angel—could handle two moves within six months.

The logistics of the move flowed smoothly, as usual, partly because I'm a Virgo and can't stand chaos, and partly because I absolutely hate the moving process. As a result, I strain to keep each room so orderly that only an experienced eye can detect that there's a move in progress. Moving completely sets the stage for what I call my "ultimate Virgo snit."

My snit goes something like this: First, I measure every piece of furniture in my home. I know that sounds goofy, but there's method to my madness. See, I create a floor plan on graph paper, *to scale*, of the new place. Then I make little cardboard cutouts of each piece of furniture. Next, I arrange and rearrange the pieces to determine their placement in the new home. (Angel always loved that part, because it was so much like playing with paper dolls.)

Finally, I tape the "furnished" floor plan on the door of each room so the movers can set the furniture exactly where I want. Hey, it's a move-me-now-or-move-me-later thing. I'm a girl! I don't want to drag furniture from one side of a room to another after I get into the new place!

My 100 moving boxes, chock-full of stuff, are another issue, but I've pretty much solved that problem, too. I take every precaution to assure that each box lands in or near its designated room in the new place.

I smack a big, laser-printed, neon-colored label on each box that coordinates with the color I've assigned to each room. That way, I can tell—even from a distance—if the movers are putting the boxes in the proper rooms. I don't want to have to move them later, either. In fact, I have the movers stash as many boxes as possible into the closet of the designated room so that the boxes don't create any clutter in the room itself. Then I can pretend—for as long as I want to—that I didn't move. Again.

It's not until I empty my bookcases that anyone ever suspects I'm in the process of moving. I'm a writer, which naturally means I'm a reader. I have hundreds of books, in bookcases all over my home.

I have no intention of picking up a heavy box of books and schlepping it somewhere out of sight, so I pack the book boxes close to the empty bookcases. In plain view. For the whole world to see. *Hate that!*

I have to admit, as much as I hate moving, I do love decorating a new place. When Angel was young, my number one priority was restoring her bedroom to its original condition. While her father and I were divorcing, our marriage counselor advised me to minimize the changes in Angel's life, and to keep her surroundings as familiar as possible.

Well, since I couldn't seem to stay put too long, I figured the least I could do for my baby girl was to minimize the changes in her personal space. The morning of a move, Angel would hop on the school bus in front of the old place. By afternoon, she'd return to find her room almost exactly as she'd left it—but in a new home.

Give me a week and it would look as if we had lived in the new place for years. I would have hung the window treatments (and wallpaper, if allowed) and repainted the rooms, if necessary. I might even have changed the lighting fixtures.

Looking back, I don't recall that Home #19 needed any major changes. To tell you the truth, it changed me more than I changed it.

What a great place it was! I wasn't expecting it to be quite so wonderful when I spotted the ad for it in the newspaper the day after receiving that goofy five-day notice.

Like they say, the best revenge is living well! Home #19 was a much larger three-bedroom apartment than #18. The rooms were huge. It had sunrooms in the front and rear, a large dining room and an eat-in kitchen. It was on the first floor of an impeccably maintained building on a lovely, tree-lined street. I even had my own garage.

The apartment's previous occupant was the building's former owner, a man in his nineties. He had just passed a few weeks earlier. All of his belongings had been moved out of the huge apartment, except a few dozen books that were left in the built-in bookshelves in Angel's room. Many of them, I tossed. Others, I simply couldn't—books about alternative medicine, metaphysics, and natural healing. I generally associated books of this type with folks much younger and a lot more hip.

I wasn't sure what to make of the metaphysical classics in the collection. There were several by Ruth Montgomery, a couple from Jane Roberts's *Seth* series, Joel Goldsmith's *Leave Your Nets,* and Allen Spraggett's *The Case for Immortality.* I relocated the books to the master bedroom.

As the weeks passed, some of the titles would catch my eye as I walked by. *Later, later,* I kept telling myself. Finally, one quiet summer weekend before Angel was due to return home, I couldn't stop staring at one of the titles: *A Search for the Truth.* How compelling—especially for a journalist who relished investigations.

When I pulled it from the shelf, the book jacket was even more intriguing: "Did you know that when you grieve for a lost loved one, you can hold him Earth-bound? Or that Jesus and other saintly spirits can be summoned to this plane for rescue missions, and that we are all particles of a perfect whole?" Then, the clincher: "Find out your reason for living."

I discovered that the author, Ruth Montgomery, also was a journalist, but on the print side. She was a syndicated columnist in Washington, D.C. whose earlier book had chronicled her political coverage of six American presidents.

In true journalistic fashion, Montgomery was a skeptic when challenged to investigate the world of psychics. After exploring the field and its practitioners with the tools of an inquisitive reporter, she discovered some charlatans. But to my surprise, she also uncovered indisputable evidence that there is a continuum of life after what we call death and that there are ways to communicate with those who leave the physical world.

Frankly, I wasn't sure how I felt about this revelation. Something more than I can touch, see, hear, taste, and smell? Life after death? Communicating with the departed? Only a credible journalist could have brought me this news, and I wasn't sure how to digest it. Yet, I devoured every page of Montgomery's book, and another. Before I knew it, I'd read seven of them. With each new book, I tried to keep my mind as open as Montgomery's, when the spiritual mysteries began unfolding in front of her.

The more I began to understand psychic phenomena, the more suspicious I became that this collection of metaphysical books had not been left in this apartment by mistake. I began to wonder if the argument with my landlord and my irrational decision to move hadn't been orchestrated to deliver me to that apartment at that time. But what in the world was I supposed to do with the startling information I'd discovered in these books?

Was I supposed to do what Montgomery had done: communicate with spirits?

It made me shudder. I had bonded with her as a journalist, but not that much. She had become so trusting of spirits from the other side that she practiced what they call "automatic writing"; she allowed her angels to take control of her hands and write the amazing content that filled her books.

That was a bit too spooky for me, but I was immensely impressed with Montgomery's due diligence. She researched and verified every fact her angels had written before printing it, and she was amazed by the accuracy of their historic and prehistoric claims.

So was I.

2. "Out of the Box"

I wondered: Was I supposed to try my hand at automatic writing? Is that why these books had landed in the lap of this journalist?

I decided to find out. Early one Monday morning, as soon as I saw the school bus door close behind Angel's Catholic school uniform, I walked into the dining room, lit a candle and prayed for God's protection from any dark spirits that might have been lurking about. Then, with a pen poised over a pad of paper, I closed my eyes and waited. And I waited. There wasn't even the slightest tremor in my right hand.

How long should I do this? I wondered. I decided to give it 30 minutes. Following Montgomery's directions, I tried it at the same time for the next few days. By the fifth day, I'd lost patience—not to mention interest.

"OK, guys, this is it!" I announced. "I'm going to try this just one more time. If you have anything you want to say, come on with it!"

I sat at the table, lit the candle, said my prayer, picked up my pen, and held it directly over the paper. After 30 minutes, the only marks on the page were dropped there when my wrist tired and I inadvertently let the pen get too close to the table.

That was it. I figured, if my guides hadn't spoken up in five days, they were just going to have to hold somebody else's hand, because I had better things to do than to be in suspended animation for 30 minutes a day.

Clearly, automatic writing wasn't my calling, but I felt I had embarked upon a path, and there was no turning back. I was ready for more answers. I searched the small library I'd "inherited". Another title called to me: *Seth Speaks*.

Whoa! Montgomery's books about psychics, séances, and stand-ins were children's primers, when compared with Jane Roberts's in-your-face adventures with a disembodied spirit named Seth. I initially had found it a little bizarre that Montgomery would allow spirits from the other side to take control of her hands and type entire books. But Roberts's channeling—allowing a spirit to take control of her entire body and speak through her vocal chords—took it to a new level. Just thinking about it made my throat tickle.

From what I could gather, spirits that have something urgently important to say find that channeling is a pretty cool way to pontificate with those of us on the slower side of the vibrational divide. Seth, it seemed, was on a mission to help those of us trapped in physical bodies to understand why we're over here, and how we fit into the Big-Picture.

Seth's messages, which were recorded by Roberts's husband while she was in trance, were so complex, so puzzling and so fascinating that I damn near had a brain cramp trying to grasp it all. I felt as though I'd been living my life in one of my cardboard moving boxes, totally unaware of everything else in the Universe, and completely clueless about the many dimensions of my own being.

I tried to think outside of the box. I attempted the exercises Seth suggested, to expand my view of reality and embrace more of the totality of life—with a capital L. I tried to see no separation between myself and other living things. I tried to envision being "one" with a blade of grass, a tree, or a flower. I strained to see myself as part of the same Life that gave them life. I wanted to believe that everything was part of one spirit, that there really was no separation between us.

Whew! It wasn't easy. Try feeling "one" with everything in nature when you're on a crowded bus. Of course, it might have been a bit easier if I had followed Seth's other direction: Try this while out in nature. But who had time for that? I had to delve into the spiritual realm on the schedule of a working mom. The ride to and from work was often as much time as I could spare.

I closed my book as the express bus stopped across the street from the television station where I worked. As I walked to the corner and waited to cross the street, someone called.

"Pat?"

I turned around. Oh, my God, it was Ellen! How many years had it been since I'd seen her? It felt so good to hug my high school friend again! Of all t1e times for me to run into her, I didn't have time to talk. We quickly exchanged numbers.

"Are you reading *Seth Speaks*?" she asked, looking at the book in my arm.

"Girl, I'm trying to," I sighed.

"Me, too." She cocked her head quizzically. "Do you understand it?"

"His concepts are way over my head, but I'm so fascinated."

"Me, too!" she said. "I tell you what: Let's figure it out together!"

"What a wonderful idea! I've got to get into the newsroom; I'm running late. I'll call you tonight."

Another hug, and I ran across the street.

Wasn't that something, running into Ellen after all these years? And she was reading the same book! I didn't know a soul who'd even heard of *Seth Speaks*.

"Hey, Carrie!" I called to the security guard, as I darted through the lobby.

I tried to think back to the point that I'd lost contact with Ellen. We'd been in a YWCA club together when we were in high school and had kept up with each other afterward, even though we'd attended colleges in different cities. Mentally flipping through my wedding pictures, 1 couldn't remember seeing her at the church or at the reception.

We'd been married three years when my husband Ed graduated from business school, and we moved to Minnesota for his first job as a food company brand manager. Minutes after I started grad school, I became pregnant. In the drama surrounding those events, I lost touch with most of my childhood friends, until my mother organized a baby shower to coincide with my holiday visit to Chicago.

I smiled, remembering that shower. Ellen had unintentionally upstaged me by bringing her infant son, Joshua. All the attention shifted from the small bubble in my belly to the beautiful bundle in the blanket. Josh must have been about four months old.

For the life of me, I couldn't recall seeing Ellen after that day. I knew she'd earned a degree in psychology, and I recalled being surprised when I heard later that she was pursuing a music career. I'd never known Ellen to be musical, but everyone said she had a spectacular voice.

As I stepped off the elevator and walked toward the newsroom, I couldn't wait to get home and fill in the blanks from all those lost years.

That evening after our nightly "hug time", I tucked Angel into bed and headed for the phone.

"Ellen? It's Pat. Is this a good time?"

"Yeah, Josh has been out like a light for about a half hour. Second grade can wear a little guy out, you know."

"I've heard," I laughed. "Catch me up. What are you doing these days? What did you do before that? I feel like I'm missing some major pieces in your life."

"Well, I tried social work for a little while," she said, "but my real love is my music. I really want a career doing that. I've done a few gigs with some bands, and I'm doing backup stuff in a recording studio. The work's not steady, but I love it! On the side, I've started a little bakery business."

"Girl, there's nothing better than loving your work," I assured her. "Ooh, and I remember how much you loved baking, too! You gotta hook me up with some of your goodies."

"No problem. I'll bring some of my white chocolate chip cookies down to the station one day. Pass them around. Once they taste them, I know they'll want to order more."

"Deal! So tell me, how did you discover the *Seth* book?"

"I can't remember, really. I was just led to it. I've been doing a lot of spiritual exploration. It seemed to be the next thing that was put on my path."

"Hmmm," I said. "That's interesting. I'd almost have to say that the book found me, too. What other stuff have you read?"

"Whew! Where do I start? I've got a whole bunch of stuff around here. I pick up more books every time I go to a workshop or spiritual retreat."

I was stunned. I didn't remember Ellen being interested in following a spiritual path. Of course, we were younger then, and much more interested in having fun. We were mothers now; times had changed.

"Wow!" I said. "You're really into this stuff!"

"Without a doubt. I don't know where you are on your path, but you'd probably like going with me to the Institute for Spiritual Healing in Evanston. I don't get up there a lot because I don't have a car, but I really enjoy it."

"The Institute for Spiritual Healing?" I asked. "Sounds...a little deep for me. Not sure I'm ready for that."

"It's far from deep. What I like about the folks up there is that they don't take themselves seriously at all. In fact, humor is a large part of their ministry."

"Huh?" That hardly seemed possible. Nothing I'd read had put spirituality in a humorous framework. Seth, for sure, was dead serious.

"It's hard to explain," Ellen laughed. "They work with energy."

"Energy?"

"Yeah. They do energy readings and spiritual healings. I don't know if any of the stuff you've read so far has explained to you that on a quantum physics level, *everything* is essentially energy.

"I don't know if I'm explaining this correctly. This is actually Einstein's theory. He was quite a spiritual dude. The way I understand it, the speed and configuration of the molecules really determine whether a clump of energy is seen as a table or a human body," she explained.

"O...K," I said, not fully understanding or accepting her explanation. In fact, I wasn't sure what to make of this energy thing. Then, something occurred to me. "Wait a minute! Is that what Seth is talking about—that we're all essentially the same thing?"

"That's the way I've interpreted it," she said. "We're all energy. We're all spirit. We're billions of different manifestations of the same thing: energy.

"Have you ever walked into a room and just *felt* the energy?" she asked.

"Yeah."

"Or have you been near a person, and you could just *feel* his vibe? That's his energy vibrating."

I'd never thought about it before, but I was anxious to find out more. Within a couple of months of moving to Home #19, my entire perspective on life had taken a dramatic shift. I was edging toward the belief that Earth is a miniscule part of the living Universe, and that life in this body is a small part of my total existence. Ruth Montgomery certainly had presented solid evidence that we outlive our bodies.

More than anything, I was beginning to wonder whether my reunion with Ellen, at this juncture in our spiritual explorations, was destiny rather than coincidence.

3. Let's Get Metaphysical

I create another drama as infuriating as moving. Maybe it's more maddening because it happens more frequently. It's my "stuff 10-pounds of activity into a five-pound bag" drama. There's always so much to do and never enough time.

I worked on the evening news shows, so I didn't have to go to work early in the morning like most worker bees. That deluded me into thinking that I could squeeze in a project or a chore before heading out of the door. The result was always the same: *Damn it!* I was running late for work. Again.

When I burst through the revolving door, Carrie greeted me warmly, as usual.

"Good morning, Pat! How's everything?" she asked with a big smile.

"Great! How's by you, Carrie?" I asked, as I impatiently waited for the elevator door to open.

"Good." Then she looked at me intently and said, "You know, you need to pray more."

My neck snapped. *Huh?* Where in the world did that come from? Oh no, I hoped Carrie was not a religious fanatic. I didn't want a sermon every morning.

The elevator came to my rescue. *Say something!*

"You know—I think, you're right," I called out, as I quickly stepped onboard. The doors closed ever so slowly before the elevator whisked me up to the newsroom. *Whew!*

My close friend Debby was the only person in sight when I walked into the newsroom. She was busily banging out a rundown for the five o'clock newscast when I arrived at my desk; she barely noticed that I was in the room.

Deb and I had met at the University of Minnesota School of Mass Communication when she was a senior and I was a grad student. She was the first person I had told that I was pregnant, although I hadn't intended her to be.

I'd gotten the news from the campus health service just before I was scheduled to meet Deb for lunch. I had stopped instantly and called Ed, but he wasn't at his desk. Since I didn't want to leave such an important message with his administrative assistant, I decided to wait.

On my way to meet Deb on the West Bank of the campus, I stopped at the bookstore and picked up a few books on pregnancy and childbirth. By the time I saw her, I was so excited that I blurted it out before I could say hello.

Debby was the only friend to visit me while I was in labor and the first person to baby-sit for my beautiful baby girl. After we graduated the following year, we worked at the same Twin Cities television station. I was a news reporter; her interest was in behind-the-scenes production. My marriage dissolved and I moved back home to Chicago. Her job in the Twin Cities imploded, and I helped her get a writing job in my newsroom.

A gifted writer, Debby's professional life was utterly joyful and fulfilling. Her personal life? Well, let's just say it was neither of the above.

Debby was a beautiful, shapely young woman with the longest, thickest eyelashes I've ever seen outside of a box in a drugstore cosmetics section. She had a head full of thick, shiny, dark brown hair that fell halfway down her back.

With Deb's brains and beauty, you'd think she'd have her pick of really great men who absolutely adored her. But, Jiminy

Christmas, each man she attracted into her life seemed to bring more grief than the last.

Debby was a very private person, although she often confided in our close friend and executive producer, Bev, and me. Often, I wasn't much help. I had a pretty sorry track record, too, but Deb could always count on me to be the first to arrive, and the last to leave her pity party.

When we went to lunch later that day, I discovered that Debby's pity party guest list was growing. She'd taken our security guard into her confidence.

"*Carrie?*" I squealed in disbelief. "Are you kidding me?"

"Uh-uh. To tell you the truth, I didn't say a word to her about anything," Debby explained. "A couple of weeks ago, she said something to me. It was like she already knew about the chaos in my personal life, and she offered to help. I'm telling you, she has been wonderful."

"Back up! What do you mean, she already knew? How the hell did she already know?"

"It was like she had read my mind or something." Debby lowered her voice and leaned toward me. "Promise not to tell anyone what I'm about to tell you?"

"Of course!"

"She's psychic."

"What?"

"Carrie has spiritual gifts."

Well, you could've bought me for two cents. I had known Carrie for almost five years. Why didn't I know that? A psychic, right in the lobby of our building!

"I don't know how many other people around here know, so don't say anything."

Deb didn't have to worry about me uttering a syllable; I was too speechless. Jiminy Christmas, I'd been greeting an actual psychic every day!

After that, I had a sense of fascination about Carrie. Whenever I passed her, I tried to act normal, but I always wondered if she were reading my mind. Did she know I knew? Would she be mad at Debby for telling?

"It's OK," Deb told me a few days later. "I told Carrie that you know."

Whew! I could relax.

"How about coming to lunch with us tomorrow?"

"Absolutely!" I said, delighted at the thought of actually having a conversation with a psychic, and eager to find out if Carrie was legit or a fake.

The next day, the three of us walked out of the station, hunting for the perfect lunch spot. I was uncharacteristically quiet, not sure what to say. I didn't want to take advantage of Carrie's spiritual gifts, but I had so many questions to ask. Had she tried automatic writing? Did she see spirits? Could she hear them? What was her take on the meaning of life?

Our lunch conversation skirted all things psychic, tilting in favor of talk about men. I mumbled something disparaging about the guy I was dating and casually said that I really thought it was time to call it quits. Carrie put down her fork and looked me in the eye.

"Don't do that," she cautioned me. "It could be the biggest mistake you ever made in your life."

My mouth fell open. If she had said that a week earlier, I would have laughed it off. But now, this was Carrie the psychic talking.

I recalled Ruth Montgomery relating a story in which a psychic told her sister-in-law not to take a trip she had planned. Her sister-in-law ignored the advice. On that trip, she was in an accident that demolished the car in which she was riding. Her collarbone was broken, and she and the driver narrowly escaped the car before it plunged over a mountain crest.

Carrie had my attention. I'd pretty much made up my mind about bailing from the relationship. Now, I wasn't so sure.

"So I should hang in there, huh?" I asked, sadly.

"I'm telling you, now is not the time," she said.

Deb gave me a sympathetic pat on the arm. She knew how dissatisfied I'd been with my relationship with Bill. He was a very nice guy and a very successful businessman, but he was quite inattentive. And I was quite sick of it. The thought of staying in the relationship made me even sicker. But did I want to ride in a car that was careening toward a mountain crest? Nah.

Deb had the utmost faith in Carrie. "There is a time and a place for everything," she said softly. "Carrie's just saying that now is not the time."

I desperately needed a second opinion. That evening, I took my problem to Ellen. She seemed to know a lot of spiritual stuff; maybe she would give me different advice.

"I'm not sure what to tell you, Girl," she said. "I've had lots of spiritual readings over the years. Some were right on the money; others completely missed the mark. Just like anybody else who gives you advice, some of these angels know what they're talking about. Others? Child, it's anybody's guess where they get the crap they're feeding into the psychic's ears. I think some of them are just practical jokers. Maybe they just tell you what they think you want to hear.

"And let's not leave out the possibility that the so-called psychics ain't hearing a thing; they're just making up stuff as they go along!" she laughed.

"Yeah, right," I snickered. "I don't know which is the case with Carrie, but I certainly didn't want to hear what she said!"

"Well, I'd rather be safe than sorry. I know you don't think Bill is Mr. Right, but something or someone could be coming to you through him—just not right now. You never know."

Time dragged. Every week or so, I'd ask Carrie, "Is it time?"

She'd flash that sparkling smile and shake her head. "No, not yet."

One night on the phone a few months later, Bill said something like, "Gee, I never said we were in an exclusive relationship."

What was I thinking? I'm a relatively intelligent woman. For nearly two years, Bill's enthusiasm for the relationship had come in spurts. What part of that had I not comprehended?

Duh. If it's possible to be relieved and hurt at the same time, I was. I responded to the news quite stoically, though. When I calmly suggested that we not continue the non-exclusive relationship, Bill appeared to be surprised and confused. He hadn't anticipated that response.

As I went to bed that night, I suddenly was overwhelmed with sadness. I didn't cry often, but sometimes, you know, it just feels good to have that release.

I wasn't sure why I was sad. I couldn't have been mourning the loss of the pitiful little relationship; I truly had grown weary of it. My best guess is that I had sunk into that pathetic "Why can't I have a really great relationship with a guy who treasures me?" space. I boo-hooed myself into a lavish, down-home pity party. After a while, I sat up in bed, knees to my chest in the dark, and sobbed, "Somebody, help me with this!"

Almost instantaneously, a spirit of calm washed over me. One moment, I was sobbing so hard that I could barely catch my breath; the next, it was as if I hadn't been crying at all. Then, near me, in the darkness of my room, I heard a kind, grandmotherly voice. I was startled, but not afraid.

"Everything's all right, Dear. This is just an opportunity for you to grow. Bill has been unfaithful to you on two occasions. You need to forgive him. This is so important. Bless him. Forgive him. Can you do that?"

Bill had been unfaithful? Twice? I wasn't sure how I felt about that. Forgive him? It was opportunity for me to grow? It was important?

All I could say was, "Yes. Yes, I can do that."

I sighed deeply, stretched out and instantly fell asleep.

When I awoke the next morning, I couldn't remember if I had dreamed about the voice or if it were real. But it was easy enough to find out.

I couldn't wait to get to work. The moment I saw Carrie, I broke the news that Bill and I had broken up. She wasn't surprised. She just nodded and smiled, "It's OK now. It's fine. Everything's all right."

Bill continued to call every evening. In fact, I think I heard from him more frequently after we broke up than I had before. I guess he thought that nothing had changed since I hadn't had a fit after learning I was his main squeeze—but not the only.

Wrong. I had agreed to forgive him; that was a big enough leap. But it certainly didn't mean I wanted to talk to his butt everyday! Clearly, we needed to have the "How will I miss you if you don't go away?" talk.

I invited Bill to come by so that we could exchange whatever memorabilia we had given each other during the two years or so that I was deluded into thinking we had been a couple. Sadly, it also meant that I had to return the Mercedes convertible he had loaned me after my car disappeared. Sometimes you have to suck it up and take the bitter with the sweet.

Bill was the picture of innocence when he arrived the next evening. I went into the kitchen to get some of Ellen's cookies.

"Bill, do you mind telling me something?" I asked, as I put the plate of cookies on the cocktail table in front of him.

"Not at all," he said, taking a bite. "Wow, these are incredible cookies!"

The brother did have good taste. Ellen's butter cookies absolutely melted in your mouth, but I was not going to be distracted by his food review.

"I have it on good authority that you were unfaithful to me on at least four occasions. Is that true?"

Bill froze, his eyes popped. *"No!* That's not true! It was only *two* times!" he protested.

Gotcha! I almost laughed out loud.

A spirit really did speak to me! I wasn't imagining it! I was so excited that I almost reached over and kissed Bill, but I quickly snapped to my senses.

After another half hour or so of small talk, I handed Bill his pile of trinkets—and his car keys—and hugged him goodbye.

He continued to call sporadically for a few weeks, even though he had absolutely nothing substantive to say. Then, one day he surprised me.

"Hey! I have a really nice guy I think you'd like to meet," he said.

"Great! If he's really nice, I definitely want to meet him."

Bill arranged for the three of us to meet for lunch the following week. As I walked through the lobby to greet him, I whispered to Carrie, "That's Bill."

Her eyes twinkled and she smiled, "Yes, I know."

I giggled. What was I thinking? Of course, she knew!

In a few months, I had evolved from reading about psychics to actually knowing one. And, for the first time, I realized that prophets didn't stop walking the planet after Biblical times.

Further evidence that Carrie may have been a modern-day prophet came moments later, when Bill introduced me to the man who would catapult me onto the greatest dramatic stage of my life.

4. Déjà Vu

It was November 13 when Bill introduced me to Louis—exactly 13 years to the day that I had married Ed. I'm sure somebody in the spirit world was jumping up and down, wildly waving a huge yellow flag and screaming at the top of her lungs, "Ooh, Child, be careful! Are you sure you're up for this?"

Nearly two years later, Louis and I were planning our wedding. But oh, the drama in between! Was he committed to the relationship? Yes, he was. On second thought, no, he wasn't. This was not for the faint of heart. I would send Louis away for weeks, sometimes months at a time, just so I could catch my breath.

Luckily, I had Ellen and Debby to strengthen my spiritual muscle and increase my endurance. Without that cardio training, I'm telling you, there's no way I could have made it to the altar.

Ellen was my guru at home. Debby was my guru at work. One morning, she dashed across the newsroom, "You've got to read this book!" she blurted.

I looked at the brightly colored paperback Debby was holding. It was Florence Scovill Shinn's *The Game of Life and How to Play It*. Flipping through it, I could see that it was an easy read. I figured I could knock it out in one day, while riding to and from work. Enlightenment on the Jeffery Express bus. Perfect!

"Mmmm, OK, I'll pick it up," I said, jotting down the title.

"You're gonna love it. She makes it so simple. I think I'm beginning to understand life a lot better; it's actually beginning to make some sense!"

"Life—make sense? Really? Child, I definitely have to read it," I said, skeptically.

Deb turned to walk back to her desk, then spun on her heels and looked at me. "You know what? We've probably been close friends in many lifetimes."

"Hmmm, that's a thought," I laughed, "but I think you're way ahead of me. I haven't read a word about reincarnation. I don't understand it, at all."

Oh, but I would, and very shortly. I was having a small gathering the following Sunday afternoon to celebrate my new place. No gifts, heaven forbid. My friends would be bankrupt if they had to buy presents every time I moved.

I was placing the chafing dishes on the dining room table when the doorbell rang. It was Ellen. Before I could get over the shock that she had arrived early for a change, she burst into the living room as if someone were chasing her. Scared me half to death.

"Quick, look at my back!" she screamed, frantically yanking off her jacket and throwing it on the floor. She spun around in one direction, then the other. She was moving too fast for me to see anything.

"What do you see? Tell me!" she yelled, her eyes bugged with fright. "Do you see it?"

My heart was pounding, as my eyes zigzagged from one shoulder to another, from her neck to her tailbone. Was something under her blouse? I was too afraid to touch her.

"What am I looking for, Girl?" I wondered. "I don't see anything."

"Is it gone? You think it's gone?" she screamed, as she jumped up and down, twisting and turning, craning her neck to see if she could look at her own back.

"Is *what* gone?" I shouted, desperately trying to figure out what we were looking for. Ellen always had been deathly afraid of bugs. Maybe she had felt something crawling inside her jacket. I looked at the heap on the floor, wondering if something was lurking inside.

"What was it?" I asked, eyeing my carpet to make sure nothing was crawling on it.

"I don't know—but I'm pretty sure it was a sign."

"A *sign*?" This girl was making absolutely no sense at all.

"That *has* to be it," she said, calming down and flopping onto my sofa.

She'd better not squish any creepy crawlies into my cushions, I thought, still looking for whatever had spooked her.

"It's the only thing it can be. It's the freakiest thing. The last two times I went to a hospital to visit a friend, the same thing happened. Did you make any lemonade?" She rambled on, "It's the damnedest thing. Both times, somebody had to save me."

My heart stopped. "Save you? In the hospital? Oh, my God! Save you from what?"

"From the big fiery pit, from Lucifer and his band of merry men. I figured I must have been wearing a big-A sign that said, SAVE ME. PLEASE, PLEASE, PLEASE SAVE MY WRETCHED SOUL!" She rolled over and pounded the seat cushion. Then she peeped up at me and flashed that dimpled grin, her charade finally over.

What a drama mama!

I howled. "Girl, you know you need to stop! You scared the crap out of me," I said as I shook my head and headed for the kitchen. I couldn't believe I had let her suck me in.

"Thanks," she said, as I returned with a glass of lemonade. "Where's Angel?"

It was easy to miss Angel. The little party animal would have been buzzing about, taking care of the little party details and greeting each guest at the door.

"She had a more entertaining option: a sleepover at one of her classmates. What exactly happened?" I asked, as the doorbell rang again.

"Well, I went to visit Rae. Oh, my goodness, did she look wonderful! I've never seen her look so good. You know, Rae and I go back to—"

"Cut to the chase, Child. What happened?" I went to the door.

"Well, I was sitting there, talking with Rae and her husband, Keith, and their minister. And then, just like a musical, where they suddenly burst into song in mid-sentence, the minister looks at me and says, 'So, Ellen, have you claimed Jesus as your personal Lord and Savior?'"

Our high school buddy, Ann-Rita, and her husband, Eldridge, were now standing in the living room. They burst into hysterics.

"That's my all-time favorite question!" Eldridge laughed.

"Yeah, it's at the top of my hit parade, too," Ellen said, rising to hug Eldridge and Ann-Rita. "How you guys doin'? I haven't seen you in a minute."

"Who asked if you were saved?" Ann-Rita wanted to know.

"Girl, the minister of some close friends—at least, they used to be close friends. Keith probably won't let Rae near me again in this lifetime. He thinks I'm an absolute heathen."

"A heathen? Why, because you said you weren't saved?" Ann-Rita asked.

"No. Because I dared to ask their minister what I was being saved *from*. Child, this preacher pointed his finger at me and said that I needed to be saved from the Final Judgment, and that I should stop turning my back on God!"

"No, he *didn't!*" I said, offended now.

"Oh, yes he did. I don't think he'll do it to anybody again, though. I started spinning around next to Rae's bed, stopping suddenly every few inches to point at a different part of the room."

She demonstrated. "I asked Reverend Walker, 'Is God here?'

"He said, 'Yes.'

"Then I turned a little bit more and I asked him, 'Is God there?'

"He said, 'Of course!'

"When I had made a complete 360-degree turn, I put my hands on my hips and said, 'Point to a spot where God is not.'

"This man looked at me like I should be burned at the stake!

"He rolled his eyes at me and said, 'God is *everywhere*, Miss Ellen!'

"Then I said, 'So how is it humanly possible for me to turn my back on God?'

"I'm telling you, Keith and Rae were absolutely mortified. How in the world were they going to explain where they met such a she-devil?"

I shook my head, laughing. "Can I get you all something to drink?" I asked Ann-Rita and Eldridge.

"No, I'm fine for now," said Ann-Rita. "How about you, Eldridge?"

"I think I'd like some water," he said, taking off his jacket.

"No problem." I was retreating to the kitchen, when the bell rang again.

"You don't seriously believe Keith would keep Rae away from you because of that, do you?" asked Ann-Rita.

"I wouldn't be surprised. The last time that happened—in

the same hospital, mind you—my girlfriend fell off of my radar screen completely. Whenever I invite her to my place, she can't make it because she's doing something at church, and she doesn't invite me to her house *at all*. So, I wouldn't be surprised if Rae started treating me like a pariah, too."

Ellen tossed her hands in the air in a dismissive gesture. "The way some so-called Christians act, you'd think that Jesus said we should be judgmental and unforgiving instead of 'judge not and you will not be judged, condemn not and you will not be condemned, forgive and you will be forgiven.'"

"Whoa! Are we talking religion at this party?" asked Marie as she and her husband, George, entered the living room. Marie also was in our Y-Teen club in high school.

"Hey, Baby!" Ann-Rita and Ellen hopped up from their seats to hug George and Marie.

"No, we're not talking about religion," Ellen said. "We're talking about the hypocrisy of religiosity."

I giggled. "You know—folks who say they're Christians, but they certainly don't act like it. It reminds me of a book I'm reading, *Non-Religious Christianity*."

"Non-religious Christianity? Sounds like an oxymoron to me," Marie said.

"It does, doesn't it?" I said. "But this British minister, Gerald Coates, contends that Christianity is a lifestyle patterned after a Jew named Jesus. Remember, the early Christians were Jews.

"Decades after Jesus was crucified, a committee created a bunch of rules and holidays, and Christianity became more about pagan myths and rituals than Jesus's teaching. Peace, love, forgiveness and healing were his lessons, not his religion."

"Wait a minute," George tossed his hands in the air. "What are you saying? Jesus wasn't a Christian? He wasn't trying to convert people to Christianity?"

"Of course not," Ellen said. "Jesus was a Jew. What was the

crown on his head about? What did the inscription on his cross say? 'King of the Jews.' He wasn't a Christian. There was no such thing; but for the past 2,000 years, people have been busy trying to convert folks into a religion, rather than teaching them to act Christ-like."

"You know, that minister's got a point," said Eldridge. "Like Ellen said, some of the most judgmental, vengeful people I've ever seen call themselves Christians. Not all Christians, mind you, but way too many for my taste."

"Well, I think it makes sense that a lot of Christians are judgmental and vengeful," Ellen said.

Eldridge frowned. "Are you kidding?"

"No, think about it: There are still a lot of people who think everything in the Bible is accurate, even though physics, geography, and ancient history have proved otherwise, right? So, to these people, if the Bible says God plays favorites, and He's violent, vengeful, and judgmental, it makes sense that they would think that God's people are supposed to be violent, judgmental and vindictive—even hate people who don't look like, think like, or act like they do. Don't you think?"

"I hadn't thought about it that way," Eldridge nodded, "but you've got a point. They think they're supposed to act like that, because the God they believe in acts like that."

"That's my take on it," Ellen said. "When you think about it, the way many Christians behave is anti-Christian: they're not loving; they're not accepting; they're not forgiving; and they certainly ain't trying to heal nobody."

"You know what's always confused me?" Ann-Rita asked. "Folks will quote the verse that says 'God is Love', and then scare you to death by quoting scriptures that describe God as doing stuff that Love simply would not do. These folks think human sacrifice is barbaric—unless God does it. For example, would Love kill its own child—for any reason?"

"Child? How about killing millions of children?" Eldridge smirked, scooping some salsa onto a saucer and reaching for a few tortilla chips. "If God is forgiving, and loves us unconditionally, then how do you reconcile Judgment Day with Jesus's Prodigal Son parable?"

Ellen giggled. "Yeah, it doesn't make sense to me, either, but I've had Christians tell me that it's not supposed to make sense. I should just have faith. They run around screaming 'You're going to burn in hell if you don't get right with God!' And they swear up and down that God is loving and merciful. Well, they can't have it both ways—unless they're saying God is bi-polar."

"Yeah, they even think He's so vengeful that he'd strike you down for saying that," I laughed, taking a dirty saucer off of the cocktail table.

"There she goes again!" yelled Eldridge. "I wasn't through with that plate, PA!"

I had to laugh. Friends always tease me about playing maid, instead of hostess. "True story—you won't believe this," I said. "I went to a Bible class last week with my friend Jim. The minister was explaining to us that there's only one path to God—through Jesus Christ. On the way home I asked Jim if he believed that. And he said, 'No question about it; there's only one way to the Father.'

"So I said, 'In the last 2,000 years has anybody come into this world and left it who never, ever heard of Jesus Christ?'

"And he said, 'Sure! There've been billions.'

"Then I said, 'So you're saying that billions of people have lived and died in the past 20 centuries without ever knowing that Jesus Christ existed, let alone that He is the only path to God. What happens to them? They just go to hell, too bad?'

"And he looked at me oddly and said, 'What? Do you think God is an equal opportunity God?'

"That's when I coined the phrase *religious schizophrenia!*

29

They want me to believe that there's only one road home, but God is so diabolical that He doesn't give all of his kids the roadmap. Needless to say, I never returned to that Bible class. I don't want to know another thing about a loving God that brutalizes His children because they don't know vital information that He withheld from them."

"I think the *real* God does love us unconditionally," Ellen said, taking a sip of her lemonade. "The God I met in church—the smitin', drownin', burnin', vengeful, angry God who punishes us to the extreme—I call him the 'Bogeyman God'. He's the dude we all need to be saved from.

"Some folks believe so deeply in the Bogeyman God that they want us to be as afraid as they are. They try to scare us into acting the way they want, or joining the religion or denomination they choose. That ain't Christlike. They can threaten me all they want, but they can't make me believe that Unconditional Love inflicts a punishment that's millions of times harsher than the crime. Folks claim they love a God that treats them unfairly, but that's not love; it's fear.

"I'm with you, Ann-Rita, I don't think that Unconditional Love judges anybody, or tries to control anybody. Love doesn't forsake. It doesn't require anything in exchange for forgiveness. Forgiveness is the nature of Love."

Eldridge laughed, kicking a leg in the air. "You're right. If they really believed God is Love, then what are they trying to save us from? Love?"

Ellen smiled. "The funny thing is that God is so big and so forgiving that He loves them unconditionally, even though they believe in their hearts that He's a dictator and mass murderer. He even forgives them for spreading rumors that He's so sadistic that He gives us free will, and then burns us in hell eternally if we exercise it.

"I love it that God gives us free will to believe in whatever we want—even Judgment Day. That's why folks want you to believe and not think. Common sense tells you that a dead physical body can't feel pain. Even if your body mysteriously reconstituted on Judgment Day, how long would it take for hell's fire to destroy it? Not an eternity. And these are folks who believe we only have one human body!"

"Wait. I was with you, Ellen, until you got to the part about one human body," Eldridge said. "What are you saying, that you believe in reincarnation? Now that makes less sense to me than the Bogeyman God. Tell me this—and think carefully before you respond: Do you think we choose to reincarnate?"

Ellen put down her glass. "Absolutely."

"We choose the country we'll live in?"

"Yep."

"The parents we're born to?"

"Uh huh," Ellen nodded.

"Well, that's where you lose me." He leaned toward her. "Why would anyone *choose* to be born to African American parents in the United States—a land where black people haven't been considered equal since they packed us into filthy cargo holds of slave ships like sardines?

"Ten million of us died on the way; many of us were thrown overboard, still alive. They made us work without pay for almost 250 years. Then they passed laws that made it illegal for us to do simple stuff—like, oh, I don't know, *read a book*," he said, becoming angrier.

George piped in, "Yeah, we couldn't look them in the eye without being hung from trees. Lynching black folks was a spectator sport. I've seen pictures where Mom and Dad and the kiddies came to lynchings with picnic baskets!"

"What are you talking about?" Eldridge said, waving his arm dismissively. "They used to close the schools so the kids wouldn't miss 'em. What kind of damn field trip was that?

What kind of people would let their children watch something that gruesome—or teach their kids that torturing human beings was a wholesome, Christian thing to do? This was in our lifetime, in the South and even right here in Illinois!

"Then, when they outlawed lynching, they found more subtle ways to hang us. They made it illegal for us to vote; we couldn't eat in public places, live in certain neighborhoods, or go to good schools. Of course, without education, we couldn't get good jobs. After giving us so few options that we had to steal to survive, they decided we were natural-born criminals!

"You're telling me that we *chose* to be dehumanized, murdered, and discriminated against for centuries in this Christian country, with its history of hate?" Eldridge scowled.

"I know what you mean, man," George shook his head. "These are folks who believe they're held accountable for Adam's ancient sin, but not for the slaveholding sins of their great grandparents. They're always wondering why we haven't pulled ourselves up from our bootstraps, yet. They just made it illegal to discriminate against us, day before yesterday. They act as if we've had equal employment and educational opportunities for as long as they have! It's so stupid. It hasn't occurred to them that until everybody has access to good jobs and good education, *nobody's* streets are safe."

It had been years since I'd even thought about the evenings I had watched the news in horror, as people who looked like me were being hosed and beaten by police and attacked by dogs, simply because they wanted to vote, send their kids to a decent school, or eat in a public restaurant.

"I can relate, Eldridge," I said, shaking my head. "Remember how tough it was for us to find jobs a few years ago? I got a classic for you. One summer, when we were in college, I went from one employment agency to another, searching for a job. The drill was the same at every agency: the employment counselors would call their clients, explain that I was a Negro, then ask if it was OK to send me for an interview. They always sounded so apologetic for presenting the client with a colored candidate. What were they to do? We just kept showing up!

"The equal opportunity law had just been signed, so I guess the agency was forced to interview us. But the client could always use the agency as a buffer to tell us that the position was filled."

"Yeah, I remember those days!" Ann-Rita smirked.

"Anyway," I said, "I had on my interview uniform–a suit I had bought at Field's and these gorgeous black patent leather shoes. Child, I was too cute. Then this employment counselor asked me to stand up and take off one of my shoes."

"Take off your shoe?" Ann-Rita asked. "For what?"

I laughed. "You won't believe it! At first, I thought she was just admiring them. They had a black patent leather gardenia covering the square toes."

"I remember those shoes!" Ellen said. "I think I had a pair, too! Got 'em at Joseph's."

"Those are the ones!" I laughed, not mentioning that I had envied her so much that I had to have a pair. "And that's the funny part. I slipped my foot back into the shoe while she returned to the phone and actively advocated for me."

Marie wrinkled her nose. "Huh?"

"Yeah. She didn't just apologize to the client because I was colored. She said, 'But this is an upper class one. She buys her shoes at Joseph's!'"

Everybody howled.

"Was that a kick in the head, or what? My shoe store made me employable, not my education or my skills. Little did she know, I had squirreled away money from my part-time job for weeks to buy those fine kicks."

"I've heard some ridiculous job-hunting-while-Black stories

in my time," George laughed, "but that one takes the cake!"

"See what I mean, Ellen? If there's such a thing as reincarnation, why would anybody choose to be Black in America?" Eldridge asked.

"I hate to answer your question with a question," Ellen said, "but let me ask you this: What do you think about God? Do you think God is fair?"

Eldridge said, "Of course!"

"Then why didn't God make us all the same color, give us all the same amount of money, and the same set of living circumstances? It doesn't seem quite fair to me that some folks are born with privileges that other folks don't have. How can you say that God is fair?"

Eldridge shrugged. "I guess I thought that if anyone would be fair, it would be God."

"Me, too," Ellen said, her eyes lighting up. "Actually, I think God is fairness itself."

"I thought you just said–"

"I asked why *you* thought God is fair, if He created a world that is unfair and inhumane," she explained. "That's really where it starts; what you believe about God is what you believe about life. I happen to believe that God is fair, so He would only create a world that is fair. That being the case, the only scenario that supports my belief in a fair God is reincarnation."

Marie gasped. "Huh? I don't get that."

"I know," Ellen nodded. "Most folks in Western society don't. Tell me this: compared with the age of the Universe, how long is your lifetime as a black man in America, Eldridge?"

He frowned. "I can't even think of a measurement small enough to compare anybody's lifetime with the age of the Universe," he said.

"Uh-huh. Hold that thought," Ellen said, as she walked out of the room.

5. Drama of Biblical Proportions

Ellen returned to the living room carrying one of the Bibles from my bedroom bookcase, which struck dread in every heart.

"Oh, Lord! Are we going to church?" Virgil laughed nervously. "Is this gonna be a long sermon? Are there enough snacks out here—or should I grab a plate of food from the dining room, so I won't starve?"

"Naw, my brother, you're not going to starve—and you're not going to fall asleep, either. We're going someplace most churches don't go," Ellen laughed, turning to Eldridge. "Now, are you still holding your thought?"

Eldridge nodded. "Yep."

"Keep holding it." Looking around the room, she said, "I think we agree that the Universe has been around a long time. What are the latest estimates, about 15 billion years, give or take a few million?"

We nodded. *Who cared?*

"OK, so do you think God's a 15 billion-year-old dude who lives light years away in a place called Heaven? Or do you think God is spirit, present everywhere in the Universe?"

"God is spirit," we all agreed.

"And He's omnipresent," I piped in. "There is no spot where God is not."

"OK," Ellen said, "if we are made in God's image, are we physical bodies or spirit?"

"We're spirit," we said.

"What's the life span of a physical body?"

"On average, 75 years or so, I'd guess," Ann-Rita said.

"And the life span of spirit?"

We all looked at each other. *Who knew?*

"Let's try it this way. God is spirit. What's God's life span?"

"There is no beginning or end to God," Marie said.

"And if you are spirit?" Ellen asked.

"There is no beginning or end to us," I said, pensively.

"So, getting back to your question, Eldridge: Why would any spirit in its right mind choose to be born in a black body in America? You did say that you believe that God is fair, right?"

"Not really. I said that if anyone would be fair, I thought it would be Almighty God."

"Does the Bible say God is fair?" she asked, holding up the book.

Throwing up his hands in defense, Eldridge laughed, "Don't ask me any Bible questions. I'm way out of my league there."

"Don't worry about it. My point is that what you believe about life and what you believe about yourself has everything to do with what you believe about God."

"I got that part," I said. "If we believe we're made in God's image, then we must believe that we're spirit and not bodies. We are like God; God is not like us."

Ann-Rita laughed. "That reminds me of something our friend Vici likes to say: God made man in His image, then man decided to return the favor."

"Ain't that the truth?" Ellen laughed. "They say God has hands and feet—and a face so frightening, you can't look at it."

"And let's not forget His violent reactions to human sin," I said. "You know what has bothered me since I was a little girl?

The flood: God was so fed-up with human sin that He killed every creature on Earth except the ones on the ark?

"When the flood hit, there were newborns, little kids, disabled, and elderly people. God just drowned them all?"

"Shoot!" Ann-Rita smirked. "Before you get there, you've got to explain the meteorological impossibility that it rained everywhere on the planet even one day, let alone 40. And if they had no instruments to determine what the weather was like on the other side of the country, how did they know it was raining all over the world?"

Eldridge stood. "OK, since we're talking impossibilities, do human bodies last 625 years? Even if they did, only a sadist would force a 500-year-old man to get up every morning for 125 years and do the backbreaking work of building a huge boat. This was Noah's reward for being the only good guy? OK, he was an alcoholic—but he was the best guy around.

"Seems to me that all the bad dudes should have had to do the hard work, and Noah should have been given a free ride," he laughed, walking into the dining room.

"Hey—look how much faster the ark would have been built, with thousands of men working on it!" Virgil laughed. "Bring me a plate, man!"

"You know, I hadn't thought about it before," I said, "but did every species of animal live in Noah's neighborhood? How do you round up a bunch of wild animals? And how did all of them survive 40 days, crammed in a boat?"

"That seems inhumane," Virgil frowned. "What did they eat? They couldn't have gotten any fresh food because everything was under water. And there wasn't a fridge or freezer."

A thought occurred to me. "Oooh! Can you imagine the filthy conditions on the ark? And, weren't some of the beasts carnivores? I guess they were the only ones who were well fed.

Can you imagine going onto the deck for fresh air and seeing nothing but floating bodies surrounding you? Gross!"

"Are you all saying that God's flood was a bit inhumane?" Ellen asked, feigning innocence.

"I could be wrong, but drowning people and making the few survivors live in filthy, life threatening conditions sure doesn't seem humane to me," Eldridge said, as he handed Virgil a plate brimming with food.

"Me either," I said. "That's why I started asking myself: What am I required to believe about God, in order to believe this? I don't care what book I'm reading or how holy it claims to be, my question is always the same: What does this require me to believe about God?"

"I hadn't thought about that," Ann-Rita said. "We've been told that it's God's way or the furnace for all eternity. What do I have to believe about God to believe that? Do I have to believe He's unforgiving? That He doesn't love unconditionally? That He's violent, sadistic, and vengeful?"

Marie was obviously offended. "You all are completely missing the redemption story of the New Testament," she said. "God sent Jesus to redeem us. He died for our sins."

"Glad you brought that up. Maybe you can help me understand it," Ellen said, leaning forward and resting her head in her hands. "First, we have to believe that God is vengeful, rather than forgiving. Right?"

"Ellen, if God wasn't forgiving, He wouldn't have sent Jesus to save us!" Marie frowned, a bit perturbed.

Ellen shook her head and blinked her eyes, confused. "That's where I get lost," she said. "Jesus was sent to take on the burden of everyone's sin so that God wouldn't torture the rest of us for all eternity? So he was saving us from God, right?"

It was one of those questions that had been lurking in my mind since childhood. Like everyone else, I anxiously awaited the answer from someone who seemed to know the Bible better than we did.

Marie hesitated. Ellen leaned across the table, toward her. "God looked at this sinful world and said, 'Hmmm, my kids are absolutely wicked and incorrigible! I've drowned 'em. I've turned their fertile land into barren desert so that generations after them would starve. Nothing's worked. What should I do to make them behave?'"

Mimicking someone deep in thought, Ellen scratched her head, looked around the ceiling and snapped her fingers. "Then He said, 'Eureka! I'll do like the gods in pagan myths; I'll impregnate a young virgin and have a son! I'll have him grow up in obscurity, and then emerge onto the world stage as a wise teacher and powerful healer.

"'Let's see, what's a reasonable amount of time for him to teach everybody everything they need to know about living a better life through love and forgiveness? Two or three years should be enough. Hmmm, he can't cover more than a 200-mile radius in that time, but that's OK.

"'These people believe in sacrificing a life to appease their angry God, so I'll give them my son as a sacrifice. A few years into his ministry, he'll challenge the authority of some important people, and I'll let my control freak Roman kids subject him to the slow, humiliating, and torturous death of a common criminal. After that, I'll cleanse the sins of everyone who believes that he's my only begotten son. The rest of 'em, I'll throw into a fiery pit for all eternity.'

"Is that essentially the logic behind it all?" Ellen wondered.

Marie was outraged. "Christ came to die for our sins. You made it sound so, so sadistic and sacrilegious!"

"But the story line—that is essentially what the Bible says, isn't it?"

"Somewhat," Marie said, hesitatingly. "It says, 'As by one

man's disobedience many were made sinners; so by one man's obedience many will be made righteous.'"

"Right. Can we apply the 'What do we have to believe about God to believe that' test to what you just said?" Ellen asked. "You're telling me that God has blamed everybody since the beginning of time for one man's sin; and He will forgive everyone because one man didn't sin? Does that seem fair? Does it even make sense?"

"You're trying to understand God with your limited brain," Marie insisted. "The human brain can't possibly comprehend the vastness of God—or the reasons He does anything!"

"True, I'll never understand a punishment that is inherited from generation to generation. If that's the way God's world works, then every child born into a convict's family should go directly from the delivery room to the jailhouse.

"But listen, didn't you get a little suspicious when that same story claimed that God *left* the Garden, and when He returned he *searched* for Adam and Eve? What do we have to believe about God to believe that: He doesn't know everything and He's not present everywhere? He only occupies one space at a time, like mortal man?"

The question stunned Marie. "The Bible says it; so I believe it," she said, curtly.

Ellen nodded sympathetically. "Tell me this: did Jesus's death bring an end to sin?"

Marie shook her head, "No."

"Did his death mean that all sins are automatically forgiven?" Ellen asked. "Everybody in the last two thousand years—are their sins forgiven because he sacrificed his life?"

"Absolutely. Everyone who has claimed Jesus Christ as their personal Lord and Savior; yes, their sins will be forgiven," Marie said, resolutely.

"OK now, I want you to go slow because that's the other

part of the story that confuses me," Ellen said. "The implication here is that we're only forgiven if we ask for forgiveness. Is that the way it works? Is that what Jesus taught?"

Marie's eyes narrowed. "Don't twist my words, Ellen. I said that if you claim Jesus Christ as your personal Lord and Savior, your sins would be forgiven."

"And, if you don't?"

Virgil butted in, to rescue his wife. "Jesus said we should forgive seven times seven. He even forgave his persecutors while he was hanging on the cross."

"Glad you brought that up. Did they ask for forgiveness?" Ellen asked.

"No," he conceded.

"But *we* have to ask, or we won't be forgiven. What's that about? Does that mean we shouldn't forgive others until they ask for it? I don't understand."

"I see where you're coming from," Virgil nodded.

"No offense, Marie," Ellen cautioned. "But I'd suggest that you do a bit of homework on the Council of Nicaea and Constantine the Great before closing your mind about what the Bible is or isn't—and what Jesus is or isn't."

"Jesus? Surely there's no question about Jesus," Marie said.

"I don't want you to take my word for it. It's better if you find the answers yourself," Ellen said. "But I will ask you this: What was Jesus's occupation before he began his ministry?"

"He was a carpenter," Marie said.

"That's another part I don't understand. Angels, stars, kings, and wise men gathered for the birth of Jesus—which, by the way, was changed to December 25th by Constantine's Council. You'll be surprised when you find out whose birthday it really is," Ellen winked. "Anyway, if Mary and Joseph were aware before Jesus's birth that he was the only begotten Son of God, why would they train him to be a carpenter?"

Marie wasn't the only one troubled by the implication of that question. It had never crossed my mind.

"I'm not trying to shake your faith. I do believe that Jesus was, in fact, here to 'save' us. I'm just asking you to consider the possibility that he was here to save us from the pain and suffering we cause ourselves due to our misguided choices. What if he was trying to teach us how to make better decisions? What if Jesus was demonstrating how powerful we are, as children of the living God?

"Why did he say that *we* would do greater things than he did? If Jesus and God were One, isn't it quite possible that we are, too?"

Before Marie could answer, Ellen asked, "Do you know a soul on Earth who seemed to know and understand God better than Jesus?"

"No," Marie shook her head.

"Then how likely is it that Jesus—of all people—would cry out, 'Father, why hast thou forsaken me?' Jesus had said that God and he were *One*. He would have to believe that they were *separate* if he really asked why God had forsaken him."

"Whoa, this is getting deep," Ann-Rita squirmed in her seat.

Ellen explained. "Did you know that Jesus's question, transcribed directly from his native Aramaic tongue, meant 'For this was my destiny?'"

"You lost me," I said. "What did Jesus mean—that he was born to be crucified?"

"I can't say for sure, but Jesus certainly understood that every human life has a divine purpose," Ellen explained. "What if the purpose of his very public crucifixion was to demonstrate to us that there is no death?"

"Huh? What do you mean?" Eldridge asked. "He died to prove there's no death? That doesn't make any sense."

"What died on the cross—the spirit that was created in the

image of God, or the physical body that was recognized as Jesus of Nazareth?"

"Ohhh," Eldridge nodded. "I get it. His body was crucified."

"Right!" Ellen smiled. "No one has ever disputed that Jesus's physical body was dead. They put a lifeless body in that tomb. Three days without refrigeration, that body had to have been stinking.

"His spiritual body, on the other hand, was very much alive. Do you think it was his physical body that appeared three days later? Did he take that physical body with him when he ascended? Physical bodies can only function in Earth's atmosphere. Why do you think astronauts have to wear space suits? Would Jesus need to cart along a physical body to ascend to the heavens? What if he was demonstrating that we live beyond our physical bodies?"

"Man!" Virgil said, shaking his head.

"We tend to read the Bible literally," Ellen said, glancing at Marie. "We don't know the culture of ancient Middle Easterners; we don't understand their figures of speech. We forget that the Bible is a written record of centuries of oral history—stories that were possibly embellished over the years, and underwent several language translations. Yet we think we can pick up their books and understand them as if they were written in English last week. How can we possibly claim that there are any direct quotes in a story that was centuries old before it was written?

In the case of Jesus's life, decades rather than centuries had passed before anybody wrote about it; but still, I think we misunderstood the most valuable lesson of Jesus's ministry."

"Hmmm, you're saying that we literally killed the messenger and missed the message," I said. "This is too deep for my little brain. I think I should eat." I stood and walked toward the dining room.

"I'm not sure I'm onboard with that, Ellen," Marie argued, "and it still doesn't explain why you think we live more than one lifetime."

"Sorry, I did digress," Ellen apologized. "How old did we say the Universe was, again? Fifteen billion years? And how long did we say God's life span was?"

"Infinite," I said.

"And how long is your life span?"

"What did we say? Seventy-five years, on the average?" George asked.

"Really? You're telling me the life span of a human body. I thought you told me that you were made in the image of God," Ellen reminded him.

"Right! Right!" said Eldridge. "So we're infinite; we're Godlike. We're not mortal beings.

"That's where you're losing me, Ellen. If I were part of the all-knowing, all-powerful, everywhere present God, why wouldn't I have sense enough to stay out of the body of a black baby born in America?"

"I ain't confusing you. You're confusing yourself," Ellen said. "Let's look at what you've said. You told me that you are made in the image of God. You're pure spirit, so you're infinite, right?"

"Right," he nodded.

"You told me that a human being lives an average of 75 years—less than the time it would take to bat your infinite, spiritual eye, right?"

"Yep."

"When you put it in the context of your infinite life, is 70, 80, or even 100 human years in the body of a black person in America such a big deal?"

He sighed. "When you put it that way, no."

"And, as spirit, if you had all eternity to live, would you

choose only one bat of an eyelash experience?"

"No, I guess not. But if I were only going to have one lifetime on Earth, I'd want to be mega wealthy. I'd want to rule a country or something!"

"Right!" Ellen squealed. "And that's where the fairness of God comes in. Suppose you were wealthy—let's say, sometime during the 200-plus years of American slavery. Maybe you supported the law that made it illegal for black folks to read, or maybe you just hated black people, on sight. Here's a good one: Suppose you were a huge plantation owner or a businessman who made millions insuring slave ships."

Eldridge shook his head in disgust. "I don't even like the thought of me doing any of that!"

The doorbell rang.

"I think we're on the same page!" Ellen nodded, as I headed toward the front door. "At the end of that one human lifetime, when your spirit lifted out of that white millionaire's body and saw what you had done to the other souls that had shared that Earth experience with you, I assume you wouldn't have been very proud of your contribution to human civilization?"

"You got that right!" he smirked, shaking his head.

"So if you were given the opportunity to neutralize the harm that you caused, by experiencing another human lifetime—*another blink of an eyelash*—as a black man who was dehumanized by white folks, would you choose it?"

Eldridge sighed. "Absolutely!"

Ellen smiled and nodded. "I thought so. God is fair. And life is fair because we get so many opportunities to balance our actions. Life is fair because we always reap what we sow."

"Deb!" I said, as she reached the top of the landing. "I guess I've officially caught up with you. I now understand reincarnation. I mean I *really* understand it. From now on, I'll be paying closer attention to how I treat other folks, so that my soul won't feel compelled to walk in their shoes later on."

She looked puzzled. "Reincarnation? How did that come up?"

I gave her a hug. "Long story," I laughed, as we walked into the living room. "I think you know everybody, right?"

Debby nodded as she glanced around the room. "Yeah, I think we met after your last move. These gatherings keep getting closer and closer together," she laughed. "By the way, don't close the door. I saw Louis parking when I walked in.

"Hey, everybody," she waved. "So you've been talking about reincarnation? Is that party talk?"

"Actually, we were talking about folks who keep trying to save my soul because they think God is a vindictive, judgmental sadist," Ellen laughed.

"Gotcha," Debby said, looking confused. Although raised in her father's Jewish faith, her mother had come from a Roman Catholic Italian home; so Debby was pretty much ecumenical.

The doorbell rang.

"I'll get it," Ellen said, rising. "I'm heading toward the dining room, anyway."

Moments later, Ellen buzzed Louis into the downstairs lobby, "Hey, Louis!" she shouted, as he reached the landing.

"Hey, Ellen. How's everybody?" Louis greeted the others, as he walked into my foyer.

I introduced him around, and then pointed him in the direction of the buffet for food and drinks. Ann-Rita winked her approval as he headed toward the dining room.

Louis was a tall, thin, handsome man with a salt and pepper gray beard that made him look very distinguished.

Soft-spoken and a conservative dresser, he was a consultant in a large accounting firm—an efficiency expert of sorts, who worked with the firm's small business clients to help them increase profitability. He was quite a technology expert, even though his degree was in English.

I think highly intelligent men are wildly attractive, and Louis was really smart. He used to read encyclopedias, cover to cover, when he was a kid. I mean, this man knew a lot about practically everything and could explain it all, ad nauseum.

But a conversation on religion? Louis wouldn't have much to contribute. He was a self-declared agnostic. Initially, I was troubled when he made that declaration.

Ellen told me to ignore it. "Girl, that's just a label," she said. "A lot of people call themselves Christians, and don't bit more act Christlike than the man in the moon.

"What counts is how Louis treats people, not what he calls himself."

Ellen was right; I was being judgmental. I had to remember: saying you're Christian merely tells others what you believe; saying you're Christlike tells others how you behave—as so dramatically demonstrated by the world's most famous Jew—loving, peaceful, forgiving, healing, and accepting of all peoples, no matter what their race, gender, or religious beliefs.

6. Marriage Made in Heaven

Louis and I had been dating, off and on, for about a year and a half. It took about that long for me to develop a severe allergy to his on again, off again, gone again commitment. Finally, I quarantined myself. To assure my peace of mind, I gave Louis explicit instructions: Don't call; don't write; don't send messages by carrier pigeon. I'd had it!

Louis was accustomed to being the one who needed space in a relationship; a woman had never spaced on him. But this woman can only tolerate minute amounts of BS, and a man who is not impeccable with his word is more than I can stand. It's an ingrained annoyance, stemming from a childhood of broken promises from my father; so when a man tells me one thing and does something else, it's time for me to grab hat and run.

Speaking of running—a couple of years had passed since moving to Home #19, and as you might have guessed, I'd moved. Again. This time, though, it looked as if I might actually sprout roots. I'd bought a townhouse, ironically, in the same condo development where I'd gotten that five-day notice a few years earlier.

After nearly three months, Louis dared to call. He'd bought two tickets to a creative visualization seminar that author Shakti Gawain was conducting at a downtown hotel. I was stunned. Not that Louis had called—he always did, eventually—but that he'd taken the initiative to actually buy the tickets! Was someone else occupying his body? Louis wasn't interested in spiritual growth, and he wasn't exactly what you'd call a generous soul; but those two go together, don't they?

Don't get me wrong—Louis was basically a very nice guy, but was he stingy! I'd never met a more quid pro quo person. This man did nothing for anyone unless there was some exchange of goods or services. He was always afraid of getting the short end of the stick, the bad end of a deal. To control his losses, he was always postured to give as little as possible.

Problem was, it made him penny-wise and pound-foolish. He would pay the minimum balance on his credit cards because he hated giving up his money to his creditors. Of course, he ended up paying his creditors more, in interest, but that's a lesson he'd eventually learn about holding on so tightly to a dime.

Spending money, being inventive, taking the initiative to find an activity that I couldn't resist—these were radical changes for Louis. He'd never gone so far to convince me to accept his surrender.

Even though I was impressed, I was also quite leery—and not about to be ambushed by any more of his crap. He'd used up his last "get out of jail" card, as far as I was concerned. On the other hand, I didn't want to pass up the chance to see Shakti Gawain; I was a huge fan of her books.

I had to be careful. I didn't want Louis to think I was agreeing to a date. I even entertained the notion of refusing his ticket and going alone, but that wouldn't work. I was bound to run into him there; that man was not about to waste his money on unused tickets.

Aha! I remembered something: Louis had mentioned that there was no assigned seating at the seminar. That could solve my problem. I decided to find a friend to tag along.

A threesome would ruin any illusion that Louis and I were

on a date. Ellen had a gig that night; so I called another close friend, my former colleague, Max.

Max wasn't familiar with Gawain and wasn't particularly enamored with enlightenment, but he was between jobs, recently divorced, and quite despondent. I didn't have to twist his arm to convince him to examine some tools that might change his life. Plus, the seminar was at a hotel within walking distance of Max's Marina City apartment.

The workshop was everything I had hoped it would be. Gawain was awesome. Louis was quiet. Max was optimistic. Afterward, the three of us went to dinner at a nearby restaurant. When we finished our meals, Max was the first to rise from the table. I was scooting out of the booth when he abruptly turned to me and said, "You—sit and talk."

Before my protest could spill out of my gaping lips, he said sternly, "You two need to talk. Sit!"

Max always vacillated between acting like my big brother or my daddy—always barking orders or offering kindly advice. Most of the time, he was right. This was not one of those times, and I was furious. A grateful Louis bade Max goodbye. A guy thing, I figured. I just stared at the wall, too ticked to utter a word. The only thing chillier than yours truly was the night air.

As soon as I thought Max had entered his building, which was about a block from the restaurant, I rose from the table. Louis accompanied me across the street to the parking lot.

His car was near the front of the lot; mine was at the far end, around a corner, so he offered to drive me there. We hopped into his car, and lo and behold, the joker wouldn't start! It was a chilly night, but not below freezing. Neither of us could understand why his battery was dead as a doorknob. We walked to my car and I drove back to give him a jump.

While my car warmed up and his battery recharged, Louis poured out his heart. He'd had an epiphany during our most recent separation. He was ready to commit. He wanted another chance to prove his sincerity.

I'm a "Fool me once, shame on you, fool me twice, shame on me" kind of gal. But to be fair, I allowed Louis the opportunity to demonstrate that he really meant it this time.

Several months later, we were planning an October wedding.

7. Open, Sesame

Since it was the second marriage for both of us, Louis and I decided on a very small ceremony and reception. He was reading the paper one hot Sunday afternoon when I screamed, in frustration. Trying to whittle down the guest list was impossible!

He looked up casually and said, "Tuesday's your birthday. Why don't we just get married then?"

Tuesday? It was a work day for both of us, but what an awesomely romantic idea! So what, if it was Tuesday? Then, panic set in: could we get everything done in less than 48 hours?

My off days were Sunday and Monday, and half of Sunday was gone. We only had one day to buy rings, get blood tests and the marriage license, and select wedding attire that also would be suitable for work. We decided to let go and let God. We would knock on each door. If we were supposed to get married on Tuesday, all doors would open.

Standing behind Door #1: Angel. She was looking forward to sharing the maid of honor spotlight with Ellen, but summer vacation with her dad wouldn't be over until the following weekend. This was problematic.

Angel had been looking through her dad's and my wedding pictures a few years earlier when she suddenly burst into tears.

"Why wasn't I invited to the wedding?" my little pumpkin

sobbed, feeling sorely rejected. Her heart was clearly broken, poor darling.

Luckily, I had a reasonable excuse: She wasn't on the planet until nearly four years after the ceremony. Angel was somewhat relieved, although not completely satisfied. As the most important person in our lives, she really thought she should have been there.

I wasn't going to marry again without her, unless she gave me the OK. I picked up the phone.

I was surprised that Angel would be swept away by the romance of a weekday elopement! She gave us her blessing; in exchange, we offered to drive up to Minnesota and bring her home, instead of flying her back to Chicago. Deal!

Door #2: The rings. As luck would have it, we already had a meeting scheduled the next day with a jewelry designer. We called and alerted her to the sudden change of plans: No time to design; we needed rings on the run. She, too, was excited to go on this romantic adventure with us. She instructed us to meet her on Jewelers' Row at our original appointment time.

Door #3: Blood tests. A physician friend told me that it would be impossible to get blood test results in a day, unless my doctor had a close relationship with an independent lab.

The next morning, I called my gynecologist and let him in on our plans. A kind, fatherly gentleman, Dr. Hankin was tickled to facilitate a love connection. He made the lab arrangements. An equally excited co-conspirator at the lab took our blood samples and ran the tests while we finished our appointed rounds.

Back behind Door #2, the search for our wedding rings was at full tilt. Unable to find a ready-made set that we liked, the designer trotted us in and out of jewelers' showrooms, trying to find the perfect diamond and setting.

We finally found the diamond at the right price, but I didn't like any of that jeweler's settings. The search resumed.

The jeweler from whom we'd bought the diamond felt very much like an accomplice in our instant-wedding caper and insisted that we come back to show him the finished ring.

Time almost had run out when I finally found a setting that I liked. Problem: Sizing the ring would take at least 48 hours. Bummer. I tried it on, hoping it would be too large rather than too small—at least that would work for the ceremony.

It was a perfect fit! Unbelievable! While the jeweler put the diamond into the setting, Louis and I ran to knock on Door #4, City Hall, to get our marriage license.

The jewelry store was about to close when we breezed back in to pick up my ring. What a day! Louis had bought my ring at the exact budget limit we had set when we drove downtown that morning. We had our blood tests and our license. There had been only one disappointment. We hadn't found a ring that Louis liked.

We dashed back across the street to show my finished ring to the first jeweler, who was very pleased, but insisted that we have a double-ring ceremony. He offered to loan Louis a ring to wear the next morning.

He put several trays on the counter. Louis eyed each ring carefully and said, "There's only one that I like."

He picked it up, and you guessed it. It slipped right on! We were feeling very much in the universal flow; this was a match made in heaven.

Weeks earlier, Louis had made dinner cruise reservations for that night, to celebrate my birthday. Instead, it became our engagement party. As we walked to the Lakefront, an inexplicably angry man leaned toward me as he passed us on the sidewalk.

"Niggers!" he screamed.

"God bless you!" I yelled back. No one could snatch our happiness. We were deliriously blessed, and a good day was about to get better. About an hour later, Louis formally proposed and slipped the engagement ring on my finger, as we floated along Lake Michigan. The boat came along for the ride.

We drove downtown the next morning in a downpour, but when we exited the parking lot, the rain suddenly stopped. Seconds after we entered City Hall to say our vows, thunder cracked and the rain resumed.

The ceremony was predictably unceremonious, until we were pronounced man and wife. The normally reserved Louis picked me up and spun me around, he was so excited. I didn't know he had it in him!

It had stopped raining again, when we walked across the street to our wedding reception: continental breakfast in the food court of the State of Illinois building. Moments later, we went our separate ways, to shock our colleagues. Mine got a double shock—I was early, for a change. I hadn't arrived early since the days when working in that newsroom had been fun.

I called my mother and Ellen, and invited them to meet us for dinner at Orly's, a restaurant down the street from my Hyde Park townhouse. They thought they were joining a birthday celebration.

When we broke the wedding news, I realized for the first time that I had totally forgotten Door #5: Ellen, who had been anticipating her maid of honor duties as much as Angel. She looked directly into my eyes, surreptitiously took off her shoe, reach across the table, and playfully beat me with it.

8. Be Careful What You Pray For

Within a few months, life with Louis changed dramatically. He went from a regular guy with a consulting gig, to become the owner of a multimillion-dollar manufacturing plant. It was the late eighties; leveraged buyouts were in their heyday. Louis bought the company with a $15,000 down payment.

He upgraded his small engine Mercedes to a big S-class sedan, and also bought a sporty Lincoln Continental. Despite my protests, he insisted that we sell the townhouse in the city, and move to the suburbs. We bought a stately, five-bedroom, four-bath English Tudor with a circular drive and a 40-foot in-ground pool. (Count that as move #21 for me.) And we hadn't yet celebrated our first anniversary.

To put it mildly, our consumption suddenly became quite conspicuous. But we had more than stuff; Louis and I had a very happy partnership. In fact, the first three years of our marriage were like a romantic comedy. During the next three years, however, everything changed.

It started the day Louis received a call from his banker, notifying him that his company's checking account was $90,000 overdrawn. Now you can just imagine how Louis took this news. How in the world could something like this happen to a guy who pulled out his money clip and counted all of his bills every time he went to a cash register? Louis always knew exactly how much money he had, down to the penny.

I actually have to peel back layers of drama to get to the heart of this overdraft. Follow this closely—it's mind-boggling.

The scene was set before Louis bought the business. He was working with a business broker on the deal when he received a call from an acquaintance, the chief financial officer for one of his consulting clients. Louis vaguely remembered meeting this guy, and although he couldn't recall that they'd had a substantive conversation, obviously they had exchanged business cards.

The guy explained that he'd been fired—or was about to be. He wondered if Louis knew of any available accounting positions. How serendipitous! Louis happened to be searching for someone to do the financial research on a manufacturing company that was for sale. Because of his full-time job, he couldn't complete the task himself.

If the numbers made sense, and Louis decided to purchase the company, there could be a tremendous opportunity for this fellow. Louis would bring him onboard as his partner, and give him a 49 percent stake in the business.

No, it wasn't that cheapskate Louis had suddenly become philanthropist of the year; there was miserly method to this madness. He was penny-wise and pound-foolish; remember? Louis didn't want to pay the full $15,000 required to buy this $8 million company. He figured that he could save about seven grand, if the other guy paid 49 percent.

So the first layer, leading to the overdraft, was Louis and his bad habit of paying the minimum. Layer number two was his so-called partner—a guy Louis barely knew. What he did know initially was that a client was firing the guy, yet he trusted this man to perform the financial research on the acquisition—and then gave him virtually half of the company.

The plot thickened: The bank officer told Louis that the company's account was *frequently* overdrawn to the tune of $90,000-$100,000.

Why didn't Louis know this? Apparently, his partner normally got these overdraft calls. But this time he was on vacation, so the call went directly to the corner office.

And there, we find layer number three: Louis. He knew that his CFO hadn't honored his repeated requests for financial statements. What he didn't know until then was that the man to whom he'd given nearly half of his company had never balanced their checkbook during their two-year partnership.

Finally, we reach the fourth layer: The partners' death-defying attempt to run a multi-million dollar company without having the slightest idea how much money they had, from one day to the next. To think, my dear husband had worked for a huge accounting firm, helping its small-business clients run their companies more efficiently. Go figure.

Now, let's see if I can cut to the chase on this sob-sister tragedy: Louis fired the CFO, who then sued him on the grounds that Louis had no right to fire him, because he was a partner.

Their largest customer was already worried that the company was unstable. The customer's fears escalated after Louis tried to negotiate a new contract with his workers' union, because he was too cheap to pay a professional negotiator. Bye, bye contract.

The morning Louis's company went out of business, the hospital called to say that my father's spirit had left his body. He'd suffered an aneurysm a few days earlier.

How much could I handle at once? My father and I had just begun to mend our relationship. Until I was a teenager, he had treated me with benign neglect. On the extremely rare occasions we were together, he was thrilled to see me, which made me feel loved. But he had never paid child support, so I never felt that he really cared about my general welfare.

It had taken a while for our relationship to heal. Then suddenly, it was over. Meanwhile, my marriage was slowly dying, as I watched Louis blow an $8 million blessing and blame everybody under the sun for his business' failure.

Had this marriage really been made in heaven, or had I missed something? I recounted each step, starting with Louis's car battery conking out. We would not have reconciled that night if each of us had immediately driven out of that parking lot. Who knows when Louis would have gotten me in the same room with him again—not to mention, in the same car?

Our dramatic path to the altar had been nothing but storybook. Even Louis's business acquisition seemed to have been divinely ordered—despite his selection of the world's-least-likely chief financial officer candidate.

Oddly enough, the business acquisition was made possible the day I bought my first personal computer and decided to sell my beloved typewriter. A friend knew a real estate broker who had just opened a new office in Hyde Park. Violet thought Jerry might need a good typewriter. Jerry didn't buy mine, but he did convince me that I should get off the rent treadmill, and build some security for Angel and me. Owning a home again made all the sense in the world, so Jerry and I searched for a condo.

One dark, rainy morning as I stood at an obscure bus stop under a large umbrella, a car passed. Suddenly, it stopped and backed up. It was a former neighbor from the townhouse development. I still haven't figured out how Van recognized me under those adverse conditions, but I did figure out why. He had a message to deliver: a townhouse in the development was on the market.

The search was over! Everything fell into place—until I tried to find a mortgage. A few years earlier, I had signed a one-year lease in a beautiful high-rise apartment building for a family member. Within a few days, she reneged on the deal. I had just accepted a reporting job in Texas; what was I going to do with an apartment in Chicago?

After I was unable to find someone to sublease the place, the management company sued me for the entire year's lease amount. I was forced to file a Chapter 13 bankruptcy. I had the option of paying only a portion of the indebtedness, but opted to pay the entire amount, thinking that it wouldn't look as bad on my credit record. But when I tried to get a mortgage, it didn't matter that I had paid the debt in full. Every bank turned me down, except one, and they insisted that I have a co-signer. It made sense to ask Louis.

OK, maybe not. Louis had chronic fear-of-loss. He was concerned that if I defaulted on the loan, he'd have to pay his rent and my mortgage. I had to explain to this accounting firm consultant that if I defaulted, he would have a highly desirable piece of property in a high demand area of the city that he could easily sell. I invited him to do the math. He was getting 50 percent ownership for 0 percent cash. That computed. Louis agreed to co-sign.

It proved to be a wise decision. When he decided to buy the manufacturing company after we married, that townhouse collateralized the loan for his portion of the cash investment. It was reaping and sowing in action. As my mother would say, "Do good; and good comes to you."

For many years after the business failed, it appeared to me that Louis's other pound-foolish decisions had unraveled everything that had so meticulously been woven together. Today, however, from my seat in the audience of that tragedy, it's very clear that Louis's business loss might have been one of my greatest blessings in this lifetime.

It set the stage for a drama of epic proportions—complete with a classic Gethsemane scene. My body cried out for some way to avoid the painful experiences that seemed to be my destiny. I would learn that these experiences were pivotal to my soul's all-important, evolutionary journey.

9. Letting Go

I have learned that it's not what happens in life that defines your outcomes, it's how you react to it. Louis had been unemployed for nearly two years when our television network offered a handsome early-retirement deal that would give me a lump sum and take a bite out of our bulging debt. I jumped on it, deciding to pursue corporate video production full-time, instead of working my day job and taking as many freelance gigs as I could possibly handle.

Unlike my day job, independent production had no income ceiling. Leaving the newsroom had another benefit: It would remove the safety net from under Louis. Perhaps his survival instinct would kick in and he'd start foraging for sustenance. Either way, in deference to my growing resentment of him, I wasn't going to work two jobs while Louis worked none.

I didn't have difficulty getting projects initially, but each of them was troublesome. Cash flow was horrible because of cost overruns or delinquent payments. The additional financial stress and my chronic lack of diplomacy made me ill-equipped for effective conflict resolution with my clients. Things simply got worse.

The one thing I thought I didn't have to worry about during this drama was Angel. All of her academic life, she had ranked among the top two percentile in the nation on standardized tests. She was the only one among her circle of junior high school friends who had been placed in honors classes and the gifted program when they entered high school. That scenario morphed into a disastrous sideshow.

Angel never liked being different. She did what all girls do at that age, to fit in: They turn into pod people. She talked back. She was rebellious, defiant. I thought it was just happening at my house, but over the years I've heard other parents' horror stories about a sweet little girl who went to bed one night, and was body-snatched as she slept. A belligerent she-monster emerged from her bedroom the next morning, foaming at the mouth and taking swipes at anything that came within arm's distance.

I was not ready for this. When I was a teenager, no one in my neighborhood had the nerve to talk back to *any* adult. Either this phase of my life was wiped from my memory like the pain of childbirth, or, like us, the body snatchers were too afraid to misbehave in our parents' homes.

I consulted with Barbara, a spiritual advisor from Philadelphia I had met at the station, thanks to Carrie. Barbara was a guest on our morning talk show, and Carrie was dying to go upstairs to the studio and see her clairvoyant sister in action. I tagged along for fun; when I left, I was a fan. I consulted with Barbara whenever she was in Chicago.

Luckily, she was in town during Angel's pod-people period. Barbara told me that Angel would soon want to live with her father. I was shocked, devastated. Angel was more than my only child—she was my heartbeat, my soul mate. I recalled looking at my little bundle the morning after she was born. Stroking her, I said to her, "You're going to be my best friend."

She had always been every bit of that. We were a team. What would I do without her? Sure, she loved her dad, her stepmother, and their two kids, but live with them full-time? I couldn't see it. I didn't want to see it.

OK, Angel was an extremely bright child who was having difficulty adjusting to her new high school, but I could not believe that she'd actually want to leave home—and leave me.

Barbara assured me that it was time for Angel and her father to work out some things in their relationship; they needed this time together. She prayed for God to show me that it was time for me to release Angel.

I was inconsolable. After the reading, Louis, Angel, and I went to Water Tower Place for lunch, trying to have a normal outing, but every time I thought about Barbara's prediction, tears would stream. My heart physically ached.

A few weeks later, God did reveal that it was time for me to let Angel go. The first marking period, my brilliant child had earned D's (for "Didn't Even Try") in every class. Ed and I immediately decided that she needed a peer group that was more passionate about success. We moved her to his suburban Twin Cities home to finish her first year of high school.

I don't know who was more upset about the decision, Angel or me. I do know that I'll never do anything more difficult in this lifetime than release her to Ed's loving care.

In previous years, I'd always looked forward to her summer vacations with Ed and the break from nonstop single parenting. Without fail, on her departure day, both of us cried. She was always in anguish about leaving, because she felt that I needed her; Ed had a new family, so she wasn't as concerned.

Summers without Angel were endless; I could hardly wait for the end of August. How was I going to handle my baby being away from home for almost a full school year? That, I discovered, would be the least of my worries. Within two weeks of arriving in Minnesota, Angel called home to ask if she could finish all four years of high school there. She loved the newly built school. She was making new friends. She had gotten a major role in the upcoming school musical.

Could she stay? "Pretty please?" she begged.

It was great to hear her so excited about school again. I was so grateful that Barbara had prepared me for this possibility. It didn't hurt any less, though. But there was a silver lining: I had Angel for summer vacations, so our time together was pure play and our relationship grew even stronger.

Best of all, Angel wasn't around the house as much during the most stressful time of my life. She wasn't there when I opened the refrigerator and had nothing to eat, while my husband sat at his computer or in front of the big screen television. Angel's role model for manhood went to work every day and took care of his family's needs. I wanted that to be her image and expectation of a man. Always.

Without a doubt, everything was in Divine Order. Painful as it was, it was crystal clear that I had made the best decision for Angel. I had been a basket case on that bitterly cold January day when she called home and asked to stay in Minnesota for the next four years. What I later discovered and have learned to trust is that our souls' primary goal is to resolve everything for the highest good of all concerned. Everything was evolving as Angel's soul (and mine) had desired and meticulously planned.

Although my body didn't realize it at the time, my soul had work to do—mentally, physically, and spiritually. I probably could not have done it, coping with the regressing Louis and pubescent Angel. Part of my work was to keep my creditors at bay, which I thought required working harder, physically. The other part was to understand life, which required working smarter, spiritually .

I know now that this was the work I signed on to do when I entered this body. And no matter what it looked like or how it felt from the outside—inside, my soul must have been rejoicing that I was getting this job done.

10. He Ain't Heavy, He's My Husband

Much to my surprise, I had gradually become more than a casual student of spirituality. One day, I noticed that the texts in my mushrooming metaphysical library were dramatically coming to life, unfolding not a minute before I was prepared to receive them—and just as I needed them.

On an intellectual level, I comprehended the concepts: We are spiritual beings, not bodies. From a spiritual level, a mountaintop level where we can see everything, we create our life experiences—our dramas. The painful nature of some of those dramas causes us to think we are victims of misfortune. We're not; we design each drama to teach us something critical to our soul's evolution to conscious Godliness. *OK, got it!*

But when I closed a book and hopped on stage, where the lights were glaring in my eyes and the other actors were screaming something else in my ears, it was difficult to really wrap my arms around spiritual wisdom. So my soul decided to help. As my mother used to say so threateningly, "I can show you, better than I can tell you."

After Louis closed the manufacturing plant's doors for the last time, he actively looked for employment by sitting at his computer, printing reams of résumés, and collecting a drawer full of rejection letters to show his counselor at the unemployment office.

After his savings ran out, he expected me to lift the weight of all of the debt that was quickly burying us. My salary comfortably had met my debt load when I owned a three-bedroom condo and a Toyota Celica; it did not have the muscle to manage a mortgage three times as large, four car notes, a variety of gold and platinum credit cards, and the lawn- and pool-maintenance folks. Choose one. Any one. My little paycheck couldn't handle them all.

Fighter that I am, I tried my best for as long as I could. I wanted to be supportive. Louis was going through a tough time. I took on as many freelance production projects as I could, in addition to my full-time job.

Back at the Tudor on the hill, Louis was still cranking out résumés, and there he stayed. When I needed his help to distribute my production company's marketing materials at a trade show, he flatly refused. What if he ran into any former business associates? They might ask what happened to his company. Nope, he couldn't be anywhere in the vicinity.

After that day, I never looked at Louis the same way. He affirmed my new perception when he made no effort to lighten my load in any way. Who had to cook when she came home from work? Louis said he didn't know how, though he was literate and I had a wealth of cookbooks standing at attention on the kitchen desk. Cleaning? My job, too, unless it was our housekeeper Theresa's scheduled day. Once, I faxed home a grocery list so that Louis could get that chore out of the way while I was at work. He picked me up from the train station that evening—and drove me directly to the supermarket. He said he hadn't wanted to make an extra trip out of the house that day.

My mother, who'd had a serious stroke the week we moved to the suburbs, was no longer very talkative. However, whenever we spoke, she'd always ask, "What's Louis doing—nothing?"

Don't remind me, Mother.

Louis typically sat at his office desk until the wee hours of the morning. One neighbor said she assumed he was developing new software, because no matter what time she passed our house, she saw him working at his computer.

A former newsroom colleague suggested that Louis might be clinically depressed. He certainly seemed to be exhibiting some of the symptoms, as far as two journalists with no medical background could determine.

When I suggested counseling, Louis was highly offended, but begrudgingly agreed to see a therapist. At his second session, he told the counselor that he no longer was depressed. He returned home to resume the stare-in at his computer.

I'm the one who probably should have gone to counseling. I was feeling unvalued, unprotected, and highly resentful that I had allowed a healthy, educated man to lean on me for his total financial support for nearly three years. By wearing the pants in the family, I had given Louis permission to relinquish his responsibility to himself and our marriage. I had enabled him and disabled me.

Back when we thought Louis would be unemployed for a brief time, we had converted enough frequent-guest points from our time-share property for the family—Louis and his daughter, Angel and me—to have free airfare and rooms in a four-star Parisian hotel near the Champs Elysées. The certificates were about to expire, but Louis didn't want to go. I badly needed a break, so I decided that Angel and I would use ours and celebrate her 18th birthday and upcoming high school graduation abroad.

April in Paris! We saw the city the way all broke folk see it: on foot. We visited all of the tourist spots, from one bank of the Seine to the other. I think I appreciated the city's beauty more by seeing it in slow motion, on the sidewalks with Parisians who couldn't have been more helpful or hospitable when we needed direction. I dreaded returning to my dysfunctional life.

As the airport bus arrived at Charles de Gaulle, Angel stood, then gasped, looking down at the top of my head.

"Mom! You've got a *bald* spot!" It was true. The stress had caused my hair to fall out in huge clumps. I was a mess!

Within 24 hours of returning home, I got the strong signal that it was time to move. But I wouldn't be doing the packing, this time. Louis made me so angry, I yanked the welcome mat from underneath him. I had hesitated to do it previously because I firmly believed that we reap what we sow. If I created homelessness for Louis, I would ultimately create it for myself. But I just as firmly believed that we shouldn't bite the hand that feeds us. When he did that, he had to go. Immediately.

Days later, I noticed that Louis hadn't cut the grass while I was away. No surprise. We'd recently bought a high-end mower to replace the lawn service. I headed to the garage, preparing to cut nearly a half acre of grass. No mower. I walked next door; maybe Henry had borrowed it. Nope, but he let me borrow his.

We hadn't even finished paying for the lawn mower, and it had disappeared! I called my brother Jerry. Maybe he'd borrowed it. No, but he knew where it was. Louis had sold the mower while I was away. Well now, why hadn't he sold the lawn, too? What did he expect to do without a lawn mower, or had he anticipated that he wouldn't be around to cut the grass?

Was it any wonder that my hair was falling out? I needed a deeper understanding of this drama, and the divine purpose for it—a task for Ellen's beloved Institute for Spiritual Healing. She and I had gone there often, to enjoy the guided meditations and energy readings from students in clairvoyant classes. We also had completed several classes over the years, often using their interactive format to test the claims made in the metaphysical books we were studying.

Like my virtual mentor Ruth Montgomery, when she started exploring spirituality, I was quite skeptical at first, but I later found the Institute's energy readings to be both credible, and a powerful investigative tool.

The Institute's teachings were rooted in the premise that everything is energy. It wasn't hocus-pocus New Age-speak; it was physics. Albert Einstein proved that what we believe is hard matter is mostly empty space with energy running through it.

At the Institute, energy isn't theoretical, it's practical. They work with it everyday. They "see" it. They "read" it. They communicate with it.

Energy vibrates. As we can hear sound vibrating with our physical ears and discern body language with our physical eyes, students at the Institute learn to read energy with their spiritual eyes.

Energy is infinite and invisible; it has eternal life. At the Institute, they say our souls, which are spirit—pure energy—retain memories of all the experiences we've ever had, just as our physical brains can vividly recall our childhood memories. They call human bodies "space suits"—equipment required to navigate through the physical planet Earth, but useless anyplace else.

Because we are essentially spirits having a physical experience, they operate on the premise that anyone can learn to see and communicate with the higher-vibrating energy of the spirit world, so they conduct an intensive series of classes to teach clairvoyance. Clairvoyant means "clear seeing", the ability to "see" with your spiritual eye.

I've never enrolled in those classes, which require many months of dedicated study and practice, but clairvoyant readings from Institute students have helped me look behind the curtain of my life dramas to find the real source of my problems—insights that physical evidence didn't reveal.

The Institute students aren't trained to predict the future. They focus on the present and past. Their aim is to help us understand why we attract certain situations and people into our lives. How? What I'd read—and what they've consistently proved over the years—is that everything starts in the spiritual realm and manifests in the physical. If you want to effectively heal a situation, you start at the spiritual cause rather than the physical effect. At the Institute, they accomplish that through what's called a spiritual healing.

I'd witnessed a lot of these healings at the Institute before I tried one. Frankly, I thought it was a bit ridiculous that someone could wave his hand near a part of my body and claim to clear blockages in my invisible energy system and aura. Initially, I watched with amusement, as the roomful of healers waved their arms. How could anyone refute or prove that they had actually healed anything? My goodness, energy is invisible!

The healers stood a few feet from the seated recipients, waving their hands up and down, explaining that they were clearing stuff in the recipients' auras. Then they'd step a bit closer, moving their hands back and forth, never coming more than a few inches from the person's body, never touching. The healers explained that they were neutralizing the energy in each chakra (pronounced *"SHAH' krah"*), the energy centers that run through the body, aligned along the spine. They also explained the characteristics of each energy center. In all, it was an educational as well as spiritual experience.

Finally, one Sunday when they asked if anyone else would like to have a healing, I decided to give it a try. They certainly couldn't hurt anything, I figured. Garrett, the director, looked at me carefully, explaining that he was reading my energy. Then he scoured the room for a student healer whose energy was a "good match". A student named John got the honors.

I'd seen John around the Institute, but I had never had a conversation with him. He knew nothing about me, or my hellish life. Since he allegedly was clairvoyant, the most he knew was that I was mentally poking fun at the arm-waving healers working nearby.

After supposedly "combing" my aura to remove any stuck energy and clearing some blocks he "saw" in my first chakra, my survival center, John bent over and said quietly, "There's a lot of anger energy in your second chakra, your emotional center. What do you want me to do with it—release it or leave it alone?"

"It's all yours!" I laughed. The cynical investigative journalist in me figured this was the part where they scheduled an appointment, for a fee. I wondered what was the going rate for disposing of "anger energy".

John knelt by the side of my chair and placed one hand about six inches in front of me, just below my navel. His other hand was parallel to it, about six inches away from my back. Eyes closed, he waved the hand in front toward my body, as if he were pushing something through me to the other side. Behind me, the other hand was catching whatever it was and pitching it downward. *Weird*, I thought.

"I'm going to send the anger down through your grounding cord, into the center of the Earth, where it'll be neutralized and recycled," he explained.

Yeah, right. Within seconds, the area just below my navel started churning. I physically felt something rumbling throughout my lower torso. I suddenly started rocking in the chair, which was not a rocker, and I held on tight. Not a fan of horror flicks, I wondered if this was like *The Exorcist*. Tears were pouring. I was petrified. What the hell was going on? In all of the months I'd been going to the center, I hadn't seen anyone react to their healing this way. What was wrong?

Garrett walked over, put his hand on my shoulder, instructed me to relax and exert no effort to help John. How did he know that I had been trying? I wanted it to end, and had tried my damnedest to help John dump as much anger down my grounding cord as I could. Finally, the churning subsided. I was wrung out and wobbly when I finally stood, but I felt about 50 pounds lighter. And why not? I'd not only lost my anger, I'd also shed my skepticism about spiritual healings.

I learned that day that anger has a personality and a power all its own. I finally understood the mind-body connection that medical doctors such as Bernie Siegel and Deepak Chopra had been writing about for years. Some of the world's most-renowned medical schools have published research linking our emotions to physical conditions. Researchers say that repressing or retaining negative thoughts and emotions can make us violently, even deathly ill. If that's true, then what they are saying is that the mind—not the brain—is more powerful than the body.

When you think about it, the mind is not a physical part of us. It's invisible. It's spiritual. It can't be spotted on an x-ray, but we know it's there.

I couldn't see my anger, either. My guess is that I had been pretending it wasn't there. I can be brutally honest—emphasis on brutal. Generally, what comes up comes out. As one of our senior reporters used to say about my feistiness, "Pat says what she thinks. And sometimes, she says it without thinking."

Knowing this about myself, I deliberately had bitten my tongue for three years, afraid that if I said something to Louis, my words would mortally wound him. Those words were not spoken, but they did not go away. Each one jammed itself uncomfortably into my bulging emotional energy center, my second chakra, and morphed into silent rage. Thank God, John released this anger before it—or I—exploded.

73

11. Spiritual Sleuthing

Like many people, when my life wasn't working the way I thought it should, when I had done everything possible, but the results didn't match my expectations, my first instinct was to ask, "Why is this happening to me?" At another time in my life, I would have blamed God. "How could God let this happen?" I would have cried. But, after much spiritual study, I've learned that nothing is ever done *to* me; I'm never a victim. Every experience is the result of my previous choices.

After that epiphany, I began to flip the script, asking: "Why did I create this situation?" or "Why did I attract that person into my life?" Old habits die hard. Most times, I forget and immediately sink into that victim hole.

Reality check: If I want the right answers, I have to ask the right questions. I began to learn those questions, as I relentlessly sleuthed for the detonators in my imploding life. I searched everywhere. Surely, there was a class I could take, or people I could speak with, to help me solve the problem du jour. If they could point me in the right direction, I was sure I could sniff out the answer.

Aside from leading me absolutely nowhere, all of these tactics had one other thing in common: I was looking outside myself for the cause and the solution. It never occurred to me to look at the soul who was impatiently patting her foot on the stage mark that I had drawn for that scene.

Hello? If I hadn't been so accustomed to blaming God when things went wrong, it would have occurred to me that it was *my* mark. I had drawn it, so that spot must have been exactly where I was supposed to have been standing at that moment.

I'm sure I'm not the only observer of far-away planets who realizes that the Universe was created with astounding mathematical precision. It is synergistic, synchronistic, and perfect in every way. Science—which, in its former life, was religion (and now is religion's greatest nemisis)—has proved that empirically.

Astrologers, for example, say their discipline is based on the precision of planet movement. They say that those born when the sun was in Virgo are, among other annoying things, highly analytical. In other words, we think things to death. I do; so is it any wonder that I sleuth?

I've spent a lot of years studying life, trying to figure out how it works, why things happen the way they do, and what I can learn from each personal experience. Now I know why they say, "Believe half of what you see and none of what you hear." I've rarely found an answer by looking at the physical evidence.

The sages say that spiritual beings, creatures made in the image of God, have all of the information we really need. It's not "out there" somewhere, it's inside us. We simply have to go within to access it. They urge us to meditate, to listen for the "still, small voice".

Yeah, right. The voice is still and small, and the volume on the dramas re-running inside my head is on full blast. How can a still, small voice compete with that kind of noise pollution?

Prior to trusting myself enough to retrieve my own answers from within, I consulted with a variety of souls who lacked neither the confidence nor the ability to commune with spirit. Like Ruth Montgomery, I stumbled across a few who had cultivated a grand pretense of possessing spiritual gifts, but for the most part, my sleuthing expeditions have been joyful and illuminating.

Because I'm trying to understand why things have happened rather than what's going to happen, I prefer clairvoyant or psychic readings that look backward from the present moment. If a clairvoyant can tell me something about my life that I already know, then I have some evidence that he or she truly is "seeing clearly".

These consultations have helped me view incidents in a much broader context than my physical eyes can see. More often than not, the clairvoyant's perspective enables me to make some sense of my life drama and understand why I create the scenes I do. As a result, I've learned how to create less traumatic scenarios in the future.

For example, a variety of clairvoyants who knew absolutely nothing about my financial circumstances, have told me that it appeared as though money was "leaking" from me. True enough, that's what was happening, on a physical level. Projects would flow in; then they'd postpone, stop prematurely, go over budget, or disappear entirely—which fanned my money woes. How did these strangers know that?

In each case, the clairvoyant would ask if I wanted him or her to plug this leak. That was a no-brainer.

They'd close their eyes, wave their arms in the direction of my first chakra, the energy zone of survival, and grin with satisfaction when they were done. By the next reading, a brand new person would announce that I'd sprung another leak. That much, I knew before I arrived.

My frustration to find the root cause of this annoyingly persistent leak directed my research to explore a variety of spiritual or metaphysical disciplines. One was numerology, popularized by the Greek mathematician Pythagoras, but studied long before he arrived on the planet.

Like energy readings, numerology is also based on vibrations. Numerology assigns a numeric equivalent to each letter of the alphabet. A is one; B is two, and so on. When you get to J, the tenth letter, the numbering starts again at one.

Numerology contends that the numeric vibration of a person's name foreshadows his or her destiny. My birth name is the sum of 41+27+28, or 96. In numerology, they reduce double-digit numbers to a single digit. Nine plus six equals 15, so I have to reduce it again to get a single digit, adding the one and five to arrive at a vibration of six.

P	A	T	R	I	C	I	A		L	O	U	I	S	E		A	R	N	O	L	D
7	1	2	9	9	3	9	1		3	6	3	9	1	5		1	9	5	6	3	4

I had to retrieve an early Seventies-vintage book by Helyn Hitchcock, entitled *Helping Yourself with Numerology*, to explain this to you. It was one of the books I found at Home #19. I'm fascinated by what Hitchcock defines as Number 6 characteristics. I found that she pretty much nailed me:

• You are devoted to your family to the extent that you often smother them with love and protection. *I might have been so protective of Louis that I disabled him.*

• Serving in the community gives you great pleasure. *I've always enjoyed community service, whether I was in the Girls Scouts, the Junior League, or working with my sorority.*

• You like to see a home run smoothly and orderly. You like beautiful things and surroundings. You also delight in decorating your home artistically. *Absolutely!*

• You are kind and tolerant. At times, you can become stubborn and argumentative. *This is especially true when I feel that an injustice has been committed.*

• Having a good sense of timing, you often gravitate to a career in music, either singing or playing a musical instrument. *Does wishful thinking count? My singing voice is more suitable for a choir, not a career; but playing the piano like a virtuoso has been a lifelong, unfulfilled dream.*

When I first heard about numerology, I was skeptical, as usual. I didn't think it was an exact science, but decided to keep an open mind and check it out with the objectivity of a journalist turned spiritual sleuth.

By that time, my sleuthing had become somewhat of an avocation. In fact, it had created somewhat of a buzz around the TV station. Our talk show host saw me in the ladies' room one morning, and asked about some of my metaphysical exploits. She thought I might be a good resource for upcoming shows. (I haven't done her numerological chart, but I wonder if her obvious destiny to become a billionaire is evident in her name's vibration.)

For most of us, though, anything outside of the physical world is taboo. Some of us have even been taught that anything that's not of this physical world is satanic. Venturing into the spiritual world is akin to plucking fruit off of the tree of knowledge—the original sin.

For me, that raises a few issues: First, both Satan and ignorance generally are associated with darkness; knowledge, on the other hand, is considered enlightenment. If God had a preference for us, which would it be? Second, if God is everywhere, where in the universe is Satan? Third, isn't it still impossible for Darkness and Light to occupy the same space?

Since I associate God with Light and believe that God does not want me to maneuver through my life in darkness, I probe. I learn. I try to live consciously. Blindly following others' dictates and beliefs can only keep me in darkness.

Being kept in the dark is typically problematic, as I was reminded after missing a couple of mortgage payments on our home. I was surprised that we hadn't heard from the bank.

It was no surprise for Louis. "Oh, foreclosure papers arrived a few weeks ago," he said, casually.

What? Had Louis withheld vital information about the roof over my head? This brother was "cruisin' for a bruisin'", as my dad used to say.

Louis spoke with the bank's attorney the day before the foreclosure hearing, and claimed that the attorney told him that there was no need for us to show up in court, unless we were able to pay the entire mortgage balance. I don't know if the attorney really gave Louis that advice; but when we didn't appear in court, the bank won an instant default judgment.

Our house was officially in foreclosure, and so was our marriage, as far as I was concerned. The only difference was that we had six months to redeem the house. The clock clearly had run out on the marriage.

I was both fascinated and frustrated by the drama—more accurately, tragedy—in my life. There was a script I was following, but couldn't see. I desperately wanted to read it, so that there would be no additional surprise endings.

Ellen referred me to a musician friend of hers who also had a reputation as an excellent numerologist. Ayana was a delightful, loving being with a gruff voice, a warm heart, and a contagious laugh.

Louis had been unemployed for about three years when Ayana made a house call. He and I were separated, living in the same house but in different rooms. In fact, I had gone to the local library, borrowed a do-it-yourself divorce textbook for broke folk like myself, and had drafted the divorce petition. After retreating to his room for a couple of days, Louis reluctantly emerged and signed the documents.

Ayana sat at the dining room table with Louis and me, and created our numerological charts. She pointed to this number and that number, and explained what they meant. Then she netted it all out for us: We were to take our home off of the market, even though we had less than six months to sell or lose it. She said God had given us that home and the bank could not take it from us.

She also told me not to file the divorce papers. She said that Louis and I were meant to be together. The numbers showed that there was no separation between our spirits. Our union was made in heaven.

Louis was elated. I was relieved. He happily took the FOR SALE sign out of the yard. I obediently retrieved my engagement and wedding rings from my jewelry box. We both wanted desperately to believe that we could save our home. And neither of us wanted another failed marriage.

A few days later, I still had no inspiration to invite Louis to my side of the house, and I couldn't stop staring at the rings on my finger. What did they signify, really? For nearly three years, Louis had treated me with benign neglect. He had not lifted a finger to make sure that I had food in my mouth, or a roof over my head. I'd been abandoned, and I was hurt beyond repair. Was this the kind of marriage I wanted?

I removed the rings; they didn't feel at home on my finger. Time had revealed the veracity of Barbara's prediction that Angel would live with her dad. I challenged time to reveal the truth of Ayana's reading, as well. It didn't; and the rings stayed in the jewelry box, where they belonged.

It took a little longer for Louis and me to give up hope on saving the home, but eventually, we put the sign back on the lawn, where it also belonged.

12. Playing the Numbers

As a seeker of truth, I must be objective. If I'm going to be open to infinite possibilities, I must embrace the possibility of false prophecies and practitioners. Ayana's reading made me skeptical. Either numerology was not a valid investigative tool, or she wasn't.

A year later, by chance, I was referred to a woman named Alzina, who lived in a small town in Indiana. She agreed to give me a numerology reading by phone. To my delight, it was her regular practice to record these sessions and send audiotapes to her clients. To me, taping expresses a metaphysician's willingness to be accountable for the information he or she gives. It also enables me to review and analyze the session later.

Alzina, whom I have never met face-to-face, proved that numerology can offer dramatic insight into the reason our lives work the way they do. Having only my full birth name and birth date, she began telling me things that had occurred in my past, phases I'd gone through during certain time frames.

She described the characteristics of my relationships with Ed and Louis. Her specificity and her accuracy utterly amazed me. The person who referred me to Alzina didn't know any of this stuff, so how did Alzina know?

"From [the age of] 31 to 36, you learned to manage, harmonize, regulate. But you did take on responsibilities of other people there—people who came into your life. Who was the next man in your life?" she asked.

"My second husband," I said, recalling that I had met Louis during this timeframe.

"His name and birthday?"

I told her. Alzina revealed something that absolutely astounded me.

"Actually, his secret agenda was to remain a child emotionally. Did you realize this?" she asked me.

"Not soon enough," I giggled.

"Of course, at that point, your secret agenda was to be in control."

Alzina was correct. I always had been the rock in the relationship, the go-to gal. I was the one who aggressively fought all of Louis's battles, even his CFO's lawsuit. I had wanted to be valuable and to feel valued, which was something I hadn't experienced with my father or with Ed. I guess I also needed to be in control—not of anyone else, but of myself. My father inadvertently had taught me not to depend on a man for my survival. My mother's independence reinforced it.

I had fallen in love with Ed because not only was he extremely smart, he was very nurturing—very much like a father, even though he was nearly a year younger than I. However, after we married, his nurturing disintegrated into condescension and criticism. I had felt superfluous, insignificant, and incompetent during the final years of our marriage. When Ed went on business trips, I'd stay up all night, painting, wallpapering, tiling, or making draperies because it was my only opportunity to decorate the house out of the glare of his critical eye.

In his sight, I rarely did anything right. By the time the marriage was over, my self-esteem could easily have slipped through the eye of a needle. I longed for a man who treasured me. Five years later, I met Louis, who thought I was brilliant, gorgeous, creative, and strong. He admired my independence.

"You [and Louis] got what you asked for," Alzina continued, "but you both outgrew it."

"If he outgrew it, I wasn't around to see it," I laughed.

"Oh, sure. He's all of 18 now!" she chuckled.

I thought she was going to say more about Louis. Instead, without any questions or additional information from me, Alzina revealed why I had felt so worthless during my marriage to Ed. She said that we had met before, in different bodies.

I sat straight up in my chair. At that time, she said, I was in a man's body and he was in a woman's.

"You treated women as if they were stupid," Alzina said.

I gasped. "*I* did that?"

"Yes. And he was one of those [women]. So, this is a karmic situation."

How did she know that Ed had treated me that way? I wondered.

This was the first time I'd actually encountered past life karma, in action. Everything I'd studied revealed that karma is not about punishment; it's about balance: it's the *natural* consequence of our actions. Everything in nature balances something else. This balance keeps the planets in their orbits and maintains the constant exchange of oxygen and carbon dioxide, so that plants and human bodies can coexist on this planet. In this case, Ed had brought balance to our previous relationship by treating me the way I had treated him.

I was so intrigued. I also was beginning to understand the synchronicity of life, beginning to grasp the natural pattern of reaping and sowing through a continuum of life experiences.

I was not being punished, I was being granted an opportunity to receive what I had given, to understand how it feels so that I can make better choices in the future. I didn't have

83

much time to enjoy that insight into the dynamics of my relationship with Ed before Alzina uncovered another one.

"You'd sail off, saying, 'I *will* return,' but you didn't return," she explained.

I was speechless. That drama also had been replayed in this lifetime. Ed and I had been through marriage counseling twice, and couldn't seem to get happy. I suggested that we separate, hoping that we might find the love we'd lost if we started fresh, dated each other again, and looked at each other with new eyes. I didn't want Angel to be a child of divorce, as Ed and I had been.

I thought Ed had agreed. But we never started fresh; he didn't return. Much to my surprise, he filed for divorce, and the karmic shoe was snugly on the other foot.

I never questioned Ed about his decision. In fact, he had to ask me if I'd received the divorce papers. He was surprised that I hadn't said anything about it. Heck, he hadn't mentioned that he'd filed, either, even though we spoke every day to coordinate Angel's nursery school pick-ups. Since it appeared to be some big hairy secret, I'd kept my mouth shut.

I also made no attempts to reconcile the marriage; I didn't want to be married to someone who didn't want to be married to me. What's the fun in that? Plus, I preferred that Angel grew up in two happy homes, rather than in one loveless one.

On a physical level, our marriage seemed dead. On a spiritual level, all was well. Our relationship simply had come full circle. Balance had been restored.

The reading with Alzina increased my desire to understand why I'd cast some of the other characters—especially the men—in my dramas. I certainly wanted to know more about Louis. I decided to follow-up Alzina's insights into my marriages with an energy reading at the Institute for Spiritual Healing.

Ellen told me that Garrett had partnered with another clairvoyant master. He and Ken had moved the Institute to another Evanston location, and had changed its name to the Psychic Institute.

As before, I was assigned to a team of students for the reading. What I like most about these readings is that the student teams are never the same. As a researcher, it eliminates any concern that someone might know me or remember something about me from a previous reading that would influence the outcome of the current one.

The way these readings work is that my energy, my spirit— my true essence, if you will—projects "pictures" or scenes that the trained clairvoyant can "see" and interpret.

I gave the students my name and Louis's, and then asked a typically vague question: Could they see a past life that would explain the karma that currently existed between Louis and me?

I said nothing more. They knew nothing of our relationship. Since I had, once again, reverted to my maiden name, Louis could have been my father, my brother, my boss or a client, as far as they knew.

The lead clairvoyant repeated my question and waited for the relevant scenes of my drama with Louis to play for her.

"He was your brother," was her first insight. "You took care of him."

The reader paused. Her eyes were closed, as she surveyed the scene my spirit was revealing to her. There was an awful knot in the pit of my stomach. *I took care of Louis in a previous life? What was this—history repeating?*

Even though a tape recorder captures the sessions, I always write detailed notes I can use as reference before I transcribe the tape, or in the event of a mechanical failure. Writing also forces me to look down so that my eyes won't reveal to the readers whether or not they're on the right track. (Not all of them have their eyes closed at the same time.)

She continued. "He's very frail, and it looks like there's something wrong with his legs. He's in a wheelchair. You've devoted your life to his care."

In this life, Louis was neither frail nor unhealthy. He was very thin and a bit bow-legged, but physically, he was very strong. On the other hand, he did sit a lot during the last three years of our marriage.

"If I took care of him in a past lifetime, where did the karma come from?" I asked.

"He was very needy," she said. "No matter what you did, no matter how much you gave, he wanted more."

Oh boy, some things don't change, I thought. Year Three of his unemployment, I asked Louis to explain the difference between him and a gigolo. (Don't gasp—you know I'm not tactful!) Louis's look told me that his response would be a no-brainer.

"I married you," he said, matter-of-factly.

Of course! What was I smoking? Since I was his wife, Louis reasoned, I should take care of him indefinitely. If the situation were reversed, he said, he'd do the same. *What was he smoking?*

"Finally, you just left him," the clairvoyant student said.

"Left him?" I repeated.

"Yeah," she responded. "You wanted a life of your own. I'm not saying you abandoned him, but you refused to be his primary caretaker."

Suddenly, I flashed back to a reading that I'd had with Barbara soon after Louis and I divorced. I recalled her saying something like, "But you didn't *leave him* this time." I didn't understand what she meant then and hadn't asked for an explanation. I was beginning to wish I had.

Interesting, I thought. Louis and I certainly had replayed that scene. As both my husband and my brother, he had become my dependent. In the previous life, my freedom had been restricted by duty; in the current life, by debt.

With all of the spooky similarities, my major concern was that Louis and I hadn't really balanced anything this time around, though the opportunity certainly had presented itself. He'd had a chance to protect me, take care of all my needs, but he didn't.

"Let me get this straight," I said to the student. "Do I owe him, or does he owe me?"

"He owes you, *Big Time*," she said, raising her brows.

Oh, no! Did that mean I was going to have to relive this drama with Louis in another body? Under no circumstances did I want to do that! What I'd learned through my studies was that forgiveness changes karmic patterns and erases the debt. Forgiveness creates balance.

I immediately closed my eyes and said a solemn prayer of forgiveness, canceling any and all karmic debt Louis owed me. I then sent him energies of Love, Light, and Peace. I gave myself closure and gave our relationship balance. I was done.

What Louis does is another matter. His soul may still feel that it needs to create a drama in which he is strong and unselfish. That's his spiritual business; I prefer not be on that stage, thank you very much. They can perform that show without this kid.

That student reading was quite revealing. I'd often advised Louis to find the lesson his soul was trying to teach him through the loss of his business and his protracted unemployment. I was sure that if he didn't learn that lesson, he wouldn't transform his experience.

Louis was paralyzed by fear, confined to a desk chair for much too long. He once said that his greatest fear was that he would lose me. His next greatest fear was that he would lose my respect. Sadly, he lost both.

He was afraid he'd have no money, so he always kept a $100 stash in several random places. He was afraid that someone would dent his car in a parking lot, so he'd park in the back of the lot, away from everyone else. He was always concerned that someone would take advantage of him, or steal something from him. If it wasn't one thing, it was another. He was always in a defensive mode.

"Fear is the opposite of faith," I kept warning him. "And fear is a powerful magnet—pulling the things we most dread into our lives."

And so it was.

13. Affirmations, Shmaffirmations!

Months after Louis moved out, I was robbing Peter to pay Paul (and creating or completing karma along the way), just to keep a roof over my head. The IRS was nipping at my heels and levying my bank accounts. Bill collectors had my home number on speed dial. Some of them were mean-spirited and disrespectful, creating more karma for themselves than collecting debts from me. Obviously, their corporate training had superceded their home training, and they had completely forgotten to treat others as they'd want to be treated if the shoe were on the other foot.

Trying to save my home and extricate myself from the quicksand of debt, I prayed and meditated. I repeated affirmations in books and created dozens of my own. I completed a 40-day course in abundance. I developed an aggressive, well-researched, 100-page business plan to launch an educational video production company. I took my plan to a couple of banks and also presented it to groups of investors.

I even entered the Publisher's Clearinghouse sweepstakes. Child, I was leaving no stone unturned.

As my financial life completely swirled out of control, I continued to search for answers. I gravitated toward the works of personal development gurus who claimed that we have the power to create our own realities. We become what we think about, they said. It's mind over matter. *Just what I needed to hear.*

Friends declared that Satan was busy in my life. I declared that since there is only One Presence in the Universe, and since Darkness and Light cannot occupy the same space, it must be God who was busy in my life. I kept affirming, *there can be no Darkness where there is Light.*

I had so many prayer candles burning around the house; you would have thought I hadn't paid the electric bill. Actually, it was one of the few I could afford. I read books and listened to motivational tapes, some of which told me that I needed a deep desire to accomplish my goals. I certainly had that.

Other authors instructed me to attach a strong emotion to my desire: how would I feel, after my accomplishment? I imagined feeling deliriously happy, once I had saved my home and paid off all my bills and vendors.

Seth Speaks was very definitive about the creative power of our thoughts: "Mental images, accompanied by strong emotion, are blueprints therefore upon which a corresponding physical object or condition or event will, in your terms, appear....

"If you are... of a highly pessimistic nature, given to thoughts and feelings of potential disaster, then these thoughts will be faithfully reproduced in experience.

"Your thoughts and emotions begin their journey into physical actualization at the moment of conception."

The Bible said, more or less, the same: "What things soever ye desire, when ye pray, believe that ye receive them and ye shall have them."

Ellen had given me a set of inspiring cards from *A Course in Miracles*. One of them said, "Miracles are natural. When they do not occur, something has gone wrong." I was ready for my miracle—natural or manufactured. Who cared?

Self-help books told me to think about every detail of my desired goal. No problem. I envisioned myself opening envelopes containing checks with lots of zeroes after the dollar sign—made payable to me, of course. I saw myself sitting at my computer with dozens of checks spitting out of the printer, paying every one of my delinquent bills, in full. I felt like squealing with delight at the mere thought of it!

What else would I do when my ship came in? I heard myself talking to the supervisor of the construction crew that was renovating my kitchen and all four bathrooms. The house was abuzz with activity. Another crew was replacing my roof. Through the library window, I could see a third crew digging up my blacktop circular drive and replacing it with bricks in a herringbone pattern. In the backyard, more workers busily installed a similarly patterned brick patio near the pool. I was one new-reality-creating sister.

Checklist: I'd made the decision. I had the strong desire and the vision. I felt the emotion, and did the work. According to everything I'd read, I should receive my desired result.

Shazzam! I was just weeks away from losing the house at public auction when several large clients contracted me to produce new training and marketing videos.

"You know, with these new contracts, you probably could refinance your mortgage and save your house," my friend Craig suggested.

He was right. With so much equity in the house, I discovered that I was eligible for a mortgage with a new lender. About a week before the deadline to redeem my home before the auction, a mortgage broker who specialized in intensive-care cases such as mine told me she'd found a lender that would refinance my home.

Prayers answered! Affirmations manifested! My miracle had appeared! Praise God! Thank you, Jesus! I collapsed into grateful tears. Ellen cried with me.

Christmas was approaching, and everything in the business world was grinding to a halt. The mortgage broker said she would need two weeks to complete the property title research. She instructed me to ask my bank to delay the foreclosure sale by two weeks, so we could pay off the loan.

Good news for me, good news for the bank. Moving ahead with the auction meant that the bank would have to purchase my home for the amount of my outstanding debt; then they'd have to wait at least a month for the court to confirm the sale. After that, they'd have to sell the home to recoup their money, and await the closing of the new sale. Waiting two weeks for me would save them a lot of time, hassle, and money. I quickly dialed the collections officer.

Just as quickly, he refused my request. They had waited long enough, he said. I was devastated. My mortgage broker was stunned. Why would any bank in America refuse to allow someone to pay off a delinquent loan? A loan officer's job was to get these loans off the books, as quickly as possible. His refusal defied sound business practice. Why were they choosing to wait months longer than it would take me to pay off the loan? It was so irrational that I was highly suspicious.

The bank's poor business judgment aside, Ellen and I were more confused by what we perceived as a mixed signal from God. Why would I suddenly be blessed with the money I needed to save my home, only to be kicked to the curb? It defied our perception of the way God worked.

The bank's decision meant that I would have to move immediately after the holidays. Within a week, I found a new place: a beautiful four-bedroom apartment in South Shore, in a six-flat building around the corner from Home #19.

I explained my situation to the lovely couple who owned the building. They didn't have fond memories of my bank's dealings with minority consumers, so they were willing to give me a lease, even if my credit scores would make anyone's heart stop.

I always have what I need had become my mantra; now, it was becoming my reality. I needed a beautiful home. I needed to feel safe and peaceful again.

Seth says that the most painful thing we humans do is resist change. I knew it was best to adjust to the loss of my home, but the thought of packing up 12 rooms and just as many closets made me choke.

The fabulous new space psyched me for the move. It was just the inspiration I needed. And it confirmed that God was still with me, after all. I admit that I had begun to wonder.

Time was running out, but I just couldn't seem to start. Nothing in my spirit was telling me to pack a box. That worried me. I don't usually freeze in times of crisis. If anything, everybody can always count on me to calmly get the job done. One of my news directors once remarked that he always could rely on me to keep my head, when everyone else in the newsroom was losing theirs. Where was that girl?

The next day, I really thought I'd be energized enough to start packing, but the urge still wouldn't come. If anything was pushing me at all, it was the urge to write a letter of protest to the bank. That sounded highly irrational, I told myself, and so I ignored it. It was time to move on. But the spirit was relentless.

True, I suspected that the bank would've have given me the two weeks to refinance if I were not playing my role in blackface, or if the props surrounding my home were not country clubs that didn't admit actors in blackface. A letter wouldn't change any of that.

The bankers and their attorneys were so offended by my attempts to save my home, you'd have thought I'd walked up to their desks and slapped them upside their heads. They were absolutely vile. The bank's attorneys treated my lawyer so disrespectfully that he decided to send a young white associate to make his court appearances, to avoid further personal confrontation and the possibility of jeopardizing my case.

With little time to spare before being evicted, I was bedridden with the flu. I hadn't been sick in a couple of years.

I don't do sick, was my mantra. And I meant it.

"I told you! I don't think you're supposed to go anywhere," Ellen insisted. "The Universe is telling you to be still."

"Riiiight. For how long—until the sheriff arrives and puts my stuff out in the cul-de-sac?" I asked. This girl was making no sense at all.

Ellie was right about one thing, though. There was a Divine Plan, a Big-Picture that this scene fit into, but it clearly wasn't created with a write-your-own-ending option. I'd never felt so powerless or frustrated in all my life. If it's true that we are wading in an unlimited reservoir of information and guidance, why was I crawling on a dry riverbed?

Adversity had never tripped me before; this time, it knocked me to my knees. And that was not a bad thing.

Admittedly, when times were good and my marriage was solid, I didn't seem to pray much. I went to church on Sundays, read lots of spiritual literature, and mouthed words of thanksgiving. But I didn't pray, because I didn't think I needed to. I was healthy; I had an adoring husband and a brilliant, talented, and oh-so adorable child, a good-paying job, and a lovely home with a driveway full of cars. *Why ask God for more? I thought. I have so much. I'll relinquish my time to someone who needs it.*

What I didn't realize then is that praying isn't about begging or petitioning. Praying is consciously making a connection with the One Presence that is always with us, acknowledging the God Light and the God Power within each of us, honoring God's Love, and expressing gratitude for God's undying presence. That's the kind of prayer Carrie had been encouraging me to do years earlier. As one of our ministers often says, prayer doesn't change *things*. It changes *us*.

The widely advertised real estate auction day arrived, and the plot became more sinister. The loan officer had told me that the bank's practice was to bid the amount of the outstanding balance. Apparently, they decided to make an exception in my case, since I had fought so hard to resist foreclosure. They bid about $100,000 below my home's market value, leaving an outstanding mortgage balance of nearly $40,000. Then they filed court documents to assign my wages for the $40,000 difference.

Score one for early retirement. There were no wages to assign. *Whew!*

On the day the court was scheduled to confirm the bank's low-ball bid, I strapped the biggest, most beautiful Christmas tree I could find onto the roof of my car. It was a full-bodied spruce that stood nearly eight feet tall. After decorating the house inside, I spent hours stringing tiny white lights in the shrubs in front of the house and in the huge evergreen in the middle of the yard, just as I had in previous years. And I sang gospel songs. Loudly.

"God is so good to me!" I sang, over and over. "He gives me everything!"

14. Word Warrior

Out of the corner of my eye, I noticed two cars coming up the hill toward my house. Because you almost needed a map to find the street, and it wasn't on the route to anywhere else, cars rarely ventured onto it by accident.

Both cars slowed when they neared the top of the hill. i pretended to be oblivious to the woman in each car who was staring incredulously at me. Finally, they passed. When they reached the bottom of the hill about a block away, one car pulled alongside the other. They talked to each other for a moment, and then drove on.

They're probably connected to someone at the bank or the bank's law firm, I laughed to myself.

"Wanted to show off your new house to your friend, did you? And you can't figure out why I'm out here decorating, instead of inside packing, huh? Now you've got something to discuss at the dinner table tonight, Girlfriend," I called out defiantly.

If this was to be the last Christmas in my beautiful home, I was determined that it was going to be my best Christmas ever. Besides, Angel was coming home; I wanted everything to be as normal as possible. No eviction drama.

"Make a sign of the cross with some salt, right at your doorstep," Barbara advised me. "It'll protect your home."

Barbara had a spiritual antidote for everything. She and I had talked at length about my tug-of-war with the bank. Like Ellen, she didn't feel it was time for me to move.

When I finished stringing the lights, I poured salt in a distinct sign of the cross in the driveway outside my front door. It was almost dusk. I walked into the foyer and flipped the switch for the outside lights. The yard lit up.

Oh, how beautiful! I thought, looking back outside. I tossed back my head, opened my arms, and said, "The Light of the Christ surrounds and protects this place. I am safe from all harm. God is with me now and always, and all is well. So it is. Thank you, God."

I closed the big double doors, trying with all my might to believe my affirmation. Then I fell against the doors and cried.

As I calmed myself, once again, an inner voice urged me to write the bank a letter. Louis had called me the Word Warrior, because I could write some ferocious letters when people got on my nerves. My family called them "Pat Letters". Recipients needed Teflon mitts to hold one of my angry missives.

This crisis, I felt, could not be remedied by a letter. "Nothing I write can stop this train. These people intend to take my house and destroy me financially for having the nerve to try to save it," I sighed as I pulled off my coat.

The bankers were playing Oscar-caliber villains. They were nasty and intimidating, and I no longer wanted to share a stage with them. I'd rather lose my house than lose my mind. Plus, I didn't have the superhuman energy required to pry my door key out of their fists.

But the urge to write a letter of protest kept nagging me. I told myself—and the spirit bugging me about this letter—that I had too much work to do to sit down and write *anybody*.

The nagging wouldn't let up. Finally, I gave in. There was only one problem.

"I haven't the slightest idea who I'm supposed to write to," I told Ellen. "And what, pray tell, am I supposed to say?"

"Got me, Little Girl. Why don't you just leave yourself open to receive whatever comes to you from spirit, then write it down?"

I agreed. After writing the words that came to me, I addressed two letters: one to the bank's Vice-President in Charge of Colored People, whose job was minority community damage control, another to its president and chief operating officer. I was sure they didn't know that the loan department wasn't acting in the best interest of the bank's shareholders.

When they didn't respond, I was infuriated and invalidated. I also was a highly skilled journalist. I faxed a news release to every member of the board of directors, complaining about the bank's treatment. My home was at stake here! I was not going to be ignored.

The news release immediately captured the attention of the VP, who called me minutes after the release slid out of his fax machine. The release also got the president's attention. I had dared to embarrass him in front of his board. After that, it was as if this man's survival depended upon snatching the roof from over my head. The fight got ugly, very personal, and was of inexplicable importance to the chief operating officer of one of the largest banks in North America. I was not intimidated.

I fought back with my full arsenal: my sharp mind, my righteous indignation, WordPerfect, and my fax machine. I called my prospective landlords and told them that I was going to stay and fight the bank. They wished me luck and told me to check back with them if I changed my mind.

I donned my armor and battled the bank through every state and federal agency, its parent bank in Canada, the Federal Reserve, and pertinent congressional committees. I even wrote Attorney General Janet Reno and President Bill Clinton.

Watching the action, my friend Sandra quipped, "Ain't nothin' scarier than an angry, educated black woman with a fax machine!"

If I was going down, these boys were going to know that they'd been in a nasty fight.

I received letters of support—OK, they were closer to gestures of empathy—from the chairman of the congressional housing committee, the congressman in my district, and both of my senators. Senator Paul Simon wrote a letter to the bank. Senator Carol Moseley-Braun called me to personally voice her concern about the situation. I'm telling you, this battle scene had all the pageantry and star power of an Andrew Lloyd Webber production!

On encouraging days, Ellen and I celebrated. Then the bank would fire its next shot and we were diving for cover. Nothing—inquiries from Congress, positive thoughts, creative visualizations, candles, or prayers—could deter this bank's full-out assault.

I tried to accept the inevitable. Obviously, it's time to leave, I told myself. It's time to move on. Moving certainly doesn't intimidate me. I've got it down to a science. But I still was very confused. Do we or don't we have the power to create what we desire in life? Are we not writing our own scripts? Do we have free will? Or is free will powerless in a duel with predestination? And where, pray-tell, is God?

Something told me to review a transcript from a research consultation I'd had months earlier. It was a session with an out-of-body being, like Seth. His name was Dr. Peebles.

I'd read about Dr. Peebles in a remarkable book that Ellen had loaned me, *To Dance with Angels*. It was the only book I'd ever read in my life that I didn't want to end. It was as if I were saying goodbye to an old friend. I had resonated so much with this wise and delightfully charming being, channeled through a gentleman named Tom Jacobson. I was so overwhelmed with sadness that I cried when I turned to the last page.

At the end of the book was contact information for Jacobson, who lived in California at the time. I called and scheduled a telephone consultation.

It was summer, and Angel was home. When the day of the consultation arrived, she, Louis, Ellen, and I had huddled around my office speakerphone. I was tickled that Dr. Peebles' voice sounded just as I thought it would—a brogue of sorts.

He wanted to know my first name, nothing more. That was less information than I'd ever given anyone. Then he absolutely floored us with his insights that were very specific, rather than vague and general, despite having such a tiny bit of data.

Now that I was being led back to the 23-page handwritten transcript of that call, I wondered if the answers to my questions were tucked inside. I've often found that something said during a research expedition blows right over my head; months later, the words make all the sense in the world.

Suddenly, there they were, three words: *safety, sanctuary,* and *security.* Wow! Like Alzina, Dr. Peebles remarked about some control issues I'd had in previous human bodies, but he went much farther than she did. He said that often I controlled large numbers of people, by creating and imposing law upon them. That could explain my current disdain for control freaks.

Dr. Peebles said that to balance my controlling role, which I seem to have played during many incarnations, I would have to "go beyond any promise of safety, sanctuary, and security" in this lifetime.

I hadn't understood what he meant, at the time, but now I was beginning to see why my life had been so unstable, why I moved so much, and why I was experiencing severe financial insecurity. Then I saw the section I obviously was sent to find:

"These are old, old chasms, repeated over again that your soul is not going to let you get away with this time. How can your soul not let you get away with that? Well, to orchestrate your life in such a way that no matter how hard you try with these [controlling] attributes, they will not work from any vantage point—forcing you to do what you are doing right now: to question, to evaluate and to create a new premise for life."

Thank you, God! I sighed as I gently put the transcript on the desk in front of me. *Thank you for that.* So, that's why my affirmations and prayers had fallen on deaf ears; my soul was in control, bringing me the lessons I needed. I immediately reached for the phone to call Ellen.

"Sometimes, the best answer to our prayers is 'no'," I sighed.

"*No?*" she screamed. "God would not tell you no. God *cannot* tell you no. You are God's child! It is His good pleasure to give you the kingdom. Prosperity is yours by Divine Inheritance!"

"First of all, I don't get the God can't tell me 'no' part," I argued. "You act like 'no' is a negative thing. 'No' can be the most loving thing we tell our children, so I'm not buying it.

"I am trapped in a body. My vision is limited. God's vision is unlimited. My God-Self knows why I'm here, and what I set as my goals when I came here. Who am I going to trust: my brain or my God?"

"Uh-uh! You have free will. You act like losing your house was predestined," she yelled back at me. "You can create anything you want! You decided you wanted to stay in the house. You claimed it; I'm in agreement; it's yours, and no one can take it from you, Little Girl!"

"Ellie, Ellie. Girlfriend, let's be real. Someone did take it from me; remember? The bank bought the house at auction." I was not getting through. So I decided to come at her from a different angle.

"Do you think we are just physical beings?"

"Of course not!" she said. "We're spiritual beings in bodies, having a physical experience."

"OK, then. God has granted free will to which part of me—the physical being or the spiritual? Which part, do you think, has the control?"

"I would guess it's the spiritual, since that's the real you," she said.

"Suppose a spiritual being decided exactly what it wanted to accomplish before stepping into the body that would be known as Pat Arnold."

"OK," she said.

"Suppose this spirit wanted to have certain experiences in that body, and even made agreements with other spirits to make sure those experiences were realized. It's like if you and I went to a banquet and I told you, 'Ell, keep me away from that dessert table. I don't care what you have to do; make sure I don't go near it,' and you agreed."

"OK, I can see where you're going with this, but even if you decide something on the spiritual level, you can change your mind!" she argued. "You can always change your mind. And you did. You decided you wanted to stay in that house."

That girl could be so exasperating!

"Ellie, what if my physical self decided to stay in the house, but my God-Self, my spiritual self, didn't want to? This body is just a space suit, after all. Its only function is to allow my soul to have the experience it wants. My body does not have the power to make my soul follow its directions.

"That's not to say that the body can't make a decision and the soul won't say, 'Cool! Let's do it!' But sometimes, the body makes a decision and the soul says, 'That's wonderful, but it doesn't suit my purpose. Maybe another time.'

"My soul knows what's for my highest good. My brain

doesn't. My body doesn't. I think my results prove that what the body does or says doesn't make the slightest bit of difference, if the soul says no.

"I prayed the prayers, said the affirmations, I made sure my thoughts were positive. I worked hard to earn the money I needed to pull myself out of this hole, Ell. I've done it all! I can't do any more!" I shouted.

"There's got to be something we overlooked. There's got to be something else you can do," she insisted.

"Girl, what you're talking about is the tail wagging the dog. Would you put on a costume and let it choose the masquerade ball, if you knew exactly where you wanted to go? Staying in this house may not help me meet the goals that I—I repeat, I— established for myself, coming into this body. No one else predetermined it for me or imposed it on me. I, as spirit, made that decision. I, as spirit, am creating my own experience. I, as spirit, am driving this vehicle."

Ellen didn't want to hear it, but I could be as stubborn as she could. We arrived on the planet only two days apart— practically simultaneously, in spirit.

"Ell, you act like you've never prayed for something and didn't get it!" I yelled. "Remember when your father was ill? You told him that he didn't have to die if he didn't want to. He said he didn't want to die. We both know what happened.

"He didn't lie to you. His physical self did not want to leave here. It didn't know anyplace but here. His soul, on the other hand, was ready to do something else, somewhere else. The soul is ultimately in charge, not the body."

I could tell that I'd finally struck a chord, but Ellen didn't want to admit it. I'm sure that part of her resistance was that she wanted a "Daniel versus the downtown lion" victory. We had become like sisters. My losses probably felt as if they were hers. I'd lost my role as a full-time mother; I'd lost another marriage, and now, this. She probably thought I couldn't bear another loss. Or maybe, she simply couldn't stand witnessing another one.

"Well, possession is nine-tenths of the law," she said resolutely. "Until the moving truck pulls into that driveway, it's your house."

Ellen was right about one thing. My frontal assault did significantly delay the bank's possession of my home. Because of the ongoing investigations of the suspicious refusal to grant me a two-week delay, the bank had decided not to evict me until the final government probe was complete.

But the bankers were busy working behind the scenes, in what had mushroomed into a teeth-clenching drama. Barbara's spiritual eye detected that the bankers were thoroughly investigating me. Later, an insider at the bank inadvertently confirmed Barbara's observation. A former colleague also reported an unusual sighting: a few of the bank's employees were on a tour of the newsroom and editing areas with the station's general manager. My friend considered it an intimidation tactic. The bankers weren't aware that I had moved to a different network. I had been freelancing at my old station when I launched my fight to save my home.

The intrigue didn't stop there. Senator Moseley-Braun's office and I had asked the Federal Reserve Bank in Chicago to investigate the matter. After waiting more than a month for the Fed's determination, I received notice that it had ruled in the bank's favor. Internal documents I later received through the Freedom of Information Act confirmed my suspicions. My case had been closed two days after it was received—without any investigation at all.

My last hope rested with the U.S. Department of Housing and Urban Development. That investigation was still pending.

It was almost Christmas again. I was suffering severe battle fatigue. It had not been a good day in the war room, my basement office. I had just received another brutal and irrational letter from the bank's attorneys. I walked across the large room to go upstairs. As I reached for the banister, my body went limp in absolute surrender.

With head bowed and tears flowing, I cried out loud, "How could they treat someone so inhumanely? How would they feel, if someone treated them this way?"

I stopped, panicked. What if I had done this to someone before? What if my soul was bringing balance to that situation?

Recalling what I had learned about karma, I added: "Mother-Father God, if I have *ever* done this to anyone else, I forgive myself. I know that you forgive me, because you are a forgiving God. I now release any karmic ties that bind me to those whom I've hurt. If this is new karma being created, I forgive those who are trying so vigilantly to hurt me, and I release them from the natural results of their actions."

I stood there for a moment, waiting for peace to be restored to my body and spirit. Then I slowly walked up the stairs.

15. To Hell and Back

Although the bank hadn't attempted to physically remove me from the house, the bankers did make it as uncomfortable as possible for me to remain. One of the collections officers put my home's gas and electric accounts in his name, and ordered the service shut off.

Barbara had told me that someone connected to the bank was planning to move into my home. Still, I hadn't expected this. They were attacking me from every angle imaginable! I had to be a contortionist to keep up.

I visited the utility companies, explained that the ownership of the home was in dispute, and requested that they restore my name to the accounts, which were not delinquent. Unlike the bank, the utilities made a logical business decision. They preferred to continue being paid for service.

Next, the bank tried to shut off my water supply. When I stopped a worker from disconnecting the meter, two collections officers left their desks, drove 45 miles from downtown, and arrived at my door with two village police officers in tow.

Were home visits in their job descriptions? Certainly, they couldn't give everyone in their loan portfolio such personal attention.

If those weren't Gestapo tactics, then the bogus real estate appraisal the bank commissioned to justify their low-ball bid on my home certainly qualifies. How do I know it was bogus? First, the bank suspiciously selected an appraiser from the northwest side of the city, instead of from the south suburbs, where I lived. It's highly irregular to engage an appraiser who's unfamiliar with a residential area of the subject property.

It was clear from his appraisal report that not only was he unfamiliar with my suburb and the property values there, this man had appraised the home without venturing into the vicinity. His map didn't even pinpoint the correct location of my home; and his list of comparable home sales was from an incomparable development, nowhere near it.

I was outraged, but my protests fell on deaf ears. The bank played crazy, and the organization that monitors appraisers said it could do nothing about that appraisal because the appraiser didn't become a member of their association until after he had done the dastardly deed. How many brick walls would I hit?

After nearly a year of combat, my domicile war drama ended as it had begun—with a fax. It came late one evening, long after the bank was closed. I held my breath as I watched the bank's logo slide through my machine. The fax advised me that HUD had found that the bank had acted reasonably. In less than 30 days, the bank would take possession of my home.

My knees buckled. My hands began to tremble. But I couldn't cry. Of all nights, my mother was visiting. I didn't want to upset her, so I couldn't reveal that anything was wrong. If I could hold it together a few minutes more, she would be in bed.

The curtain finally had dropped on this very painful scene. The fax in my hand felt like discharge papers after a long, embittered military engagement. I walked slowly into each room, surveying my fort and beginning to let go of it.

They say that if you expect one outcome and plan for another, you get what you plan for. As a consequence, I'd been very careful not to make any moving plans. Now, I had no choice. However, I knew that if it was time to move, God already had picked out a perfect spot for me. I was more than ready to be led from the battlefield.

I've always been a city mouse. Moving to the suburbs had been Louis's idea. It would feel great to go back home.

I searched the real estate section of the neighborhood newspaper from my favorite part of the city, Hyde Park-Kenwood, and within a few days, I found it: a gorgeous, newly rehabbed three-bedroom coach house, nestled among some historic mansions.

The owner told me that someone else had rented the place, but he took my name and number and said he would give it to his wife, who handled their real estate transactions. The next day, I received a call that the woman who had rented the coach house suddenly had changed her mind. Did I still want the place? *Absolutely*—as soon as I could organize the move from Home #21.

Again, the thought of packing up a 12-room house sucked the wind out of me. On the other hand, the vision of the Cook County Sheriff's band of merry men packing for me quickly put the wind at my back.

They say that every thought is a prayer. Like a lot of people, it wasn't until my happy life was threatened that I began to pray in earnest. I called on God from the moment I opened my eyes in the morning until I closed them again at night. I took on prayer partners, went to prayer meetings.

I loosed my grip on the house a little more each day, by reading something spiritually uplifting. One night, I plowed into a book Ellen had loaned me, *Dialogue on Awakening*. She was very excited about it. Authors Tom and Linda Carpenter claimed to have captured channeled messages from Jesus of Nazareth.

One message, in particular, hit home: "Exercising the Will of God can only be recognized...as your own expression of peace and harmony. There is nothing for God to take over, as you surrender to His Will. God's Will now, as it always has been, is for you to experience only that which is for you to experience: ... be only Love with the ... knowledge that you are ... an extension of His perfection. There is nothing for you to do to accomplish this because it is your natural state."

Most of my life, I had thought that God was someone else who lived someplace else. However, as I seriously studied the teachings of Jesus and others, I discovered that God is where I am. We are one. If God's will had been done, *my* will had also. I certainly needed confirmation of that.

Everything I read during that period seemed to have the same message: God and I were on the same page. God's will was for me to accomplish what I intended when I entered this body. Those accomplishments would bring me peace and harmony, and that was God's will for me.

Fighting to stay in my home had given me neither peace nor harmony. Should I have surrendered before the enemy took me captive? I wondered.

I dropped to my knees, calmed myself, and took a deep, cleansing breath. Almost immediately, tears began to stream down my face. Perhaps it was remorse for not surrendering sooner. Maybe it was sadness for the predicament in which I found myself. I began to pray positively, thankfully, as if I'd already received my heart's desire:

"Mother-Father God, I surrender my will to you. I know right now that Your arms are open to receive me and direct me along the path toward my Highest Good. I thank you, Mother-Father God, for loving me so unconditionally, and for patiently waiting to direct my path. My only desire is to follow that path. I release this house and all my possessions, knowing that You are the source of all I have and all I need. I relinquish the desire to hold onto anything that is not truly mine.

"I ask that You light that path, so I can clearly see where You want me to go. I hold no expectations of any particular outcome. I know that by walking according to Your Will, everything will resolve itself perfectly, for the Highest Good of all concerned. I thank You for this Truth. I accept it as The Truth. And so it is."

I remained in the moment, feeling such a sense of relief from having stripped myself of everything that was creating stress and tension in my life. I visualized my body meeting my God-Self on the street, handing over all my bills, my house, my troubles, and walking away with my burdens lifted. What an incredible release! For the first time in months, I slept straight through the night.

As I tried to organize the move, I recalled how long I had held onto the hope of keeping my house. Much of that hope had come from Barbara. She had told me any number of times that my battle with the bank would end in weeks, days, even minutes. She also told me that I would win—and that my story would be in newspapers and magazines.

Ellen had no confidence in Barbara's readings. "Either she's wrong—or you were Don Quixote in a past life!"

I certainly felt as though I had been swinging at windmills. "Well, Sancho Panza, I guess we'd better find out."

A few days later, the two of us headed to the Psychic Institute. I was looking for a deeper understanding, the root cause of the battle with the bank. As usual, I didn't give the students any specifics. I just asked about the disharmony between the bank and me.

The lead clairvoyant student said that I was showing her a past life that could hold the answer: I was a knight whose duty it was to seize the land of those who owed money to the monarchy. On occasion, she said, I would convert the land for my personal use.

I shuddered. The clairvoyant student had no idea that the medieval land grab she saw was such a chilling parallel to my current life struggle.

When I told Barbara about the reading, she was horrified, and vehemently disagreed. This was not a karmic situation, she insisted. My history was fighting for those who couldn't fight for themselves.

I knew that certainly was my history in this body, but I couldn't be as certain about previous excursions during my soul's eternal life. Maybe medieval debauchery had made an indelible impression on my soul. Maybe I wanted to know how it felt to lose my home, so that I could have a deeper understanding of what I had done to others. In this broader context, the bank's callous refusal to let me save it, the cruelty of its attorneys and executives, the extraordinary visit from the loan officers, as well as the fruitlessness of all the investigations made sense.

It wasn't until I removed my art from the walls that the impact of the drama finally hit me. Bare, the walls screamed, "this is not your home," triggering an emotional meltdown.

I managed to get the bulk of my possessions out of the house a couple of days before the sheriff was scheduled to evict me. I had sold or given away a truckload of furniture, appliances, and clothing. Still, it took me a week to get everything out. The movers filled up their huge van twice. Much of the stuff went into storage because it wouldn't fit into the cute little coach house.

For several days afterward, I returned to clean my former home. It was a matter of pride. Mother had taught us to leave a place in as good or better condition than we found it.

This home had been good to me. I was not going to dishonor it, or my upbringing, by damaging it in any way.

I left with my head held high, not as a defeated soldier.

A few days later, I returned to pick up a mirror I'd forgotten on the wall in my office. As I rounded the corner into the cul-de-sac, I pushed my garage door transmitter. Nothing happened. I pushed it again as I pulled into the driveway. Nothing.

It was the final blow to my gut. I was officially a visitor at that address. I took a deep breath, fought the tears, and drove back down the hill.

16. What Goes Around, Comes Around

The coach house had been impeccably restored and updated. The architect, my landlady Petronela, had done a superlative job of keeping the best of the old and adding the best of the new. The place not only had warmth and charm, it was cozy and isolated. I felt so blessed!

After I'd arranged my furniture and hung my precious artwork, the space was breathtaking. Somehow, I'd managed to fit select pieces of furniture from the living room, family room, den and dining room of Home #21 into the large living/dining room of the coach house.

On the interior wall sat my piano, which the movers almost didn't get up the narrow staircase. I prayed the entire hour that they struggled with it. The piano had been my refuge from stress. I needed it with me.

Shortly after moving, I learned that Louis had been calling the bank repeatedly for months, trying to get his name deleted from the defaulted mortgage note. Since he had signed a quitclaim deed when I was trying to refinance, he felt that I should be solely responsible for the entire $40,000 shortfall from the foreclosure sale. I guess he reasoned that he shouldn't be penalized, because he had done absolutely nothing to block the bank from seizing our home—and I do mean nothing.

Louis's role is one of the more intriguing aspects of this drama. On the surface, it appeared that he'd fed me to the wolves. But if I'd learned anything, I'd learned not to confuse the action on stage with reality. Life is synchronous. Everything serves a purpose. I had to think more universally.

The picture of my medieval land grab popped into my mind. I gasped. What if Louis and I had agreed, before we came into these bodies, that he would do precisely what he did—set the scene for the vicious battle over the home? If he was playing that role at my request, he was merely fulfilling an agreement. In that case, he had created no new karma through his actions (or, more accurately, inaction).

True, Louis's later attempts to shift, rather than share, the entire mortgage and delinquent tax debt certainly could be characterized as overacting. Even spiritually, there is absolutely no way I would have scripted or agreed to that, his bankruptcy filing—which eradicated the divorce court's order for him to repay the $80,000 he owed me—or his covert seizure of the balance of our frequent hotel guest reward points, with which he took an all-expenses paid trip to San Francisco. My script wouldn't have directed him to use my American Express corporate account to pay for his hotel room the night I ordered him to leave, either. Yeah, I definitely think he used his free-will to do a bit of karma-creatin' improv.

But the reason I'm entertaining the possibility that Louis and I agreed to the core drama—but not his karma-creating scenes—stems from a discovery I made later, during another sleuthing session at the Psychic Institute.

I had returned to my research after I was safely settled into my new place. I wanted to look behind the curtain of my eviction drama. Previously, I had asked about my relationship with the bank, but not about the bankers. I asked first about the president.

"I need to understand the dynamics of my relationship with Rick Peck." I said nothing more.

"Give us your full name, then his," I was instructed.

I did.

"Once more."

I did it again.

"OK. One final time...."

I must have looked shell-shocked when I walked out of the room.

"What the hell did they say?" Ellen gasped.

"You're not going to believe this. This is deep," I said as we walked to my car. "Remember the last reading, when I asked for information about the bank and me? This time, I asked about the dudes at the bank, starting with my fave, little Ricky Peck. You'll never guess what pictures my spirit showed them: a lifetime when I was a knight."

Ellen spun around. "Like last time? These were different students?"

"Yeah. I'd never seen these folks before in my life. You know they don't take notes, and I have the only tape from that last reading."

I unlocked the car doors. "I've never had two different teams of students dig up the same response, let alone the same lifetime."

"Except the leaking money thing—and your father being in your space, trying to keep you from running too much male energy," Ellen corrected me. She was right. Those had been recurring messages over the years.

"Yeah, but this was different. Plus, I never said that Rick Peck was involved with the bank. Even if they had notes from my previous reading, they wouldn't have known that the two questions were related.

"But they said that I was showing them pictures of a lifetime when I was a knight. They told me I was very well known in the kingdom, one of the king's favorites. I was rugged. Women loved me, and I loved battle. I felt it was my duty to do whatever the king told me to do—even if it meant killing people."

"Hmmm, didn't Dr. Peebles say that you used to use the law to justify all kinds of behavior?" Ellen said, recalling the reading she'd witnessed a few years earlier. She buckled her seatbelt. "Remember? You thought it might be something bad that you did. So where does Peck fit in here?" she asked.

"From what I could gather, his family was indebted to the monarchy. Apparently, you could wipe out your debt if you won a duel with one of the king's knights," I said as I pulled away from the curb. "Peck had to fight me—the meanest son of a bitch in the kingdom. I killed him. They said it disgraced his family. And guess what else?"

"What?"

I had to catch my breath before I could repeat it. "They were tossed off their land."

"Whoa! Sounds like a karmic debt!" she yelled. "Let me get this straight: Last time, Peck was fighting you for his land. That could explain why this battle was so bitter and personal. He's subconsciously avenging his previous death and the loss of his family's land?"

"That's what my spiritual history seems to say."

"Did the students see anything else?"

"Well, I asked them to relate that incident to present time. The first thing one of them saw was that Peck was out of his mind with rage. Actually, she said it was a combination of rage and fear. He vacillates between the two. She said he is so furious with me that he can't contain himself."

"That's 'cause you kept messing with him. He couldn't scare you. Every time he thought he'd knocked you out, you bounced

116

right back. That would be scary—and infuriating. He probably hadn't considered you to be such a mighty warrior." Ellen paused, smiling with feigned sympathy. "Po' thang."

She was right. A pen is a mighty sword, if you know how to use it. My caustic-but-reasoned responses to the attorney's illogical excuses for the bank's action must have been one of the greatest frustrations of their lives. One of the bank's attorneys had even told me that I was "a worthy adversary."

"Yeah, the clairvoyant student even mentioned that I had been condescending to Peck!" I laughed, recalling the day I walked into his office.

I had expected Peck to be a big brute of a man. It was quite empowering to look down on the bully who was trying to take my home. I was about a head taller.

The clairvoyant student had nailed it: I was irate and condescending. I thought the bankers were goofballs for not waiting two weeks for full payment of the delinquent loan, and I didn't hesitate to tell them so. Months later, I was in the house, at their expense. I didn't have a mortgage; I didn't have a lease. They were receiving neither principal nor interest. I couldn't find a brain cell among the bunch.

But winning the battles and winning the war were two different things. I sighed.

"What goes around comes around. This appears to have been a rematch," I said as the traffic light turned red. "Only the roles are reversed. Now Peck's part of the establishment, and he's got them to support his irrational behavior, just like I had the monarchy to support mine.

"But here's the kicker; this one almost knocked me out of my chair."

"Girl, don't tell me there's more!" Ellen closed her eyes and threw her head against the headrest.

"You know why Peck is really ticked off?" I hesitated. "The student said that it's because I released the karma."

Ellen opened her eyes and frowned at me. "What did she mean by that?"

"I was confused by that too, for a moment. Then I remembered. One day while I was still in the house, I wondered whether this situation might be karmic. I stopped, prayed, and forgave myself, just in case I had ever brutalized anyone the way the bank was brutalizing me. I very specifically released any karma attached to that past situation.

"Now, how did that student know that? I was in my basement. Alone. After it happened, it didn't cross my mind to mention it to anyone—not even you."

Ellen's jaw dropped. For once, she was speechless.

"So, Girl, it looks like Peck and I were locked in a battle that he had waited centuries to have with me. And in the middle of the fight—*snip!* I cut the karmic cord that had bound us together all of that time. I changed *everything*.

"Think about it, Ell. The worst that could have happened to me didn't happen. I was in that house for a full year longer than anyone had anticipated—without a mortgage or rent payment, and barely any income. On the other side of the battlefield was a beautiful home.

"It just goes to show you: Forgiveness is powerful, Ell, *powerful!* And forgiving yourself changes *everything*."

17. An Eye for an Eye

Life is great! It's such a persistent and demonstrative teacher, always reinforcing and graphically illustrating the truly important lessons. My soul was determined that I would experience the dramatic effect of forgiveness, on the worst possible karma. I discovered that forgiveness not only neutralizes karma, it alters our destinies.

Forgiveness is so simple—and so powerful. You have to wonder why we keep holding onto the anger, meditating on the hurt, feeding the resentment, because we think forgiving the other person empowers them and weakens us. We star in a glorious variety of walking wounded dramas with a plethora of *How Could You Do This to Me, I'll Never Forgive You,* and *I'm Gonna Get You, Sucker!* scenes.

Ah, yes! That's what it's all about, isn't it? Controlling by fear. Guilt-tripping. Getting even. And there we go—spinning around on the wheel of karma, judging everyone, and forgiving no one.

My dear friend Reverend Vici told me something that has stuck with me for years: "Hurt people hurt people." And let's not forget: Hurt people hurt themselves. It's impossible to hurt someone else without hurting yourself. Why? Because for every action there's a reaction—a *natural* consequence.

It's a law more ancient than the Old Testament's "eye for an eye", and its New Testament update, "you reap what you sow".

It's nothing but karma, the *natural* consequence of our every thought and action.

Here's how the karma drama is enacted on the typical stage: You and I disagree. You're frustrated because I don't see things your way, so you hit me. I decide to even the score, and I hit you back. You hit me again—this time, with a more powerful punch. I'm not intimidated. To prove it, I pop you really hard. So it goes, until one (or both) of us gets tired, or seriously hurt.

While I'm engaged in this onstage battle, where's my focus? Right, I'm concentrating on landing a good blow to mitigate the hurting you put on me. But if I were to watch that duel from the audience, I would see a different dynamic:

Your first blow set the stage for a natural response from the Universe. We won't call it good; we won't call it bad. It's simply the natural response: karma. Again, the emphasis is on the word *natural*. If you sow cabbage seeds, you don't naturally reap oranges. If you sow war, you don't reap peace. If you sow deception, you don't reap honesty. You get my drift.

Now, when I chose to hit you back, that decision and action triggered its own natural eye/eye, reap/sow response: *Someone* is going to hit me. You have the option of deciding whether that someone will be you.

Whatever choice you make will have the appropriate natural consequence for you. If you choose to land another blow, you must understand that it will trigger a natural response: Someone is going to hit you. I decide whether I will be that someone.

That's what free will is about: choices. We always have choices, and each choice comes complete with its own consequence. If we understood consequences, I don't think the Bible writers would have felt the need to devise commandments. If we understood consequences, we wouldn't need man-made laws. If we understood consequences, we wouldn't need so many prisons.

Tell me, what's a greater deterrent to crime: prison, or the realization that whatever you do to others will be done to you? Would you lie, cheat, or steal? Would you disrespect someone else's property or violate a trust? Would you abuse another in any way? Would you launch an attack? Would you commit adultery, murder, deny someone's human or civil liberties—or steal a vote, if you were sowing the seed for it to happen to you?

Have you ever wondered why most murder victims are killed by people they know? Is it possible that this is not the first lifetime in which the victim and perpetrator have met? Since it's impossible to kill spirit, do murder victims really die—or do their murders haunt the souls of their killers until the act is balanced, an eye for an eye?

In a society that thrives on blaming others for everything that happens to us, it's difficult for us to believe that we authored all of the scenes in our dramas. But, as Kahlil Gibran reminds us in *The Prophet*: "The murdered is not unaccountable for his own murder and the robbed is not blameless in being robbed." He's talking about natural consequences: karma.

The concept of natural consequences may be totally unacceptable to you. Perhaps any attempt to make sense out of life is ridiculous. That's OK. You may continue to make decisions that cause you to tumble around in a karmic cycle for lifetimes, bumping into walls like gym shoes in a clothes dryer. It's up to you.

If you're not knocked senseless when your head rams into the wall, you may be conscious enough to recognize that you alone have created all of your joyful and painful dramas through your thoughts, choices, and actions. And you're creating your future dramas the same way.

I'll demonstrate. Let's rewind the tape on that fight scene: I hit you. Now, you are keenly aware that what you do comes back to you. You stop and think. You may even look at me as if

I've lost my mind (or my awareness of how simply life works). This time, you restrain yourself from your learned response (retaliation), because you realize that it's impossible to inflict pain on me without inflicting it upon yourself. To demonstrate your power, you turn the other cheek, as suggested by Jesus of Nazareth, and you leave me standing there with karmic egg on my face.

Now what? If you are angry or resentful because I hit you—even if you did nothing to physically hurt me—the energy of that anger forms a karmic cord that ties you to me. If you want to rid yourself of me (and my ignorance of Universal Law), you can take control. How? Simply forgive me. The cord evaporates; you are free; and I'm left, spinning around in the dizzying karmic cycle, alone.

When we sow forgiveness, we reap what? Forgiveness. How many times have we deftly said the words, "Forgive us our trespasses, as we forgive those who trespass against us"? Do you have any idea what we have been saying, all of these years? "Forgive us to the same degree that we forgive others." In other words, "If we are unforgiving, don't forgive us."

When we forgive, we're not doing the other person a favor. We do it for our benefit. We're not letting them off the hook. We're releasing ourselves from their karmic cycle. We're cutting the cord that binds us to them and their ignorance of The Law. *A Course in Miracles* says that all forgiveness is a gift to yourself: "You accept God's forgiveness by extending it to others."

So tell me, how did forgiveness come to be considered an act of unselfish generosity? Come on! Forgiveness actually is a highly selfish act, because it ricochets back to the giver.

I spotted a story in the newspaper recently about a family that had refused to forgive their relative's murderer. Whom were they hurting? If I'd had the slightest idea where they lived, I would have sent them a copy of Colin Tipping's *Radical Forgiveness*.

I stumbled across this marvelous book in a very dramatic way. (How else?) I was sleuthing, trying to find out why I'd been so consistently unable to create steady income, so many years after Louis's business failure. Angel referred me to a young clairvoyant named Tony.

As is my practice whenever I'm doing spiritual research, I gave Tony very little information and didn't tell him what I was researching. Early into the reading, he observed that I had no money problems. Money flowed to me freely, he said.

I doubled over with laughter. *What in the world was this child talking about?* Was Tony looking at my life, or had someone else slipped into the room? Although he clearly seemed to have spiritual gifts, he was either too inexperienced or just dead wrong.

Tony was dumbfounded and embarrassed by my hysterics. Even with his eyes closed, I looked like a wealthy woman. In fact, he was adamant: I was wealthy. That was his story and he was sticking it, no matter how outrageous I thought it was.

I loved Tony's vision of me. He hadn't been the first clairvoyant to tell me that. Yes, on a spiritual level, I had access to all the wealth in my Father's kingdom. However, on a physical level, I was forced to employ a trick my friend Max said his accountant taught him when his lucrative broadcasting career imploded: Throw your bills into the air and pay all of the ones that land on their edges.

It works like a charm. This clever sleight of hand makes expenses match revenue every time, guaranteed.

Poor Tony. He'd never been stumped like this. He decided to take a more in-depth look at why I wasn't fulfilling my destiny as a wealthy woman.

"Why is Pat broke?" he lightheartedly asked his spiritual guides.

Some spiritual teachers say that "why" is never the correct question. But "why" clearly was a good question to launch that particular session. The floodgates opened and almost swept me into another zip code, dragging poor Tony along for the ride.

"I'm seeing a lot of anger," he said. "You feel as though you've been jilted in a relationship. I hear you saying, 'He took my home. He made things happen to me.' Who are you talking about?"

"I can only imagine that it's my ex-husband Louis," I said, stunned that Louis would have anything to do with my lingering failure to attract and hold onto money after nearly a decade. I had not mentioned Louis to Tony, or the circumstances surrounding my financial collapse. Neither had Angel, who adheres to the spiritual sleuthing rules.

"There hasn't been a lot of forgiveness in that situation," Tony told me. "You need to snip the karmic wire connecting you to him."

It was my turn to be stumped. It had taken many years, but I really thought that I had forgiven Louis. Forgiveness didn't require me to like him or even want to be around him, but I certainly thought I had released him.

What more could I possibly do to free myself? I wondered.

18. Shaky Chakra

Tony suggested that I perform some exercises to clear the blockages, and increase the flow of positive, light-filled energy through my chakras. Years earlier, before life cracked my mind wide open, I would have dismissed his remedy as New Age hocus-pocus.

You might be wondering: exactly how do you increase the flow of energy through your chakras? Let me 'fess up: Despite years of study, I'm not an expert on chakras or energy. I leave that to quantum physicists Albert Einstein and Deepak Chopra and their genii brethren. All I really want to know about energy is that when I flip a switch, the lights will come on.

I have about the same interest in knowing the DNA of spiritual energy. I want evidence that it works—not the how or why. I don't want to be a spiritual engineer. I've learned enough to be functionally literate, and that much I can pass on to you. If you want to know more, I can point you in the direction of the Information Superhighway or your nearest metaphysical bookstore.

Here's what I do know: All of your energy isn't in one place. There are centers, "specialty departments" called chakras, and each handles only one type of energy. Yeah, there's more than one type.

The first chakra, at the base of your spine, focuses on Earth-related survival issues: food, shelter, clothing, and income. As you might imagine, many of my issues surround blockages in energy flow through this chakra. Oddly enough, I've also been told that my money leaks out of this chakra. Wouldn't it be nice if the blockages would sit right on top of the leaks? My problem would be solved! Apparently, it's not that simple. My luck.

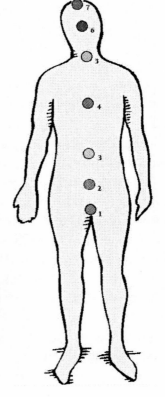

Remember that on a quantum physics level, everything is energy; it just vibrates at different rates. For example, when your first chakra is vibrating at its optimal level, it's red (the same color as the bottom line of my balance sheet).

At the opposite end of the first chakra is the seventh. Contrasted with earthly survival issues, this energy center relates to your openness to and your communication with the God of your heart. It vibrates royal purple.

In between is everything else: The second chakra, located just below your navel, is your emotional and sexual center. Here lies your ability to "feel" the energy around you. The color orange is associated with this chakra.

Your third chakra is located in your solar plexus. This is your energy distribution center. It determines how you "run" your energy throughout your body. It's the home of your "gut" feelings. This chakra's color is yellow.

The fourth energy center is your heart chakra. It is here that your attraction to and affinity for certain things and people are born and maintained. To my surprise, the color of the heart chakra is not red; it's a fertile green.

The focus of the fifth chakra is communication: hearing and speaking. If you're having trouble speaking your mind, chances are that something is blocking your fifth chakra, the light-blue energy center located at the base of your throat. No blocks there, for me.

Your sixth chakra is located in the center of your head, between your eyes. The energy flowing through this so-called third eye determines how clairvoyant you are, how well you can "see" energy. This chakra is blue-violet.

I don't think about chakras, as a general rule, but after Tony diagnosed trouble in my first and second chakras—my survival and emotional centers—I couldn't think about too much else. I wanted my energy to flow at an optimal level all the time so that I could get optimal results. I didn't want any blocks, anywhere.

A few days after consulting with Tony, I was scheduled to attend a financial planning seminar. OK, I had no finances to plan; in fact, I barely had bus fare downtown. But they say that what we think about, we bring about, so it made good sense to me to maintain a prosperous attitude. I needed to know how we rich people are supposed to manage our assets if we're going to enjoy a leisure class lifestyle during our golden years.

At the end of this particular seminar, I overheard someone say that a major bookstore chain was closing, and the bargains were astounding. *Hark? Did I hear the "B" word?* I couldn't get my coat on fast enough.

The nearest store was only a few blocks away. With Tony's advice on the brain, I hoped to find an audiotape with a guided meditation to help me increase the flow of energy through all of my chakras.

I burst through the door of the store, only to be accosted by a thick cloud of misery energy wafting through it.

The atmosphere was depressing. The shelves were in absolute disarray. Employees could not have cared less about customer service. I could tell that the store manager was not a Virgo; otherwise he or she would have wound down the store's operations with a lot more dignity—and order.

Unable to find a salesperson, I muddled through the mess until I spotted the books-on-tape section. Among the audiotapes, haphazardly tossed on the shelves, was a book. *A book?* What was that doing there? I looked closer. The title took my breath away.

It was *Radical Forgiveness*. Who knew there was such a thing? I never would have searched upstairs in the stacks for it. I assumed that it had been placed there for me.

As I reached for the book, something else caught my eye. It was a tape: "Chakra Clearing" by Dr. Doreen Virtue. There was only one. I grabbed both of my treasures and bolted to the cashier, almost faint with excitement.

About a week later, as I was organizing a closet, something fell on the floor. It was a business card. I stooped down and flipped it over. *Where did that come from, after all of these years?* There, in the corner of the card was the embossed logo of the bank that foreclosed on my home. In the center was the name of the bank president.

It suddenly hit me! Maybe it wasn't Louis that I hadn't completely forgiven; it was Peck. Just in case, I held the card to my heart and said a prayer. Then I put the card in a spot where I'd encounter it frequently. Today, every time I see that card, I send Peck blessings, forgiveness, and thanksgiving.

His card reminds me that every painful situation or relationship represents karma that I've either created or am completing. It also reminds me to make a conscious choice to always act in my best interest. That means: Do nothing that I would not want done to me. Treat others only the way that I would want to be treated. In other words, create no unpleasant karma.

Most important, the business card reminds me that when I forgive others, I heal myself. I free myself of karmic consequences. What more inspiration do I need to forgive absolutely everything and everybody? It's not rocket science. In fact, it couldn't be simpler. We make life more difficult and more painful than it has to be because we think that we are our bodies. We think that we are mortal. We think that everything that's going to happen to us will occur during the lifetime of our mortal bodies. We see people around us lying, cheating, stealing, backbiting, and unjustly attacking others. We don't always see them experiencing any negative consequences; so we think there's no such thing as reaping and sowing. Life's simply unfair, because God lets bad guys win.

When no one's looking, we think we can lie, steal, or deceive, and get away with. Guess what? Someone's always looking. It's your soul; and the tape that records all of your thoughts and actions is rolling. Playback may occur when you least expect. As I discovered in my rematch with Peck, our inescapable, natural consequences don't fall on our bodies; they stick to the immortal part of us, until neutralized.

Those in Western culture view reincarnation as a New Age phenomenon. It's not new at all. Some find reincarnation unfathomable because, they say, it is not mentioned in the Bible—or what's left of it, after so many human errors in language translation, idiomatic interpretation, geography, astronomy, and oral history.

Others claim that, during the many revisions of the text, Bible writers exorcized all mention of reincarnation from the Scriptures, to control and scare followers to follow a strict code of behavior because they thought that the world would come to a violent end during their lifetimes. No one could have made them believe the world would still exist 2,000 years later.

A third group cites several instances disproving both viewpoints—references to reincarnation in the Bible, indicating they were not all exorcized. One of those citations is found in John 9:1-3, a dialogue that appears to indicate that Jesus's disciples believed that the consequences of our actions follow us, from one body to another: "And as Jesus passed by, he saw a man which was blind from his birth. And his disciples asked him, saying Master, who did sin, this man, or his parents, that he was born blind?" (John 9:1-2)

The belief of that time—and still held by fundamentalists today—was that God routinely punishes one person for another person's sins. In fact, history tells us that some children were even killed for their parents' misdeeds, as devout believers mimicked what they thought was God's modus operandi. Blindness or any serious illness was seen as punishment for sin.

The story of Jesus' encounter with this blind man—which was written several decades after Jesus' crucifixion, so quite possibly is not a direct quote—*begins* with the disciples' assumption that our lives do not begin in our current bodies.

Why do I say that? The disciples had established that the man had been blind since birth. The only way the man could have sinned *before* his sightless birth was if he had done so in a different body. In other words, had he created karma that was being balanced by blindness?

Jesus responded that the man's condition was not karmic. Blindness served his soul's purpose: "Jesus answered, 'Neither hath this man sinned nor his parents: but that the works of God should be made manifest in him.'" (John 9:3)

Jesus's response seems to indicate that everyone is here for a unique purpose, and has unique experiences that serve each soul's history and desires. This blind man's God-Self, his Spirit-Self, his Divine-Self, his soul, or whatever you want to call it, found some value in not having sight in that body, just as my God-Self found value in financial instability, eviction, and indebtedness. On the physical stage, these experiences appear to be debilitating or tragic. Behind the curtain, metaphysically—beyond the superficial physical level—they reveal themselves as blessings, "works of God" that are manifesting within us.

Earth is merely a physical creation, just as our bodies are physical creations. If we come here for a reason, do you think it's possible that we decide, before we get here, what roles and with whom we'll play? Does it make sense that we make agreements with our co-stars, supporting actors, day players, and extras to assure that our dramas are portrayed the way we want (or need)? Can you imagine that you decided in what part of the world you wanted to live, which family you wanted to join? *(Yes, you chose those people. Don't ask me why.)*

Then go a step farther and see yourself jumping into a costume and—*cue the music*—the curtain rising on a dramatic series that was pregnant with possibilities as you exited the birth canal!

19. Loaves and Fishes

A few weeks after I was settled into the coach house, Angel returned home for semester break. It was her second year at a private East Coast college. Each time I saw her, I was reminded that allowing her to attend high school in Minnesota was the right decision. She had been surrounded by a wealth of talented students and gifted teachers. In addition to the superlative academic environment, she received phenomenal acting and vocal training—a real blessing for a diva who'd maintained her desire to be a singer and actress since she was four years old.

I never missed one of her high school's productions. The students were megatalented, well directed, and highly disciplined. It was grand entertainment, professionally staged, and always worth the drive to the Twin Cities.

Angel, who'd been a drama queen since before she was able to utter a word, was charismatic on a musical theater stage. She also won national awards for dramatic interpretation, and was offered a full academic scholarship to an excellent university. Of course, her school of choice was a more prestigious college that offered hardly any money, but she deserved the best.

Having grown quite accustomed to a big house in the suburbs, Angel wasn't sure she'd like my new place in the city. After running through the coach house and twirling around in every room, she made up her mind.

"I *love* this place, Mom! Let's stay here forever!" she squealed, jumping up and down. I smiled and shook my head. Angel was always such a gleeful child. The moment her legs were strong enough to stand, she would jump up and down with delight, whenever Ed or I approached her crib. She still hops like a little rabbit whenever she's happy.

I was thrilled that Angel liked our new home. I was sure that knowing I was comfortable and secure would give her peace of mind when she returned to school. But live over a garage forever? Nope. This was purely transitional.

My stay in the coach house actually lasted five months. Yep, five months later, I was packing boxes again. Blame Petronela, this time. She had restored a beautiful four-bedroom home a few blocks away, and its current tenants were divorcing. Blame the house. (*I'll tell you about that drama, in a moment.*)

Anyway, Petronela knew that I had just left a big house, and had lots of stuff in storage. She also was very pleased with the way I had decorated and maintained the apartment in the coach house, so I was at the top of her list of prospective tenants for the much larger home. Having a home again sounded like a dream come true—planting flowers, having more space. But I couldn't bear the thought of another move. I'd lost count. Would it be Home #23? *Jiminy Christmas!*

"Just come see it," Petronela insisted.

I reluctantly took the short ride with her. When she parked in front of the six-foot wooden fence surrounding the property, I had no idea what would await me on the other side.

The front yard was massive. The house sat on the back of the large lot. Cement benches sat on each side of the yard. One was near the gate, beside the long walkway to the front door; the other was near the driveway—two tire-wide strips of concrete bridged by grass, leading to the parking pad adjacent to the house.

Nearly a century before, the two-story prairie style cottage was the carriage house for the mansion to the west. Next door to it was the stately mansion of a soon-to-be named Nobel Prize winner. Petronela also had meticulously restored and renovated that home.

She had done as magnificent a job with the grounds of the carriage house. It was an eyesore when I saw it a decade earlier. Now, its huge oak trees stood guard near a sprawling red brick veranda that stretched the entire width of the home. Eight French doors replaced barn doors that once had welcomed horse-drawn carriages. A lush, manicured lawn, ground cover and other foliage set off the home beautifully.

I was still admiring the grounds when we walked into the front door. Petronela had done it again. She was masterful! She had restored this place so impeccably that she was able to obtain historical status for it. There were leaded stained glass windows, and interesting nooks and crannies, blended with new appliances, fixtures and modern cabinetry in the kitchen and the three baths.

I wanted it badly, but it meant a rent increase of more than 50 percent. Petronela instantly dropped the rent. Even with the money I'd save by eliminating a furniture storage bill, I couldn't justify it, so I turned down her offer. She insisted that I think about it.

I decided that if God wanted me in that place, I'd get a very clear sign. It came the very next day. The news manager at the station where I was freelancing asked if I could work more days each week. The extra income would cover the rent increase to the penny. I called Petronela, and said yes.

Angel came home for summer vacation a few weeks after I was settled into Home #23. After running upstairs and down and twirling around in every room, it was final.

"I *love* this place, Mom! Let's stay here forever!" she squealed, as she clapped her hands and bounced on her toes. I smiled and shook my head. Some things, I never want to change. My baby girl's childlike enthusiasm is one of them; my twice-a-year celebration of New Year's Day is the other.

As the summer drew to a close and my birthday approached, I announced to Angel, "It's time to send the Universe a signal that the penniless, unstable phase of my life is over. It's about to be a new year. It's time to pay all my bills in full, and spend the rest of my life with my perfect mate. Let's have a party!"

"What? A birthday party?" Angel asked, her eyes darting around the kitchen for paper and pen. There's only person I know who loves entertaining friends more than I, and that's my baby girl.

"Um-hmm."

"I'm up for that!" She ran upstairs to her room to get a notebook to start her list for the menu and party decorations.

A party was not in my hand-to-mouth budget, but Angel and I planned anyway. I mentioned my party idea to a friend whom I'd let stay in my home when she was between jobs. Now back on her feet, she offered to buy all of the food.

Another dear friend was just as responsive. When Charlotte heard that I was low on funds, she offered to share a writing project with me. She arrived with a retainer—not from the client, but from her personal checking account.

"This is the loaves and fishes party!" Ellen exclaimed as she pumped helium into the elegant gold and silver balloons that we were placing throughout the yard.

She was right. We were miraculously prepared to feed the multitudes. There were several long tables on the expansive front lawn, laden with food. There were tubs of champagne and soft drinks, and more of everything in the kitchen.

Since my birthday is the beginning of my personal new year, it seemed appropriate to reenact one of the New Year's rituals performed at my church: the Burning Bowl. It's a classic out-with-the-old, in-with-the-new ceremony.

Each of my guests received a pink note when they arrived at the gate:

> *Dear Friend,*
>
> *Because you were gracious enough to share this day with me, I'd like to share an important part of my "New Year" with you: It's called the Burning Bowl.*
>
> *If, during the past 12 months, there were things in your life you'd rather not take into the next 12 months (e.g. financial woes, health challenges, heartaches, disputes with friends or family), write them on this sheet of paper. Fold and drop it in the bowl. Later, we'll all watch our troubles go up in smoke.*

As my guests dropped their lists into the bowl, they were given a blank sheet of paper. On that sheet, they were to write a letter to God that detailed the new conditions they wanted to replace the old. Then they addressed an envelope to themselves, and put that letter inside. As is the tradition, I promised to mail those letters to them in about 12 months to remind them of their affirmations.

Friends of all religious persuasions were at the party: Catholics, Protestants, Jews, Muslims, and everything in between. Everyone enjoyed the spirit of the burning bowl because all of us had conditions in our lives that we were eager to torch. No one was more eager than I to light that fire. *Goodbye* to the battle over my former home. *Toodles* to the large companies that had postponed or canceled big training video projects. *See ya* to clients who were nearly two years delinquent in paying me thousands of dollars.

Two checks from one client had bounced, which made several of my checks bounce—including my rent. American Express and Citibank had gotten wind of my financial trouble and canceled my corporate executive and Diners Club cards, even though those accounts never were in arrears. *Burn! Burn!* I was ready for a fresh start—and quickly, please.

A week before the party, I had been dealt the latest blow: I would not be able to pay my half of Angel's backbreaking room, board, and tuition bill for the upcoming school year. I was in an odd predicament. Based on my income, she would have qualified for significant financial aid, but because of Ed's income, we qualified for very little. He refused to pitch in more than half of Angel's college expenses, so I was forced to pay a lot more than I could reasonably afford. Talk about a no-win situation!

Last-minute miracles had saved me the two previous years, so I was hopeful. If my luck didn't change immediately, Angel would have to sit out her junior year. She was furious! I'm not sure who she was angrier with, Louis or me. I had set aside $40,000 for her college education, but because of Louis's three years of joblessness, that money evaporated before Angel graduated from high school.

On the surface, we appeared headed for disaster, but I was confident that everything was in Divine Order, working out according to the script. If Angel was supposed to return to campus, I knew the money would come.

I believed that her God-Self knew what best suited her purpose; but I couldn't coax her into the audience of her drama so that she could see beyond what appeared to be a great tragedy, and trust that all was well. As *A Course in Miracles* says, "It takes great learning to understand that all things, events, encounters, and circumstances are helpful."

We were bracing for the inevitable when I spotted a newspaper ad for evening classes at a prestigious local university. Tuition was a small fraction of Angel's East Coast campus's. She enrolled for a full course load and worked full-time in a Chicago-based research project conducted by an Ivy League university.

That year, Angel built self-sufficiency biceps, much to my delight, just as I had done by working full time and carrying a full course load, as an undergrad. The survival skills were invaluable. Angel had lived the ask-and-you-shall-receive life that I'd dreamed of as a little girl, so her self-sufficiency muscles had no opportunity to develop; but pushed to perform, she excelled.

Angel made the dean's list both semesters and earned stellar reviews at work. Because she had planned well, she was able to transfer all of her credits back to her home campus, which allowed her graduate with her class the following spring. The experience was pivotal to her growth, and it gave Ed and me confidence that she had the wherewithal to live independently in New York after graduation.

However, the summer before her junior year, before everything unfolded so perfectly, Angel could not believe that anything about my negative cash flow was a blessing. As we prepared for the guests to arrive at my birthday party that August afternoon, it was difficult for her to stop thinking about friends returning to campus without her.

Angel spotted Ellen across the yard and joined her at the table where the materials sat for the Burning Bowl. She took a sheet of paper and began to write. I knew what her letter to God would say, my poor baby.

Ellen was wrapping up the list of conditions that she wanted to release from her life. She had been going through a rough time for a lot longer than I. Singing gospel songs is what she loved to do, but unlike the self-help gurus had promised, the money had never followed. Keeping a roof overhead had been a constant challenge throughout her adulthood.

We thought her life was turning around when good ol' Bill, who loved Ellen's gourmet cookies, transformed her sideline baking business into a real corporation with a number of store locations. He gave her a small lump sum for her recipes and hired her to run the kitchen. After she'd set up the baking process and trained the workers, he gradually reduced her hours. Then, one day he told her that she no longer needed to report for work. To add injury to insult, he and his attorney diluted Ellen's stock in the company until they had edged her out of the business completely. We both were devastated.

Ellen was as unlucky with romance. For years, she'd been deeply in love with a fellow musician who seemed to love her just as deeply—but he married someone else.

Despite her painful circumstances, Ellen sang and sang. She never stopped giving glory to her Mother-Father-Everything-God.

20. Oh, So Healing

There's no doubt in my mind that if God appeared on the Earth stage as the Father we've been taught to envision, most of us would run, scared to death, screaming bloody murder. Think I'm kidding?

OK, close your eyes. Clear your thoughts. Now, imagine God knocking on the door of the room where you are. What happened? Did you feel tightness in your chest, your gut, maybe even in your heart chakra? Were you panicked by the thought of seeing God? Perhaps it's because you've been taught that He will judge or punish you because you're so sinful.

Ellen had a different image of God. God was the go-to guy. If "He" really was created in man's image (We first have to believe spirit has or needs male genitalia, hands and feet), and paid her a visit, Ellen probably would bolt to the door, leap into His arms, give Him a big hug and demand to know what took Him so long to get to her place.

I've never known anyone who loved God as intensely as Ellen. That girl sang her love for God with every fiber of her being. She was in and out of one church (and soprano section) after another, trying to find one that snugly fit her beliefs about God. She struck pay dirt one New Year's Eve, in a large Pentecostal congregation in Chicago's Woodlawn neighborhood.

"Girl, I've never experienced such joyful praise!" she told

me. "My spirit was lifted high.

"It was like I was floating on holy ground. I rejoiced and rejoiced!"

That night, she also cast off her fear of baptism.

"Girl, they gave me this white gown and swimming cap, and I was ready to be cleansed, healed, changed and Holy Ghost-filled. I dipped one foot into the water.

"Oh, my God, it was ice-cold! I was ready to bolt back down the aisle when, *splash!* They dunked my entire body into the pool. Whoa! The supersonic drop in my body temperature scared away the Holy Ghost, or anything else that might have taken hold of me!"

Going limp, she demonstrated how she'd reacted to the dunking. "When they lifted me out of that water, my eyes were rolling to the back of my head. I was stiff as a board, and my teeth were chattering out of control. They stretched me out on the floor."

She bent over. "Folks gathered around me, thinking I had gotten the Holy Ghost and was speaking in tongues."

I laughed, enjoying her little show.

"One lady kept asking, 'You got it? You got it?' All I could say was, 'Child, I'm f-freezing!'" she said, her teeth chattering. "I've never seen anyone more disappointed. I mean this sister was really bummed out. When it was her turn, I know that getting the Holy Ghost was the farthest thing from her mind, too."

Only Ellen could make baptism sound like an adventure movie! What was I going to do with her?

Everyday, whether she left home or not, Ellen went to "church": The morning started with a chat with her Mother-and-Father-God and her brother Jesus. Next, she meditated. Finally, she set the color for the day at "bright", and the tone at "joyful".

It's probably Ellen's outlook on life, and the warmth and playfulness of her spirit, that attracted so many people to her. Rare was the time when I was with her in Hyde Park or downtown that someone didn't run up to us and hug Ellen— people of all races, all ages, straight, gay, rich, broke, able-bodied, and otherwise. She had more "best friends" than the law allowed.

Many of her newest friends were clients that she had helped through her latest passion, massage therapy. I always envisioned massage therapists as much larger, and a lot more muscular than Ellen's diminutive frame. Her graceful, tapered fingers didn't appear to have strength enough to deliver a great massage. And looking at her, you would never suspect that she was a spiritual healer.

Oh, I forgot to tell you about her healing work. This is quite a drama. Let me see: Ellen discovered, quite by accident, that she had hands-on healing power. She revealed it to me one afternoon when she dropped by, unannounced.

Nothing irks me more than people who drop in without calling. I was especially irked when Ellen did it, because we typically talked at least three or four times a day. You'd think it wouldn't hurt her to mention that she was coming by.

Shortly after I returned to Hyde Park, she rented an apartment a few blocks away. Whenever the spirit moved her, she'd be at my front gate, ringing the bell. If I'd been able to see her on the sidewalk—or if she hadn't been able to see my car through slats in the fence—I would have left her butt at the gate, to break her of the habit.

This day, I buzzed her into the yard. Although it was quite a distance between the sidewalk and my front door, Ellen could tell that I was irritated.

"What do you have your mouth all poked out for, Little Girl?" she yelled with a half-grin and half-scowl.

"Ell, you know how I hate it when folks just drop by!"

"Why? You havin' sex? If you ain't havin' sex, I ain't interruptin' nothin','" she laughed, barging right in. Ellen could be so incorrigible. It was impossible to stay mad at her for more than a few minutes.

"First things first. Before we get to sex, I'd have to get a date, wouldn't I?" I laughed.

It was no secret that I'd had only a few dates since my divorce—and those were with a guy we had dubbed the Nutty Professor. This man was a brilliant author and college professor, but he was crazy as a betsy bug. I don't know how else to describe a 48-year-old man who wanted to start a family, then pursued a relationship with a 48-year-old woman. *Duh.*

After that fiasco, I really had to examine the type of men I was attracting. I decided to make a "perfect mate" list, so I'd know my man when I saw him:

Like Ed, Louis, and the Nutty Professor, my perfect mate must be highly intelligent. Physically, I want him to be proportional in weight and height, with a healthy body and attitude. Psychologically and emotionally, I want him to be a man, not an overgrown boy. He also must have tons of common sense and lots of genuine friends.

My man is refined, well educated, well groomed and has impeccable manners. He has an easy laugh and a keen sense of humor—he's playful, but not a player. He is a nice guy and a good man. (Louis taught me that the two are not synonymous.)

I also learned from Louis that I prefer a man who wants me, but doesn't need me, and who absolutely treasures a good woman. My perfect mate is a verifiably single, heterosexual man who loves himself and me unconditionally. He's warm and self-confident.

He's creative in a lot of ways: has "a slow hand", likes giving and receiving pleasant surprises, and knows when to plan and

143

when to be spontaneous. He is attentive and committed to our relationship, has a negative BS quotient, and enjoys cooking and entertaining friends. He has achieved most of his career goals, is financially secure, and rebounds quickly from failures or disappointments. (I added these criteria for obvious reasons.)

My perfect mate's ex-wives and ex-girlfriends don't hate his guts. He can lead without being domineering. He's so secure and self-confident that jealousy is not part of his reality or his act. He likes to travel to fascinating places, has discriminating taste in women, clothes, cars, and his environment.

He has integrity; his word is his bond. He keeps his commitments and lives up to his responsibilities. He is a great role model for young men and boys, and is admired and respected by others—especially by his children.

Right, this is no ordinary dude, which meant that I might have to wait a while; but I'd rather be alone, than settle for less than I deserved.

It appeared that my wait might be even longer than I thought. The feng shui experts who blessed Home #23 reported that there was "a corner missing from the marriage house". Sure enough, the southwest tip of the cottage wasn't there. It created a charming angle for the kitchen door, but a not so charming outlook for my love life. Did that missing corner doom the previous tenants' marriage? I wondered.

"If you didn't intimidate men so much, you'd have a date, Little Girl!" Ellen mumbled, as she walked past me, toward the sofa.

I rolled my eyes. I didn't need the reminder. I'd been told repeatedly that I intimidate men. They say that I have a presence that says, "I'm strong, independent, and very capable. If your act's not together, don't break your stride."

On the other hand, I'd also been told that I'm the kind of woman many men dream about. I guess that can be intimidating, too; but surely, there was a man who could rise to the occasion. Until he did, the likelihood that Ellen or any other dropper-inners might be "interrupting anything" was, let's say, extremely remote.

Ellen plopped down on the sofa in a flurry of color, as if she'd had the weight of the world on her small feet. She had such a talent for mixing and matching stylish separates. She looked like a Caribbean diva, her vibrant colors complemented her sunny disposition.

"What's for lunch?" she asked, as if she'd been invited.

"I hadn't thought about lunch." Meals have never been a high priority to me. "I'm sure there's something I can rustle up. How much time do you have?"

Ellen looked at her watch. "I have about an hour before my next appointment. It's just about five minutes from here; that's why I stopped by."

"Lucky me. I get to stop working and fix you lunch."

"Hell, I can fix it, Little Girl. Don't get your panties all in a bunch."

"Cool." I was happy to let her do the honors; Ellen was a much better cook than I. We walked toward the kitchen.

"Sit down," she said.

"Let me see what's in the fridge first."

"No. Sit *down*," she insisted.

I was in no mood for arguing with Miss Ellie. I promptly sat. Instead of walking to the fridge, she circled around and poked me right under my shoulder blade. I damn near jumped to the ceiling.

"Owww, Ell! What are you doing?" I jerked away and turned to look at her. Ellen's eyes were closed. She reached for my shoulder and started digging deeper into the area.

"I don't know," she said. "Something just told me to touch you right here. Has it been sore in this area lately?" Her little fingers continued to work the muscle.

"Uh, yeah, now that I think about it."

"Uh-huh. Bend forward. I'm going to move that tension out of there."

I was puzzled, but did what I was told. I began to feel some relief.

"Move your shoulder," she directed.

I did. It didn't hurt. "That was amazing! What did you do?"

"I don't know," she said. "I just did what I was told."

"What do you mean, you did what you were told."

"Just that. I did what I was told. I heard a voice. It told me to touch you there, and it told me how to manipulate the area to bring you some relief."

"Get outta here! Just out of the clear blue sky, something told you to massage that area of my back? Girl, please!"

"Well, you asked. And I told you."

"I don't understand."

"That makes two of us. It's been happening for a few weeks. I was doing a massage on a client who's had an almost crippling stiffness down her right side for years. No one has been able to figure out what it is, but she seems to relax a bit more with regular massages. This was our first session.

"I was just getting into the rhythm of the treatment when I heard a voice telling me to touch her in a certain spot. At first, I ignored it. I heard it again. I looked around. No one was in the room but us. I heard it again—clear as a bell.

"Finally, I said, 'OK, what the hell?' Girl, I touched that woman where I was told to, and she broke down and cried like a child. Scared the crap outta me. The voice told me to stay calm and to tell her that everything was all right. I was directed to do a series of therapeutic techniques that I'd never been taught.

146

"I closed my eyes, so I could focus on the instructions as they came. Then I really freaked out. Girl, you wouldn't believe what I saw!"

"What?" I was beginning to freak out, too.

"It was like a movie. I saw this woman as a little girl, hiding under a porch. It seemed to be a big, old farmhouse. I didn't get the sense that it was a neighborhood in the city.

"A man seemed to be looking for her, calling her name. I could feel her little heart pounding and she was afraid to answer. When I looked closer, I could see that her little dress had been ripped. She had been sexually assaulted. This child couldn't have been more than six years old."

I clutched my heart. "Oh, my God! Then what happened?"

"The woman on the table kept crying, and I kept doing what I was told until I felt this sudden surge of really heavy, dark energy drain from her body. Spirit told me that this woman had held the pain and guilt of that assault in her body for more than 60 years.

"She obviously felt the release, too, because she started sobbing, 'It's over! It's over! Thank you, God, it's over!' She got off of that table and stood erect for the first time in I don't know how long. She reached over and hugged me like I had resurrected her from the dead. Child, I didn't know what to do."

"Oh, my God," I said, wringing my hands. "It gives me goose bumps. There's an eerie Edgar Cayce vibe in this. Did you tell her what you had seen?"

"I was afraid to. I didn't want to traumatize her. Frankly, I was traumatized enough for the both of us. While she was getting dressed, though, I did talk with her sister. She was sitting in the waiting area.

"I had heard an unusual name in that vision. I asked her sister if she knew anyone by that name. She looked at me very strangely. She said they had an uncle with that nickname, who had stopped coming around the family when they were kids. She hadn't seen him in years."

"Get outta here!" I gasped.

"Girl, it sent shivers through me."

From that point on, Ellen massaged her clients with her ears open and her eyes closed.

21. Everywhere, Everyone God

hy didn't I let this call dump into voice mail? I moaned, as I hung up the phone. I had planned to chill out and enjoy the rainy Sunday at home, but one of the other freelance writers had called in sick; now I was headed into the newsroom.

A few blocks after I got on the bus, we stopped in front of a church, where a woman in her Sunday hat waited to board with her two daughters. The younger child, a beautiful wide-eyed preschooler, had to be coaxed onto the bus. Reluctantly, she hopped onto the first step, then immediately turned around and waved a gloved hand toward the church.

"Goodbye, Lord!" she called to the building, as she was led to her seat. Several blocks later, this child's sweet little voice was still calling out wistfully, "Goodbye, Lord!"

Obviously, the child had been told that the church was the "house" of God; she thought she was leaving Him behind.

Say something, my heart cried out to her mother. Are you going to let this baby think that God is a person who can only occupy one space at a time? Are you going to let her think that "He's" going to piddle around at "home" until she comes back next Sunday? The woman did not open her mouth. I wanted so badly for her to tell the child the truth that I almost could see her lips moving, Clutch Cargo-style.

Girl, mind your own spiritual business, I scolded myself, as I shifted in my seat and stared out of the window. Isn't that what I thought when I was that age? That's how myths survive from generation to generation. Grown-ups tell us about a faraway God who looks and acts like a man, who's hard to please, judgmental, unforgiving, and has a grisly temper. Once it's been firmly implanted in our minds, it's difficult to dislodge. I looked at the cute little girl. How thrilled she would be if she knew that the God she obviously loved was sitting in her seat.

I suddenly was reminded of the day that I field-produced an interview with the Reverend Dr. Johnnie Colemon, founder of Christ Universal Temple, a large Christian teaching ministry on the far South Side of Chicago. We were featuring Dr. Colemon as the "Queen of Positive Thought" in a special series for the ratings period.

By the time I arrived at her home that day with my film crew and our principal anchorman, I already had been on the clock six hours. I had another six hours to go. I'd spent my only day off entertaining then three-year-old Angel, who had read all of the books in her library and impatiently announced that she was bored. *Let's do something, Mommy!*

I was still recuperating, as the crew set up for the interview. Dr. Colemon cordially asked me how I was feeling.

I said, "I am absolutely *exhausted!*"

Earth to Pat: Wrong response to the "Queen of Positive Thought".

Dr. Colemon gasped. "Words have power, my dear. You must be very careful about the words you attach to 'I Am'. 'I Am' is God's name."

It is? Then I remembered that when Moses asked God what He should be called, He said, "I Am." But I'd never heard anyone actually call God that.

"Whatever we attach to 'I Am', we are claiming as a

condition," she explained. "God is within you, and believe me, God is *not* exhausted!"

I was speechless and confused. As a Baptist-turned-Catholic, the thought of God being *within me* was unfathomable! In fact, the distance between God and me had increased exponentially with my religious conversion. As a Baptist, I could pray directly to God. As a Catholic, I needed someone to do it for me.

All my life, I had been taught that God was somewhere else. I was unworthy to be in His presence, or for Him to be in mine. I had absolutely no context for what Dr. Colemon was saying. I sat at her kitchen table and respectfully accepted her scolding. Inwardly, I totally dismissed every word, considering it positive thought, run amok.

Today, her words simply reflect common sense. If God is all knowing, all-powerful, and present *everywhere*, why is it so far-fetched that God would be in *every* soul?

Even if she were wrong, what would be the harm? Is it possible that we might treat each other with more reverence if we thought we were good enough to house God? Would we re-direct our focus from externals, such as skin color or bank accounts to the God Light within others? When we look within ourselves, would we see God, and strive to be more honest, more forgiving, and more loving? Would we be less manipulative, controlling and judgmental? Would we perform our jobs more excellently? If we thought that God was within us, would we make any important decisions with our brains without first consulting our God-Selves?

Would we be more interested in resolving disputes in our personal best interests, or for the Highest Good of everyone concerned? Would we attack others, based on the fear that they were going to hurt us? Or would we be strong and fearless, because we have faith that the all-powerful God is protecting us at all times? Whom would we trust—God or man?

My reporter's notebook was full of these kinds of questions, as Ellen and I searched for God's presence in our hard-knock lives. Traveling together, sleuthing as partners on this spiritual path, brought us closer than we'd ever been as teenagers. We talked every day. I knew where she was, where she was going, and what she was doing almost every minute, and vice versa. No day started until we'd checked in with each other.

There was one exception. For several years, Ellen went to Europe around Thanksgiving on a gospel singing tour. She and the small troupe traveled throughout the continent until just before Christmas.

Holiday parties and shopping kept me so busy that I didn't miss her as much as I normally would. On occasion, she'd call for a few minutes. But it wasn't the same. We never had enough time to catch up. I missed her terribly.

That year, I could have wrung Ellen's neck on departure day. She had to be the least-organized Virgo sister on the planet! It was the major reason the man who loved her couldn't handle her on a day-to-day basis. Until she moved into her new apartment, her home was always disorderly. For some reason, she typically kept the new place nice and neat.

Ellen's preparations for this trip constituted a disorderly relapse. She had waited until the last minute to complete her chores. That forced me to run hither and yon, trying to help her get everything done before I dropped her off at O'Hare. Since my car had been acting temperamentally, she parked hers at my house so that I wouldn't be without transportation while she was gone.

The last few hours before she left were tense. For a moment, it looked as if we weren't going to make it to the airport on time. When we arrived at the terminal, Ellen bolted from the car, grabbed her bags, and was inside the door of the vestibule before she realized that she hadn't even hugged me goodbye.

She turned around, jumped up and down blowing kisses, and screamed, "Bye, Little Girl! Bye, Little Girl! I love you!"

I shook my head, laughed, and began the countdown to her return.

22. Every Goodbye Ain't Gone

A week before Ellen was scheduled to return home, I realized that I hadn't heard from her since she'd left. I looked at the clock. What time was it in Switzerland? Or was she in Sweden today? I couldn't wait to tell her how grateful I was that she had left her car with me. Mine had completely conked out.

My friend Kate was visiting from San Francisco. Instead of tooling around the city in my S-Class Mercedes, we were in Ellen's no frills Toyota Tercel. Not fancy, but it beat the bus by a long shot.

Kate rode with me as I delivered Christmas gifts to my clients. She was still coming to grips with her father's recent death, and wanted to talk about it.

I'm never quite sure what to say when discussing death. Most people's perspective on it is so different from mine that I run the risk of seeming insensitive, if not insane.

I was a little girl the first time I thought about death. I had spotted a drawing in a religious magazine. There were two scenes. One was a birth; the other was a funeral. The caption said something to the effect that we should celebrate when a soul leaves this world, and mourn when one enters. I was quite grown when I finally understood the meaning of that drawing.

In Western culture, death rarely is a celebration. There generally is a tremendous amount of pain, grief, and fear

154

surrounding it. Sometimes we're so grief-stricken that it's difficult to resume our normal routines—as evidenced by a scene I recently witnessed after attending a graveside service. As we left the cemetery, I spotted a young woman sitting in a lawn chair, lunch in a cooler by her side, talking to—well, I'm not sure who she was talking to. I am sure that her loved one didn't live at the cemetery where his or her physical remains were buried. Something about the scene told me that if I returned to that spot another day, I'd find that young bereaved woman in that lawn chair, talking to the ground.

Isn't it interesting that we believe we were made in God's image, but we think we're mortal bodies rather than eternal souls? When someone's body stops functioning, we think he or she has ceased to exist; and we sink into despair.

Human bodies, like boots or furniture, don't last forever. (Name one thing on planet Earth that does.) Physical life is fleeting—with good reason. The experience is so much more confining and restrictive than the spiritual experience. I would imagine that no soul would want to spend eternity cooped up in a physical body, any more than a scuba diver would want to spend eternity in a wet suit. It's fun for a while, you can see and do some things you couldn't before, but then you urgently want to come out of the water and peel off the suit.

Think of the sacrifice it requires to shrink your powerful, unlimited self into a body that has only five senses, and functions within three measly dimensions. How long would you want to relinquish your unlimited nature for such a limited and limiting experience within a human body, in a heavy atmosphere, weighted down by gravity? Six days? Seven months? Eighty years?

How many people go to school, and stay years after they've met the requirements for graduation, refusing to accept their diplomas? How many people go to work, and refuse to go home at the end of the day? Once your job is done, once your learning is over, what do you naturally want to do? *Grab hat and run!*

If you have evidence that Earth is Home, I'd like to see it. Isn't it possible that the souls that are our departed loved ones might prefer to be more like their God-Selves—expansive and unlimited? When a soul decides his or her work or schooling is done here, how should we react when it slips out of the body—with inconsolable grief, or with unconditional support, maybe even congratulations?

Just as that drawing indicated so many decades ago, death may be cause for celebration. No matter how the spirit freed itself from the confines of the body—whether through illness, murder, suicide, execution, or accident—it now has more freedom, more options than it had within a body.

In the case of murder, natural consequences will always balance the killer's disrespect for that soul's physical body. But the attacker didn't take that soul's life. If that soul wants another body, it will find one that provides the dramatic experiences it desires. Plenty are being created every second of every day. At least, that's what I believe.

I wasn't sure if I could share that belief with Kate. But as she began to weep about her father, I thought that my perspective might give her some comfort. It did, although it didn't make her miss him any less. I didn't expect that it would, or that it should.

A year earlier, my older brother Spencer had transitioned out of his body. He was a college professor in his mid-50s, handsome, debonair—and suddenly gone. In his eulogy, I recounted his many graduations: elementary school, high school, graduate school, graduate school, and graduate school. (Spencer had tried three times to capture his Ph.D., stopping short with a master's degree on two occasions before he ultimately succeeded.) We were gathered again to salute another graduation—his promotion to pure spirit.

We never stop missing our loved ones; we never stop cherishing them. Our physical limitations prevent us from seeing them, but they're not "dead". They're as much alive as they ever were. They've simply left our view, walked out of our particular theater.

We experience a lot of anguish when we witness the end of a physical life, because we don't realize that:
- Endings are beginnings;
- Bodies and personalities aren't real or eternal;
- Evolving requires leaving one level and going to the next.

As I parked in my driveway, I told Kate about one of Ellen's recent encounters with death. Ellen had a terminally ill friend, Venus, an artist with whom she'd instantly bonded. As a healer, Ellen fervently believed in the healing power of God. She was at Venus's bedside every day, tending to her physical, emotional, and spiritual needs. She prayed for and fully expected a miracle.

"I'm going to be real mad at God if He lets her die," she fussed one day.

"Mad at God?" *What was she talking about?* "Why would you be mad at God?" I asked her.

"Venus doesn't want to die, and I don't want her to die!" she pouted.

Ellen had been a spiritual student longer than I. She intellectually understood life and death as well as I did. But when the rubber hits the road, I think we all have a tendency to revert to our childhood, to that time when we believed that God was a Superhuman Being who lived in a place called Heaven. If we petitioned the right way, through the right person, or with enough people, we believed that He would intervene on our behalf.

Typically, what happens when we don't get the response we

want is that we feel abandoned and disillusioned. We lose faith; or, as in Ellen's case, we get mad.

It always comes back to what we believe about God, doesn't it? Based on our traditional beliefs, life on Earth is complicated, painful, unfair—even diabolical.

"I hear what you want," I said. "I hear what Venus says she wants. But that's her ego talking. What does her soul want, Ell? After all, it's running the show."

Ellen frowned, wishing Venus's soul would get with the program. She didn't want to accept the possibility that God would not answer her prayers.

"Nothing outside of Venus's soul is going to make that decision," I reminded her. "Her soul has free will to go or stay. You can't impose your will. Even if you could, you wouldn't want the karma that comes with disrespecting her soul's desires."

"She has a right to live!" Ellen shouted, angrily.

"Nobody's robbing her of that right," I argued. "She was alive before this world was created. She'll be alive whenever they dispose of that body. This isn't about *whether* Venus is going to live. It's about *where* she's going to live. Her soul may have decided it no longer wanted to live on this planet, in this country, in that body. Are you saying it doesn't have the right to make that decision?"

"No," Ellen conceded. "I guess I just don't like that decision."

"Well, Sister Girl, you aren't the first, and you won't be the last to be unhappy with those decisions. The bottom line is that Earth is not Home. I don't know a soul who has come here and stayed. To me, that says a lot. One of the things it says is that this ain't all there is. And thank God for that, 'cause this certainly ain't enough!"

That summer, Venus's soul transitioned out of her body.

Ellen wasn't happy, but eventually, she accepted it.

As soon as Kate and I walked into the house, I prepared dinner. We had a big weekend ahead. We had joined a company that produced personal development programming for a private satellite television network. Our sales group had established a tradition of conducting a weekend of marketing meetings at a downtown Chicago hotel each December. Our colleagues—especially those who hailed from warm places—always got a kick out of having a brief White Christmas experience, holiday shopping on the brilliantly lit, often snow-covered Magnificent Mile.

We turned in early so that we could get to the hotel in time to stake out some great seats in the meeting room. Several hours later, I heard the phone ringing down the hall in my second floor office. I always turn off my bedroom phone's ringer because I hate being startled out of a sound sleep by the noise.

My initial thought was that the call was for Kate; someone from the West Coast probably didn't realize they were calling Chicago at an ungodly hour. I hoped she'd pick up the guest room phone. When she didn't, the caller phoned back again. And again. And again.

Finally, I sat up in bed and looked at the clock. It was after 3:00 A.M.! *Who would be calling at this time of morning?* I turned on the lamp next to my bed.

Probably Ellen. There's a seven-hour time difference. This is probably the only time she had available. I reached for the phone.

"Hello?"

"Pat? This is Sasha," the voice said. Sasha was a close friend of Ellen's. I didn't know Sasha well—certainly not well enough for her to call me before the crack of dawn.

"It's about Ellen," she said calmly.

My heart began pounding.

"She's dead, Pat," she said. "Ellen's dead."

I was trying to wake up, trying to comprehend what Sasha was telling me, and trying to keep myself together so I could get all of the facts. Surely, there must be some mistake.

"Was there an accident? What happened?" I asked. "Was anybody else hurt?"

"She seems to have had a heart attack. They found her in the tub at the hotel. I have a lot more calls to make. I'll call you later."

I collapsed into tears. No, this couldn't be possible. Not Ellie. Not gone. Not now. Not so soon. We were going to celebrate our 50th birthdays together in eight months.

I walked into the bathroom. Over the mirror sat two little cards that Ellen had given me. One said, LED BY SPIRIT the other, TOTALLY UNLIMITED. Now, she was both.

"Ellie?" I said to the mirror. "Ellie, were you through? Were you done? Did you finish everything you came here to do? I can't believe you were done!"

I returned to bed and cried myself to sleep.

The next morning, everything felt surreal. My caller ID confirmed that Sasha really had called, but I still couldn't believe what she'd said. It didn't make sense.

I walked downstairs to the kitchen. Through the window, I saw Ellen's car, sitting on the carport. I quickly looked away. As I lit the burner under the teapot, I suddenly recalled a conversation Ellen and I had, a couple of weeks before she left for the gospel tour.

There was no hello.

"I died," she said, as soon as I picked up the phone.

"You *what?*" I yelled.

"I died," she repeated.

160

"What the hell do you mean, you died?"

"I mean, I died," she said pointedly. "I was in deep, deep meditation, and I guess I went so deep that I must have left my body. I was in a panic. I couldn't find my body anywhere! Suddenly the phone rang. Betty called me, and it jolted me back. Girl, I've never been so scared in all my life!"

I could imagine—and then again, I couldn't. "I guess you won't be doing that crap again," I said.

"You can bet I won't, Little Girl."

Now Ellen had left her body permanently. I sighed, fully turning my back on the kitchen window. I didn't want to see her car in my peripheral vision. I didn't want the phone to ring again. I didn't want to talk to anyone.

Kate already had left for the hotel. I just wanted to be in the silence. I wanted to pretend that this hadn't happened.

How was I going to tell Angel? She loved Ellen so much. They hadn't seen each other in almost a year. Angel's decision to live in New York permanently meant that she hadn't come home for summer vacation after her college graduation.

Oh, my God! How was I going to tell my mother, who was recuperating from a second stroke? Ellen used to lay her healing hands on Mother when she was in pain, and had brought her body great relief. I decided to wait until I could calmly tell both of them without dissolving into tears.

I reminded myself that Ellen was more accessible to me now than ever. I didn't need a telephone to talk to her. Still, I wanted to see her face, taste her delicious cooking, and marvel at her latest creative project.

I walked to the closet and pulled out my winter coat. Draped over the shoulder was a large black scarf with a mud-cloth design, laden with cowry shells and other beads on each end. Ellen had sewn each bead onto the scarf in an exquisite pattern. People raved about it, wherever I went.

161

Yesterday, it was a limited-edition conversation piece. Now it was a collector's item, an heirloom from my best friend.

The great thing about living on the financial edge all of her life was that it made Ellen creative. Since she generally didn't have money to buy gifts for those she loved, she'd make original creations. *Thank God for negative cash flow. Because of it, I now have so many treasures,* I thought.

I walked over to the beautiful hand-painted tray Ellen had given me for my birthday, and picked up each of the finely detailed, hand-painted shells. It already was in the perfect spot, on the mantel of the living room fireplace, beneath a large painting of a praying black woman. I gave the tray a loving tap.

I didn't want to think about it anymore. It was too painful. I put on my coat, and went to catch up with Kate at the meeting.

23. The Message from Home

My grieving process fluctuated between denial and avoidance. While I was cocooning, Ellen's army of best friends caucused with her brothers, arranging for the return of her remains, and finalizing the plans for her memorial service. Occasionally, someone would call to update me after a meeting. That was good enough.

Finally, it was decided that Ellen's body would be cremated in Europe. The gospel troupe would bring the remains back to the States in two weeks, at the end of the tour.

Good, I thought. That's exactly what Ellen wanted. She once told me that she never wanted people to look at her body lying in a casket.

"I'd be too embarrassed," she said. "People walking by, looking at my body like that."

Everything was in Divine Order, even the trip overseas. I wouldn't be surprised if her soul had arranged for her to leave her body while she was in Europe, to make sure it was cremated. Wish granted.

For the next few days, I fussed at Ellen's spirit, mad that she had left so quickly. How dare she leave me here! Who was going to be my sleuthing sidekick? What was wrong with her, doing this to me?

"I'm kickin' your butt the minute I see you, Ellie Mae Sing-Song Wang-Wang Spice!" I screamed. "Just you wait."

I loved calling her that. Joan, a close friend of Ellen's who practiced Siddha Yoga meditation with her, had written a children's story by that name, in her honor.

As angry as I was with her, I knew how much Ellie was enjoying her newly found freedom. She no longer was trapped inside a physical body; now she could be more than one place at a time. I knew she was deliriously happy. She had been more in sync with the spirit world than this one, anyway.

Still, I missed her physical presence, missed hearing her voice. Weeks earlier, she had given me an audiocassette of her singing *Worship Him*. I didn't have the courage to play the tape, but several times, I picked up the phone and called her number, just to hear her spiritually uplifting voice mail greeting. It was so wonderful to hear her again. If I hadn't had a clear understanding that Ellen's body had died, her soul—her *real* self—had not, I don't know if I could have raised my head off of the pillow each morning.

One day, shortly after Ellen transitioned out of her body, my chores took me to a neighborhood copy shop to duplicate some documents for a meeting. While I waited for the copies, I spotted Joan. When I caught her eye, her face brightened. She walked over, arms extended, warm and motherly.

"Ellen wants me to give you a hug," she said. As she hugged me, she said, "She says for me to tell you, 'I love you, Little Girl.'"

It was all I could do to maintain my composure. How did Joan know Ellen's pet name for me? Did she call anyone else by that name—or was she trying to confirm for me that she was still alive?

24. Life after Life

There were two services honoring Ellen's soul's latest visit to planet Earth. One was a Yoruba service to release her spirit from this plane. I'd never attended a Yoruba service before, and I'm not sure that Ellen had either, but these were friends who loved her and wanted to honor her in their special way.

The service was in South Shore, in a space on a high second floor. I couldn't believe how many stairs I had to climb! I took a seat, grateful that I didn't know anyone in the room. I didn't want to talk about why I was there.

While we were waiting for the service to begin, I heard an elderly woman's voice at the foot of the stairs.

"I don't *need* any help!" she fussed. "I can make it up these stairs. Before Ellen laid her hands on me, I couldn't even walk. I am going to make it up these stairs *by myself*. I owe her that!"

She arrived on the second floor minutes later, with a victorious grin on her face. What a joy to see what a difference Ellen had made in that woman's life.

The second memorial service, held in a city college auditorium, was a testimony to the number of lives that Ellen had touched. It was a standing-room-only crowd. The service was more like a pep rally than a memorial. Clusters of balloons and posters of Ellen were scattered throughout the room. The mood was uplifting and celebratory.

Sasha, an event planner and theatrical producer, had organized a fantastic show that evoked no sad moments, only fond, funny memories. No doubt in my mind, Ellen loved every minute of her home-going ceremony. There was a slide show, a video, testimonials, and a full-out musical concert. The closest I came to tears was after one of her friends sang a powerful, heart-felt rendition of *I Believe I Can Fly*. The entire service was a rousing tribute to one of the most loving spirits that ever visited this planet.

I didn't attend the graveside service days later. First of all, I had ostriched to such a degree that I completely forgot about it. Even if I had remembered, I probably would not have gone. I would have had to drive Ellen's car, since mine still wouldn't start. That ride would have taken me—and a whole lot of other people—someplace we didn't want to go.

Ellen had owned the little economy car for just about a year. I had been so excited for her. It was her first car and the most expensive item she'd ever owned. The car and her cute, tiny apartment were by-products of returning to social work. She had resorted to doing what she didn't love, since the money wouldn't follow her any other way.

Her car sat in my driveway for more than a week after the the service. I could hardly wait for her brother to pick it up, so that I could stop remembering that she wouldn't. Of course, I'll never forget.

On New Year's Eve, a few weeks after Ellen's departure, Ed's mother also left the stage. People often thought Marj was my mother, because I resembled her a bit. I could talk to her about anything. It was she who originally introduced me to metaphysics.

For years, Marj had sent Ed and me gift subscriptions to *Science of Mind*. For quite a while, neither of us was quite ready for a different way of viewing life or our relationship to God, so the booklets piled up until I finally was willing to open the pages, as well as my heart and mind. Divorce triggered the awakening.

A few months before Marj made her transition to spirit, I picked up Deepak Chopra's *The Way of the Wizard*. After reading it, I realized that Marj had been my wizard. I sent her a copy of the book, with the deepest love and gratitude for her enlightenment. By that time, her health was in decline. She had suffered many years from respiratory disease.

I was still numb from Ellen's departure when Angel called that New Year's Day to tell me that Marj had left. Within a month, two bright beacons, spiritual seekers, and dearly loved ones were gone from my stage. How could I possibly adjust?

A few months later, my mother suffered another stroke. A few weeks after that, she suffered a fourth.

After the last stroke, Mother lay motionless, except for the slight movement of her torso, as she breathed. My brother Jerry, my sister Mickey, and I took turns sitting with her in the hospital.

As I sat in her room one day, I wondered: Is her spirit still in there? Why was it staying, if the body is no longer of use to her? I began to contemplate the mystery of comatose bodies.

As I left the room, I walked to Mother's bedside and prayed, sending her Light and Love. Aloud, I said, "Mother, if you're staying because you're worried about us, I just want you to know that we'll be all right. We will be all right. If you want to let go of the body, I support you in that. I want you to be happy, and you can't be happy, trapped in that body. You can let go."

Two days later, it was my turn to sit with Mother again. En-route, I decided to stop at the hair salon across the street from the hospital. I was sitting my stylist's chair when I heard a voice whisper, "I just wanted to say goodbye."

Instantly, tears streamed down my face, and they wouldn't

stop. I was so emotionally drained when I got out of the chair that I decided I couldn't go to see Mother that day. Instead, I drove home.

When I arrived and checked my caller ID, I noticed that the hospital had called while I was at the salon. I didn't listen to the message. I already knew: She had left.

I'd never had a close relationship with my mother. We never communicated well, and I'm not sure we ever really understood each other. Our first misunderstanding came when I was a toddler, after she had read Mother Goose stories to me. Since her name was Alyce and she was my mother, I deduced that she was Alyce Goose. She became "Abbis Goose" until my toddler logic and tongue matured.

Relatives have told me that Mother was in the hospital, seriously ill, when I was about three years old. My aunt says that at the moment when the doctors thought they'd lost Mother, I stood at the kitchen door, crying, "Don't go, Abbis Goose! Don't go!" She returned and stayed more than 45 years.

When we were kids, Mother rarely took us to funerals. When she did, she would make us stand in front of the casket and view the lifeless, gray body. *Gross!*

Now, as the handsome young mortician guided Mickey and me into a claustrophobic room, lined with fancy boxes in a variety of finishes, I discovered that viewing empty caskets wasn't pleasant, either. He invited us to select the one we wanted for Mother's body. It was much too morbid. We quickly selected one and scurried out of the room.

Next, we were asked if we had a dress for Mother's body. It had to have a high neck and long sleeves. I looked at Mickey. She looked at me. We tried to visualize whether there was something that met those requirements in Mother's impeccably organized closet. Maybe we'd have to buy an outfit.

The mortician thought he might be able to spare us the

trouble. He had someone bring in a couple of dresses for us to consider. Again, I looked at Mickey. She looked at me. This time, our eyes said, "Mother would kill us, if we put anything that cheap on her body!"

Once the burden of feeding and clothing six children lifted off of her, Mother was able to live a comfortable, middle-class lifestyle. She loved shopping on North Michigan Avenue and collecting shopping bags from the finest stores, which made her the butt end of a lot of family jokes. We knew she would want her body buried in an outfit with a designer label.

As I hung up my clothes that evening, I spotted it, the perfect outfit: a beautiful, white wool Tahari suit with a high collar. The bottom of the jacket's right front panel was designed to drape over the shoulder. It was so sophisticated that I rarely had anyplace to wear it, so it had been sitting in the cleaning bag for at least a year. I called Mickey and described it to her. Our search had ended.

I'm not a fan of funerals, so we decided to have Mother's memorial service in one of her favorite spots: in the shade of the powerful oak trees in my front yard. The preceding evening, we had a visitation at the funeral home for traditionalists who prefer to see bodies in caskets.

The evening of the visitation, I sat in the hallway outside of the chapel—ostriching, of course. I didn't want my last visual image of my mother to be a lifeless body in a box. I could see it, from a distance, through the back window of the chapel. To blur the image, I didn't wear my glasses. *Thanks for myopia!*

Friends and relatives passed by, and tried to coax me to come inside. After about an hour, I relented. I was beginning to feel silly.

I entered the chapel slowly, took a seat several rows away from the open casket and refused to look in that direction.

Aunt Doris, Mother's best friend since before my birth,

approached me.

"Paaat?" she said in her soft, lyrical whine. "Alyce came to visit me yesterday."

"Yesterday?" What in the world was Aunt Doris talking about? I'd never known her to be delusional, and she wasn't senile.

"I happened to open my front door and she was just standing there," she said. "She didn't say anything. She just stood there."

Mother had a lot of goodbyes, I thought, recalling the words I'd heard in the salon at the time she left her body.

"I was so shocked when I looked at her body in the casket tonight," Aunt Doris said. "Pat, she was wearing *that suit!*"

25. Bent, but not Broke

I am not stupid. Intellectually, I get it: Earth is not Home; for all intents and purposes, it's just theater. Souls can choose to exit the stage anytime they want. I truly understand that. Others are on planet Earth to fulfill their agendas, not mine.

That doesn't mean that I have to be happy about their departures. Of course, I'd like to be supportive. When I can't, I dig in—head first.

A year after Ellen left, my head had been buried in the sand so long, granules poured out of my ears and eye sockets. I had avoided everything and everyone that reminded me of her: power walking along the lakefront, visits to our favorite naprapath. I didn't call mutual friends. Consultations at the Psychic Institute were out of the question. I avoided all potentially painful reminders.

Thanks to my first chakra, I had plenty of survival issues to distract my attention. My newsroom freelance gig ended abruptly. Initially, that was OK; I had just secured two public relations consulting retainer clients. But a few months later, both of my clients cancelled—again, abruptly. One had cash flow issues; the other suddenly left his body. There was a lot of that going on in my roller-coaster world.

I beat on the walls and screamed at the top of my lungs for answers or an escape hatch. My life seemed to be in a one-step-forward, two-steps-back cycle. Sasha suggested that I consult with her spiritual advisor for clues.

I visited Dr. Crawford in his downtown office a few days later. He explained that he'd done a meditation the evening before my consultation. In that meditation, he said, my landlady and I had appeared to him.

"She wants you to move, and what she's going to do is harass you. She's going to harass you to the max."

"But I am so tired of moving!" I protested tearfully. "And it's such a beautiful place!"

"You know what?" he said. "This was not your place. This was only temporary. The spirit shows me here that the façade of beauty is there, but inwardly, it's not beautiful. It leaves a lot to be desired. There are a lot of things that need to be corrected there—and she's not going to correct them."

How did he know that? It was eerie. As he'd said, the beauty of the house had proved to be skin deep. Winters were especially brutal—not because I had to shovel hundreds of feet of snow-packed sidewalks, I actually enjoyed that part. The problem was indoors; I couldn't warm the first floor of the home to a comfortable temperature.

Petronela had added a forced-air system to the original steam heat, and I had installed a ceiling fan to blow the heat downward. But eight French doors with non-insulated glass panes spanned nearly the entire expanse of the northerly facing home. I was f-f-freezing; my heating bills were f-f-frightening.

Warmer weather ushered in a different problem: raccoons. Every night, I'd hear three or four raccoons galloping or fighting on the roof. My guess is that they had staked a claim on the place during the years that it was vacant. It was still home, as far as they were concerned. One summer, I caught nine raccoons in the humane traps. Petronela could not have cared less about my problem.

Dr. Crawford said, "All she wants is—"

"*The money!*" we said in unison, laughing.

"So the spirit is moving you from there," he said, "but the spirit has another place for you. And I'm hearing the spirit say to you here that eventually, you're gonna move closer to downtown. Eventually."

Downtown? Gross! "I like the area where I am," I pouted, thinking about the stark contrast between a neighborhood of gracious mansions, manicured lawns, and tree-lined streets, and the concrete and steel downtown high-rises. *Yuck!*

"You may be able to stay in the Kenwood or Hyde Park area—for now. I see that. I don't see you staying there for the next five to 10 years, no. I feel that you're moving downtown, near the lake. For some reason here, as you become more prosperous, you are going to gravitate toward the water.

"I hear the spirit saying to you that you've been wondering: When does my success take place?'"

"Uh-huh!" I laughed. Now, there's a spirit that's been paying attention.

"The spirit says to change that to: 'My success is right here and right now, and I claim it by Divine Right. As a child of a rich and loving Father, I claim my good, right here and right now, and no one on this Earth can keep me from my good.' When you hear this tape, recite that; and let that be your affirmation."

"OK," I nodded.

"You have to learn to—as we used to say in the spiritual church—you have to *decree*. In the Book of Job, in the 22nd chapter, it tells you: 'Thou shalt decree a thing; and it shall be established unto thee. And the Light shall shine upon thy ways.'

"You have to decree—*declare*—that it is so. *Affirm* it! And the spirit says, 'As you do this, you are loosening your money substance.'"

I had tried affirmations. I had loosed nothing but frustration, but I knew that at the most perfect time and in the most perfect way, I would be able to shake the money tree and

173

its leaves would shower me. I claimed my readiness to receive my bounty—when my soul determined that the time was right.

Until then, there were more pressing concerns. This man had just said that I was going to move, and my lease was scheduled to expire the following month. Would I be packing my boxes again in a couple of weeks? Dr. Crawford had said, "All of this is going to be done quickly, very quickly."

It didn't happen for another 18 months, but as he predicted, it was done *very* quickly. It was winter again in many areas of my life. We'd had back-to-back, near-record snowfalls. The house was a veritable icebox. I was warmer when I was outside shoveling snow. There also had been very little work, which meant that I was barely able to pay my rent. I don't know who wanted me out of that house more, Petronela or me.

Because of my persistently unsteady income and late rent payments, Petronela had given me a month-to-month lease a few weeks after my consultation with Dr. Crawford. I couldn't blame her. On the other hand, I wasn't at all happy with her lackadaisical attitude about the heat, the repairs, or the gigantic creatures frolicking on the rooftop.

One day, a new client miraculously materialized. It gave me the financial freedom to consider some options. A friend suggested that I speak with a mortgage broker she knew.

Who was going to give me a loan with my credit record? I wondered. It was the most ludicrous thing I'd ever heard, but my friend insisted. She said it probably would be easier for me to buy than to rent.

After running a credit check, the broker said my credit scores were strong enough for her to find a lender for me. I was utterly speechless! The report didn't list the foreclosures of my home or time-share condo, not to mention the $40,000 deficiency judgment from my buddies at the bank. There also was only one delinquent credit card that showed up!

Eighteen months earlier, Dr. Crawford had said, "I'm hearing the spirit say to you that you are going to rise again." *Could this be it?*

On the Internet, I found a huge two-bedroom condo in an elegant vintage high-rise, my favorite building in Hyde Park. I fell in love with the place in one visit, signed a contract and gave the agent the earnest money deposit. The end of the month was four days away, and my closing was scheduled for two weeks later.

My attorney had told me that if I stayed in the house even one day into the following month, I'd have to pay Petronela the entire month's rent. I needed someplace to stay for two weeks.

I contacted the relative for whom I'd paid the one-year lease. She responded, "Mi casa es su casa." All systems were go.

I filled Angel's room with furniture, clothing, and appliances that I couldn't or didn't want to take with me. Then I blasted an e-mail message to friends, announcing that they could have anything they wanted in that room, if they helped me pack. The place was swarming with activity for the next three days.

Several times during that weekend, I called the relative who'd agree to let me crash at her place for a couple of weeks. No response. By the time the moving van had pulled off, I still hadn't heard from her. When I closed the door behind my friend Badriyyah and her husband Abdul, the last of my wonderful helpers, I was straining to hold back the tears.

I ran upstairs, sat on the edge of the tub in the master bathroom and cried. I had nowhere to go. I hadn't felt that lonely or empty when I lost my home in the suburbs.

After a few minutes, I pulled myself together and called Abdul and Badriyyah, who lived down the street. Overhearing my futile attempts to reach my relative, they'd offered me their guest room.

After piling the last of my belongings in my car, I drove to their home for the night. When I packed my car to leave their home, it was almost a year and a half later.

26. The Longest Night

My hospitable girlfriend and former newsroom colleague, Karen, loves to invite overnight guests to her beautiful St. Louis County mansion. But she fondly quotes Benjamin Franklin: "After three days, guests, like fish, begin to stink." I've allowed people to stay in my home much longer than a few days. In fact, on several occasions, relatively new friends asked if they could stay in one of my spare bedrooms for a couple of weeks—and stayed for months.

One friend left without as much as a goodbye. Another found my home so comfortable, after two weeks, she changed the address on her driver's license to mine.

I vowed that I would never be that kind of guest in someone else's home. So how did my "overnight" stay roll into a 450-day odyssey?

Short answer? I absolutely, positively couldn't avoid it, and nothing I did seemed to change it. That's quite a predicament for a staunchly independent girl, accustomed to calling her own shots and having her own space.

In a world of reaping and sowing, you'd think that someone who always welcomed others into her home would never be homeless, wouldn't you? It certainly didn't make sense to me.

So I did what Dr. Peebles had years earlier predicted: I sleuthed for the underlying answers to my predicament. I needed to know why my life was unfolding as it was.

The process, which always gives rise to great drama, starts by evaluating all of the clues at hand. Two months into my residency at Abdul's and Badriyyah's, there were many.

Clue #1: My relative's inexplicable silence, after agreeing that I could stay in her home during the two weeks I awaited my closing. I certainly didn't want to be anywhere that I was unwelcome. And I didn't have to. That leads to...

Clue #2: Abdul's and Badriyyah's unconditional hospitality. Badriyyah and I had worked in the same newsroom for years, and we'd been neighbors on three occasions, but we'd never been close, socially. Consequently, I was uneasy staying at their home more than a couple of nights. I felt as if I were imposing. They didn't, and invited me to stay as long as I needed.

Clue #3: The cancelled condo purchase. A week prior to my scheduled closing, Abdul and Badriyyah accompanied me to the condo to meet a housing inspector. The place hadn't been occupied for nine years. The inspector's report revealed that a lot of work had to be done.

I called my mortgage broker to determine whether the mortgage could include a construction loan to rehab the place. She didn't think it would be a problem. At worst, she thought that I simply could move into the condo, and then apply for the second loan.

Was she kidding? I was lucky enough to get initial approval on the first mortgage. There was no way I was going to move all my furniture into a place that needed major repairs from the floors up—only to find out that I couldn't get another loan.

For weeks, long past my closing date, the broker searched for a mortgage with a construction loan to no avail. Then she discovered that construction loans could be tied to the first mortgage of a single-family home, but not to a condo.

I didn't want to close the deal on this purchase, hoping to get another loan later. In the meantime, I was living in my friends' small guest room with my laptop, printer, fax machine, and enough clothes to last two weeks. And I was beginning to know this Muslim family better than I had in the more than 20 years that we'd been acquainted.

After the first month in their home, Abdul stopped calling me by my name. I had become "Sis". It was the highest compliment I'd ever been paid. I had never felt the intense kinship in my birth family as I did with my friends.

Perhaps the oddest thing was that although we were the same age, Abdul and Badriyyah sometimes fussed over me like doting parents. Their teenage son, whom I barely had known before, seemed like my little brother. There was a loving, familial spirit in their home that nourished me. Despite that, I was a grown up who wanted to be in her own space.

That would have to wait. In addition to the rehab dilemma, a more thorough credit check prior to closing coughed up all of the dirt I had expected initially, which added a new twist to my home-buying drama.

"No problem," said the broker. "Just increase your down payment—and find a place that doesn't require any major repairs."

I recalled that I had phoned Barbara in Philadelphia prior to moving. She was puzzled when I told her that I was buying a place in a vintage building. I would be closing in a few weeks? she wondered. She didn't see me moving there soon, if at all.

"The place I see you moving into is a tall building," she said. "And there's something black all around it."

A building with something black around it? I couldn't envision such a place. I wondered if I should have paid more attention to Barbara's prediction, instead of pursuing the ill-fated vintage condo purchase.

Luckily, it was time for my annual appointment with America, a remarkable spiritual advisor closer to home.

Meeting with America is like going to the opera with a girlfriend who is fluent in Italian. You may have a vague idea of the story line, and you hate diverting your attention to the subtitles above the stage. Your girlfriend, on the other hand, comprehends every word. She gives you insights and a new appreciation for the skillfully crafted plot that would have otherwise whizzed over your head.

In the opera that is your life, the odd twist is that the playwright is you, the spirit part of you. Either before you entered the body, or during periods of sleep, your spirit develops a plot, contracts all of the characters, and designs the sets and the props. Your physical self can't remember any of it, and the language couldn't be more foreign. What you need most, at a time such as this, is a guide—an interpreter who understands things of spirit. Ideally, this interpreter would have a lot of talent and a lot of patience. For me, that would be Miss America.

Warm, soft-spoken, and dressed like a schoolteacher, America ushers you into the audience of your life drama from the desk in her small, neat office. There's nothing to distract you—no candles, no incense, no crystals, no hocus-pocus. You get the information you need, delivered with amazing clarity by this petite woman with a loving, knowing smile.

She opens each annual session by telling you about the growth opportunities you will be facing during the upcoming year, and offers suggestions for getting the best results from those opportunities.

I'd first heard about America after Ellen consulted with her, on a fluke. A friend couldn't keep her appointment, so she gave the time slot to Ellen.

Odd, I thought. *Why didn't the friend simply reschedule her appointment?* What I didn't know was that it had taken Ellen's friend three months to get an appointment with this phenom.

She didn't want to waste the time she'd already invested, so she passed on the appointment.

At the time, I wasn't in research mode, so when Ellen raved about her consultation, I did nothing. Later, another friend had a consultation with America because a friend couldn't keep her appointment. She also raved about the visit and insisted that I schedule a consultation. By that time, the wait was six months, and I found out why: At the end of a consultation with America, clients typically schedule the following year's appointment. As a result, new clients have a long wait for their initial consultation.

This was to be my second appointment with her. It couldn't have come at a better time. I needed to understand why I had been in my friends' home for two months, instead of two weeks. I was stressed, quite frustrated, and on the brink of something completely foreign to me: fear.

27. The Guardian Angels

America told me that several angels had appeared to her when she meditated about me prior to my arrival. She said that these angels represented qualities within me. Each of them had a personal message.

The first one was the Angel of Humor, who urged me to laugh at situations in which I find myself, and to be empowered by finding humor in them. *That'll be a neat trick*, I thought. There was nothing funny about my situation.

Next, there was the Angel of Possibilities, who reminded me that the unknown is just God's opportunity, waiting to be discovered. America explained that these first two characteristics work together. There is a quality of humor in me, as well as fearlessness of the unknown. So often, she said, I've been in the "Blankness."

Blankness? Before I could ask what she meant, America explained. "These periods remind us that sometimes we cannot force our agenda. Sometimes, it is just not what is meant to be. Sometimes, we have to step into the Blankness. And out of that Blankness, the agenda is revealed. There's always some value to every experience."

I recalled saying something similar to Ellen when she insisted that I had the power to save my home. I'd also said it to Angel, when she was unable to return to campus her junior year. Now, someone was saying it to me; and I felt the same resistance to the idea of powerlessness that they had felt. America could sense that, and was compassionate as she tried to help me understand the script I was being forced to follow.

"Your life is in the Unknown right now, in the Blankness," she said. "The symbolism that kept coming up was that you are standing in a desert. What you can see is the sand and the dryness. What will be revealed to you is all the fruitfulness below the sand.

"God is getting ready to reveal the fruitfulness to you. It's not what you will reveal to yourself, but what will be presented to *you*. There is not much, really, that is in your control at this point."

Where had I heard that before? Years earlier, Dr. Peebles had said that my soul would orchestrate the circumstances in my life so that my physical self would not be in control. The problem was that my soul didn't need shelter, my body did. I was not on the street—but I was virtually homeless.

"Why am I not allowed to have control right now?" I asked.

America looked down at the notes from her meditation. "There was another angel, the Angel of Home. This was the message: 'Trust that where you currently are, you are supposed to be. For we have taken you somewhere safe, a place where the Spirit of Home truly lives, a place where you can feel, once more, a spirit of belonging—*and* be with those who need your spirit of belonging. You are in a place where you are being met with *heart*; and in turn, you are offering *your* heart.'"

Though we hadn't discussed that aspect of my experience in my friends' home, America was absolutely right. Abdul and Badriyyah had given me an opportunity to see what a truly loving family relationship looked like. More than that, it was an opportunity to be in the midst of that love, breathe it in and be nurtured by it.

I was with a very close, caring family. Badriyyah and Abdul were as much in love as they'd been when they met in college. Their teenage son, Jaiz, was as devoted to them as they were to him. Their older son, Jamal, attended college, out of state.

Until that moment, I hadn't focused on the atmosphere of their home. It certainly hadn't occurred to me that I had been sent there purposely. I couldn't see it because I was fixated on the sand, the dryness—what I didn't have, rather than the gift I'd been given.

"It is no coincidence that you're there," America said, as she resumed the message from the Angel of Home. "I said to the Angel, 'Well, if this experience has been brought back into her life, maybe this is the experience that will allow her to attract the energy that she needs to find and create that for herself.'

"If you're with happy, empowered, loving people, that's going to rub off. They're giving you a home. It's giving you the experience, once again, of knowing what being a *daughter* feels like, of being taken care of in that way. The Angel said, 'We have provided for you a place where you will be held in love and in a strong embrace.'"

It certainly was true. Although I hadn't mentioned it, that's exactly the experience I was having: I was loved, accepted, embraced, and taken care of like a daughter.

It also was apparent that my angels were holding me in a strong, loving embrace, as well. How comforting! No matter how chaotic my life looked on the surface, no matter how impatient I was to find a home, my needs were being met—in body and in spirit. I exhaled.

America looked at me, smiling, "And I said to myself, 'Well, maybe she's somewhere with friends where she feels accepted, and loved, and understood.' They're not *doing* for you, but they're giving you what you need so you can go and do for yourself—like nice, healthy parents do.

"This is really what you're experiencing. If God wants to give you this, enjoy it. I'm not saying take advantage of it. I'm not saying stay there beyond the time you should. What I am saying is: *enjoy* it."

America's counsel reminded me about something else Dr. Peebles had said about my history in various bodies: I was always so much in control that I never allowed the Universe to give me gifts. The Waheeds certainly were a gift that I would have missed if I had stayed with my relative or had swiftly closed the deal on the beautiful-but-decrepit condo. Still, I was disappointed about that deal. I described to America the floor plan and all of the work that need to be done in the place.

"Was this an apartment?" she asked. "I did feel that the place you would go after this warm, safe place is an apartment. I saw more of a modern apartment, though. Something that maybe already is rehabbed. I really felt you could move into this space without doing any work on it.

"I did not see it as a huge space. How big was this place?"

"It was a two-bedroom unit," I said.

"That's what I saw. I saw a space where there would be room for you to have an office and room for you to have a bedroom. So I figured, OK, this is probably a two-bedroom— not huge, but not super small; a simple place, but safe and secure. I did see a large living room. I saw a smaller dining area. I saw a simple kitchen, very functional and actually updated, not old."

That didn't sound like my vintage condo at all. It had a sizable dining room, and the kitchen hadn't been updated since the Fifties or Sixties.

"I did, interestingly enough, see it facing the lake," America continued. "But it doesn't appear to be as old as the apartment you're describing."

I whined. "I can't stay with these wonderful people forever.

It's already been two months!"

"I'm not saying stay there forever," she assured me. "But while you're in that space, know that the angels sent you there. They sent you there, again, to get back in touch with what home and safety feel like, so that you can actually attract that space into your life."

She could see the disappointment on my face. "Do yourself a favor," she said, leaning toward me. "First of all, feel *good* about being in the house with these people. These people *like* having you there. They know you will be there *only* the time you need to be there. You won't overstay your welcome. You wouldn't do that. Give yourself that break."

I was willing to try. Still, I was obsessing over being in my dear friends' home so long. But America was right—they seemed to be delighted that I was there, and certainly had made me feel as though I already had found a home.

Sometimes we don't understand why things happen. Certainly, when we're wrapped up in the details, we can't see the Big Picture. Sitting in the audience of that drama now, I see myself dangling from a high wire, holding on tightly. The God of my heart is urging, "Let go! Trust me, Pat. Just let go! I won't let you fall. Just trust me, and let go."

Why do we need to be reminded that within us is all the power of the Universe—and all of the wisdom? Why can't we simply trust that we're always exactly where we are supposed to be to learn the lessons we're supposed to learn, no matter how wacky it looks, on the surface?

In this case, the clues were all there. Everything had unfolded in the most perfect way to lift me out of the superficially lovely cottage, and gently place me into the deeply loving home—where I obviously *belonged*.

28. Mind over Matter

Moments after the first flash of lightning, the rumble of thunder churned beneath the pulsating rhythm of the jazz band. I wasn't surprised. Rain had been predicted. That's why only a few hundred, rather than the typical thousands, had turned out for the free jazz concert. For the past hour, clouds had slowly slipped between the sun and the crowd gathered on the lawn at the South Shore Cultural Center Park.

"*Go back*—in the name of Jesus!" a young woman screamed, thrusting an arm skyward, to push the impending rain back into the clouds.

"Amen!" one of her girlfriends piped in.

"Lee God binness *alone!*" scolded an elderly man sitting a few rows behind them. "This is *God* binness! He know what He *doin'*."

"Well, I don't want to get wet," the young woman scowled, rolling her eyes at the old man. Her reason was obvious. Dressed in a pale-peach silk dress, its long skirt sweeping the ground around her chair, the sister was a poster child for femininity. A matching silk scarf and a wide-brimmed straw hat sat patiently in her lap.

"This ain' about you, Missy!" the old man argued. "God got thousands of trees and acres of grass and flowers to water. How'd this get to be about little o' you?"

He paused. "And why you think you can stop it, inny ha?"

Once again, the woman rolled her eyes. She fidgeted with the brim of her hat. This time, she said nothing.

I quickly looked the other way, so she wouldn't see my big grin. She wasn't the only one having trouble sorting out what she could and couldn't control. With continued help from our friends—and a few outspoken strangers—I figured that she and I both would learn that lesson, eventually. I hoped it would be sooner rather than later.

There I was, a highly skilled 50-year old woman with a great academic background and professional credentials, living in my friends' guest room! How's that for out-of-control? No matter how hard I tried, the Universe seemed to block every attempt to move to my own place. What was that about?

I met the same resistance when I tried to attract viable, income-producing projects. The latest vacuum was sucking money from my bank account more efficiently than my Aunt Helen's old Hoover.

God is so good! I kept telling myself. It could have been so much worse. What if I'd had a mortgage and condo assessments due, with no income to cover them? Was a much wiser part of me aware that this drought was on the horizon? Is that why I couldn't seem to find a place of my own? In reality, my continued homelessness had helped me dodge a bullet.

True, I didn't have the home I wanted, but I seemed to have everything I needed. Realizing that, I created a new mantra: *I always have what I need. If I don't have it, I must not need it.*

Many times, I wondered if my life would have been more stable if I hadn't quit my job, or if I'd more vigorously fought Louis's decision to exchange my affordable townhouse in the city for the sprawling home in the suburbs. Did my body create this predicament, or my soul?

I frequently pondered these questions as I prepared dinner each afternoon for my new family. Abdul worked nights and was often stirring about when I was in the kitchen. Many days, he would sit at the table and we would chat about the directions our lives had taken, in the context of the bigger spiritual picture.

"I am absolutely stumped," I said, one afternoon. "I have never been unable to find a home. In fact, I've almost been led by the hand to my perfect home. This time, I keep knocking, but the doors aren't opening. What's that about?"

"I don't know, Sis, maybe you're just not supposed to go yet," Abdul said, shaking his head.

"What? Do you think this is my fate?" I asked.

"Could be."

"You don't believe in free will?"

"Sure I do, but I'm not sure it's an either/or situation, Sis. I know that I've badly wanted some things to happen, but was totally unable to bring them to fruition. They simply were not meant to be. Then, there are other choices I make—and *snap!* Everything falls into place."

I sighed. "Me, too. I remember complaining about my job a few years ago. I missed the days when going into the newsroom was so much fun. My coworkers were dedicated journalists who worked together as a team. We cared about each other, and cared about doing a good job. We often socialized together on weekends. I could hardly wait to get to work each morning. I plowed my heart and soul into my work.

"Then management changed—and kept changing. There was a constant parade of new bosses, and each new management team seemed to be more disrespectful and condescending than the last. I absolutely hated going into that newsroom! I felt unappreciated; eventually, I stopped caring about my work."

"I can understand that," he said, glancing down at the sports section of the newspaper.

I shook my head. "One day, I made an off-handed comment to my minister about hating to get up and go to work the next morning. He looked at me and said, 'It might help if you learned to love your job.'"

"Love it?" Abdul looked up, amazed. "Was he kidding?"

"I know! It was the goofiest thing I'd ever heard!" I laughed. "Then he explained the power of thought. He said that what we think about, we bring about. If my constant thought was that my news managers were mean-spirited, that's what I'd experience. He also said that the ill feelings would mushroom.

"I thought about it on the way home, and I realized that he was right. It had already happened. The staff's relationship with management was in the toilet. Morale was ridiculously low. TV news is a team sport. When deadlines hit, it's critical to have folks who are fired up and willing to go the extra mile to get the job done. There was less and less willingness to do that.

"After a while, our collective malaise attracted a news manager who literally would cuss people out in the middle of the newsroom. This man would cough and spit in your face, rarely covering his mouth. If you made a mistake, he'd scream across the newsroom that you were a bleeping idiot.

"One night, he was loudly humiliating one of the other writers. You know me—I have a bad habit of speaking up, especially when people are being mistreated. I screamed across the newsroom that the rest of us should not be privy to our colleague's reprimand. The manager rolled his eyes at me and told me to go home, if I didn't like it!

"This man hated me—still does, in fact! And despite the way he treats people, he's continued to rise through the ranks. I guess it simply means that other people are unwittingly attracting dehumanizing energy into their workplaces."

Abdul shook his head. "That's unbelievable!"

"What's unbelievable is that, until the minister explained it, I didn't realize that our hatred for management was actually attracting more managers that we loved to hate," I said, shaking my head.

"That never would have crossed my mind, either," Abdul said, setting the paper aside.

"I think it's because we don't understand the creative power of our thoughts." I explained. "My minister told me to see what I could create with love.

"He suggested that I meditate, and visualize myself inside the newsroom. Instead of seeing disrespect and dehumanizing behavior there, he suggested that I see it as a perfectly peaceful and harmonious place where people respected each other and worked together as a team to produce the world's best newscasts."

"Who was he talking to, Houdini?" Abdul laughed.

"Right!" I laughed. "I decided to try it, though, just in case he asked me about my results. Plus, I had done a successful creative visualization a few years earlier, out of desperation."

"Desperation?"

"Yep. I was a special segments producer, and had to go to Los Angeles every three months to shoot stories with TV stars. Almost every trip, I either lost my wallet or it was stolen."

Abdul's eyes bugged. "Are you kidding, Sis?"

"It happened three or four times in a row! It was like I had on a homing device for pickpockets!'"

"Man, that's weird!" Abdul shook his head.

"I was so tired of replacing my ID, I wanted to scream! The last time it was stolen, I had just read Shakti Gawain's *Creative Visualization,* so I decided to visualize myself pulling my wallet out of my mailbox.

After a few weeks of doing the visualization with no results, I gave up. Then about two months later, I opened my mailbox, and there, in an envelope, were the contents of my wallet! The wallet wasn't there—and of course, the money wasn't there, but everything else was!"

Abdul threw his arms in the air. "You're kidding! After all that time, Sis?"

"Yep! So when the minister suggested doing a visualization, I was game. Before I went to bed that night, I sat down and imagined the newsroom in great detail. No one was there, because it was after the ten o'clock newscast.

"I worked on shifting the energy in the room, making it a loving, peaceful, harmonious place. You know me—I got a little carried away with my decorating. I cleaned off all of the desks and even painted the walls pink, the color of love. I could actually feel the energy calming down.

"Then I threw a party in one of the studios for every misanthrope who'd ever worked at the station. I had a fountain overflowing with pink champagne and everyone had a large glass of it.

"I stood in the front of the room and toasted them, individually and collectively, thanking each one for coming into my life. I sent them Love, Joy, Peace, and Prosperity. I forgave all of them for the way that they treated others. And I blessed 'em real good."

"Whoa! That's deep, Sis."

"No, what was deep was what happened the next day. When I went to work, the energy had actually shifted. The way people interacted with me was totally different.

"It didn't last. But it happened. Maybe if I had focused as much on the peaceful newsroom I had created in spirit, rather than the unkind interactions I was watching with my physical eye, it would have lasted longer."

"Hmm," Abdul said, giving it serious consideration.

"That exercise demonstrated to me that our thoughts are very creative, and they're very powerful. I created peace for myself in what I believed to be a mean-spirited newsroom environment.

It didn't happen for everyone; it happened for *me*. Those thoughts were in *my* head. I should remember that, so I can be more conscious of what I'm creating. It might even help me understand why I haven't been able to create a home."

29. Whose Life Is It, Anyway?

My overnight stay at the Waheeds was in its seventh month when it finally looked as if things were about to change. After an extensive search, I had signed a contract on another fabulous vintage condo in the Hyde Park-Kenwood area, this time in an art deco building on the lakefront. In my tier, the elevator opened onto one apartment per floor. The unit had beautiful hardwood floors and an expansive view of downtown.

I loved everything—almost. The building's condo board appeared to be a refuge for Peeping Toms. My real estate agent told me the members wanted their own credit and background checks, and that I should expect them to grill me about my personal life: both marriages and divorces, my daughter, the schools each of us had attended, my investments, and God knows what else. It sounded more like a co-op board inquisition. They weren't loaning me any money, and I wasn't sharing ownership of the building, so I was not going to invite these strangers to pry into my personal life. I withdrew my contract. No wonder the unit had been on the market for more than a year!

Next, I tried a condo development that was under construction, one that was farther away from the lake than I had ever lived. Waiting until the building was completed meant that I'd have to stay at Abdul's and Badriyyah's a few more months, but at least I had a moving date to anticipate. Things seemed to be back on track.

Meanwhile, life with my new family continued to feed my soul. I was included in all family activities, even the "family hug". Badriyyah and I power-walked along the lakefront. Her three sisters adopted me, too. I went with her and Abdul to Jaiz's baseball games. We rented movies and passed popcorn around the family room on Saturday nights.

One month before my planned move, the real estate agent called to notify me that construction wasn't moving as quickly as anticipated. Occupancy would be delayed a month. When that delay stretched into three months, I threw up my hands in frustration. I couldn't impose on this family that long! The builder allowed me to get out of the contract.

I had to keep reminding myself that I was living the drama I had created, but I was feeling like a washed-up playwright who could only create variations on the same tired plot.

Instead of complaining, I decided to go with the flow. I created another mantra: *If it's mine I'll get it; if it's not mine, I don't want it.* However, that mantra wasn't adequate when an attempt to rent a condo closer to the lakefront turned into one of the wackiest dramas of my life.

It was time to look beneath the surface, time to rustle up the courage to go back to what was now called the Midwest Psychic Institute. The budget-pleasing student readings had served me well over the years, but my circumstances required an expert. I went for a big gun: one of the administrators.

I'd never met Amy. I explained why I'd stayed away for nearly two years. She nodded, understanding.

As I settled myself into a chair facing her, she said, "In the corner, to your right, there's some very vibrant, colorful energy. I'm seeing oranges and purples, a beautiful array of colors. I believe it's Ellen's energy."

195

No doubt about it, if Ell were to show up in something other than a body, she'd be in Technicolor, I laughed to myself.

Amy paused. "She says to tell you, yes, she was done."

I didn't know whether to laugh or cry. Did Ellen do what I thought she did? Did she just answer the question I had asked her two years earlier, after hearing that she had left her body?

I hoped Ellen would say more, but she didn't—at least, Amy didn't tell me that she said anything. Still, I was comforted, knowing the answer to my question, and receiving further confirmation that although Ellen's body was gone, she was still alive. And close.

"She was done," Amy finally said. "But she was surprised to find herself out of the body. Ellen had trouble being free inside the body."

She was absolutely right. In fact, it probably was the reason Ellen spent so much time meditating, transcending the confines of her body. Only someone who knew Ellen well, or was able to read her energy, would know that about her. As far as I knew, Ellen and Amy had never met, either. And Amy certainly didn't know I had asked Ellen that question two years earlier.

Amy segued into my reading, talking at length about my history as a soul and past experiences that correlated to this lifetime. When it was my turn to ask questions, she explained why the condo rental deal had been such a debacle: It was not the right place for me.

"Your body would have been happy, but your soul would not."

Another body and soul collision. It was the kind of news that would make a sister put her hands on her hips, snap her neck and scream, "And whose life is it, anyway?"

Ah, yes! I remembered—it's my soul's. Why do I keep forgetting that my costume ain't running the show? I could have relaxed, trusted my soul's wisdom, and gone along for the ride, but after another two months passed and I was still living in my friends' guest room, it was time for my soul and me to have a heart-to-heart.

America had said that my angels had sent me to the Waheeds', and they'd given a plausible reason. Had they forgotten I was there? Where'd they go? Could I wait until my annual appointment with America to find out? My goodness, that was six months away! I needed information *now!*

Guardian angels were a great discovery for me. I was thrilled to learn that we all have angels that accompany us on our journeys, give us advice, and direct our paths. They're the ones who whisper in our ears, prompting us to say, "Something told me to do this, that, or the other thing." When we ignore their advice, we typically wish we hadn't.

I'd met my angels during my first visit to America's office. I'd waited six months for that appointment. When the time came, I went to the wrong address, two doors away. No one was there to redirect me, and I didn't have America's phone number with me, so my long wait went right down the drain.

When I called her from home, it really got interesting. Knowing that there are no accidents in the Universe, America realized that there was a reason I had missed my appointment. She wanted to know why, so she meditated about it.

In that meditation, she said that she found herself in nature. That wasn't unusual; but for the first time ever, she said, she was standing on a paved road.

Why would there be a paved road in a nature setting? She wondered. Then she realized what the path represented.

"This well-paved road was your path," she explained. "It held every experience that was necessary to assist your soul in its learning process, to assist your soul in fulfilling its contracts and the delivery of its contributions, and to assist your soul in receiving the blessings that are yours.

"I thought, 'Oh! Pat has a well-paved road. There's sound footing.' And I think this message was important, because it was inviting you to look at it that way, as: My road is safe. My road is perfectly designed."

America said that she ventured onto my paved road. Along the way, she met a half-dozen angels who seemed to be waiting to speak with her. Each angel told her about a characteristic in me that he or she represented. One of the many things they told her was that I was not yet ready for a consultation with her, but would be within three weeks.

She said that she thanked them for the information, but advised them that she didn't have an opening in her schedule so soon. They instructed her to look in her appointment book on a specific day near the end of the month. She said she was stunned when she looked in her book. There it was—an available appointment, just as they'd said!

Now, whenever I'm scheduled to see her, America visits first with my angels and delivers special messages from them that always give me tremendous insight into my progress along my well-paved road.

In turn, I always write questions and read them out loud a few days before my appointment. As was the case with Ellen, the angels typically answer my questions during America's meditation, and she relays their answers at the beginning of my consultation.

I needed those answers most urgently. I called America. Hearing the desperation in my voice, she once again found a spot in her very tight schedule.

30. God, Bless America!

I drove home from America's office on automatic pilot, still trying to digest what she'd told me—or, more accurately, what she said my angels had told her: "We need her to stay until after the first of the year."

My heart sank when she broke the news. Tears streamed down my face. It was September; I'd been there nine months! How could I ask these generous friends to let me stay in their home until after the first of the year? Why in the world couldn't I have a place of my own?

I didn't need to ask the questions out loud. America knew exactly what I was thinking. She picked up the box of tissues on her desk and handed it to me.

"I know these people have been very good to you," she said. "Now, they need you. It's time for you to come through for them."

My eyes widened. I was suddenly relieved. "Do something for them? Oh! Of course! I'd do anything! I'd be happy to!"

As I put the Waheeds' key into their door that evening, America's words replayed for the 100th time: "We need her to stay until after the first of the year."

I wondered if I should say anything. What if America was wrong this time? See, that's why I don't like spiritual advisors to make predictions. It makes me perch on the edge of my seat, anticipating the predicted outcome instead of tending to that day's business. I decided to go with the flow.

Two days after my emergency consultation with America, I was walking up the stairs to the third floor guest room when Abdul called out.

"Sis?"

"Yeah?"

"I need you to do me a favor."

"Sure, what's up?"

"I'm taking a part-time job for the holidays, to help us with Jamal's college bills. Could you stay until after the first of the year, to keep Badriyyah company?"

I damn near fell back down the stairs. *"Stay until after the first of the year,"* he'd said. Those had been America's exact words.

"This second job means that I'll be working every day of the week, so I won't be able to spend much time with her," he explained as I was trying to maintain some composure.

"Of course. I'd be glad to." It was so typical of Abdul to think about how his decision would impact Badriyyah. He loved her so much, and he would turn heaven and Earth to make sure his two sons had everything they needed to prepare themselves for adulthood. Getting them through college was of primary importance.

"I really appreciate it, Sis," he said. "I know you're anxious to move on. Jaiz is home, of course, but I would feel so much better if you were here, so Badriyyah would have another adult to talk to."

"Don't even think about it. Consider it done," I said, happy to be able to give back some of the peace they had given me.

God, bless America! She had averted a disaster. What if Abdul had made his request before I'd been warned? What if I had cried? Would he have felt as if he were imposing on me? I'd never have wanted him to think that. I was too indebted to him and Badriyyah for taking me into their home and their hearts.

The first of the year came and went. Abdul didn't quit his second job. I still didn't have any work, which said to me, *be still.*

I took a deep breath. *I always have what I need. If I don't have it, I don't need it,* I kept repeating to myself. By March, it was time for my regularly scheduled consultation with America. I could hardly wait to get in her chair.

"When I meditated, I did feel that things were finally coming together for you," she said. "What you've *needed* to attract and what you've *wanted* to attract, in terms of opportunities and abundances, are really going to reveal themselves this year."

I was relieved.

"I feel that you made a lot of progress last year, even though it didn't always feel that way. But psychospiritually, you did. Psychospiritually, you really positioned yourself to do a lot of healing, and you facilitated a lot of healing for those around you—more specifically, the family that you are with.

"I tell you, Pat, I know they did you a great favor, but as I've mentioned before, you did them an equal favor. You really did."

That was so wonderful to hear. "I hope that's true, because they have been *terrific,*" I told her.

She smiled. "Well, the angel said, 'Know that you have been a mirror for them. Through you, they've been able to learn more about themselves and learn more about their capabilities, their abilities, and their greatness. If the experience kept *you* whole, so the experience empowered them and connected them more consciously with their strength."

"*Great!*" I squealed. I was so glad to hear I had made as much of a difference in their lives as they'd made in mine.

"I think it's very important that you know that, and own that, because part of being abundant is being able to own the ways that *you* are abundance itself. Part of what generates abundance in our lives is for us to hold a space of: 'I *am* abundance. I *am* value. I *am* worth. I *am* the gift. I *am* the prize.'"

I felt empowered, simply repeating those claims as she said them.

"As you own that reality, then you attract waves of abundance that are out there, because similarities will attract each other. Abundance will come toward you because you're claiming your own inner abundance: 'I *am* abundance. Therefore, I will attract similar abundance.'

Come on, abundance! I thought, envisioning waves of abundance emanating from within me and attracting more to me, like a huge magnet.

"When you went to their home, you all thought it would be four months, maybe six months."

"No, we thought one *night*. Then we thought two *weeks*," I laughed.

"But you know, I don't think you could have taught what they needed to learn from you in two weeks. What you taught them was really through role modeling and conversations that you had on an on-going basis, in an unfolding kind of relationship. Had you been there for two weeks, you would not have been able to deliver the message. *Nobody* would have been able to deliver the message in two weeks.

"The 14 or 15 months—whatever amount of time you were there—was so that you could be situated. It was so that you could heal and situate yourself actively in your abundance. And they could—and when I say *they*, I know it's *everyone*, but much more specifically, it's the *man*."

"I *knew* you were going to say that!"

"It's the man. You went to that house to help that man find his power again."

202

"I believe that. He and I really connected. He calls me Sis. And as you said, he and I have had these conversations. A relationship has unfolded. He's just a *terrific* guy. He's just a *wonderful* family man—*crazy* about his family. That's been such a delight, for me to see that kind of dynamic."

I was beginning to realize that the fabric of life is intricately, meticulously woven. I'd known Abdul merely as Badriyyah's husband for more than 20 years; yet as spirits, we'd been so close that I had agreed to come help him if he needed me, and vice versa. Perhaps he'd really been my brother in another physical incarnation.

When I arrived, Abdul was despondent about his career achievement. He was a Big Ten college graduate who'd been underemployed all of his adult life. Just as America had said, he had become more empowered while I was there. Badriyyah and I had remarked about seeing a shift in his energy. She said he was more like his former self, strong and upbeat. It never occurred to me that I might have had anything to do with that.

"You went there for him to realize how his worth is designed, because everyone's worth looks different. It's like a different coat, you know. Everybody wears a different coat of empowerment. I think you went to that house to help him understand what his coat of empowerment looks like and how it works, how it moves, how it contributes. He had lost sense of that. He had lost connection with that.

"So that was a mission that you were sent on; it's done. Now, you need to get a place. And that takes time, too. It doesn't mean the relationship is done."

"It certainly isn't! They are my *family* now!"

"Yes," America said, nodding her head. "But the angels are saying that you don't have to *live* there anymore."

203

31. Right Time, Right Place

My day-to-day dramas were graphically demonstrating the synchronicity of life. I'd never heard the term before Dr. Peebles introduced it to me through my office speakerphone. I didn't have a clue what he meant. Now, within the context of my life experience during the years since that consultation, I was beginning to understand his words:

"You come into this lifetime as a healer, Pat. You come into this lifetime with a great fascination of law and then justice, but for the most part, justice. You come into this lifetime with a fascination of synchronicity, the larger laws of the Universe, what it is and why. You come into this lifetime as a mystical student by nature and inclination, now, to recognize your prowess—your prowess and power, which you will find to the degree you are willing to suspend and then disallow any need to be in control of yourself or the world around you. And accordingly, you will find joy and happiness in this lifetime, Pat, as you recognize your vulnerability—when you are able to be so open that you are open to attack."

Open or not, I certainly had been under attack—from my mortgage lender, my company's vendors, my creditors, and even from Louis. And let's not forget good ol' Petronela. I was catching hell.

What Dr. Peebles had predicted was that through these experiences, I would find happiness. At that point, I was not so

204

naïve as to assume that my body, rather than my soul, would be the one to experience that happiness. Lordie, wouldn't it be great to *feel* happy, for a change? I embraced the possibility that my life would take a more joyful direction.

A few weeks after my consultation with America, I was at the hair salon when I spotted a former newsroom colleague-turned corporate communications executive. Moments later, as both of our heads were hanging backwards in shampoo bowls, she screamed. Everyone's head turned.

"Of course! Pat!"

Huh? She'd had a eureka moment. It had occurred to her that my writing skills were precisely what her department needed. She followed up a few days later. Afterward, she awarded me one-year consulting contract. Just like that, I had the green light to start searching, once again, for a place of my own.

As was my habit, I poured over rental ads in the *Hyde Park Herald*. There it was: a recently renovated one-bedroom penthouse condominium unit with a den. It was north of Hyde Park, as Dr. Crawford had forecast a couple of years earlier.

I called and left a message. After a week had passed and my call still hadn't been returned, I assumed the place had been rented. It had sounded too wonderful to last.

The next week, I searched the ads again. The penthouse unit was still listed. Once again, I called. This time, a woman responded to my message.

"I didn't have an ad in this week's *Herald*," she said, puzzled. "I ran an ad last week, though."

I was just as perplexed. "Well, it's in there again," I said. "Is the place still available?"

"Yes, it is. When would you like to come and see it?" she asked.

Oddly enough, she hadn't received my previous message.

And, just as she had said, I discovered that there hadn't been a second ad. I had mistakenly picked up the previous week's paper from my desk and had spotted the ad again. *This was meant to be,* I thought.

I arranged to see the penthouse the next evening. As the owner walked me through the unit, America's words echoed in my head: *"This isn't huge, but I can work with it."* Just as she had predicted, the kitchen and bathrooms had been tastefully renovated. All this place needed was a fresh coat of paint.

I explained my situation: the loss of my home, my horrific credit report. The owner understood, only too well. Her financial life was upside down because she recently had lost a big client. I was the answer to her prayers, while she decided whether she wanted to sell the place.

She handed me a lease to sign. I was stunned and unprepared. I hadn't yet drawn my first paycheck, and wouldn't have the security deposit and first month's rent for another two weeks. She didn't care. It was my new home, as far as she was concerned. I was ecstatic—and astounded.

Had another home been chosen for me? I wondered. Was I being sent to another place to fulfill a mission? Was it going to be as challenging as the last?

I walked through the penthouse unit again, marveling at the hardwood parquet floors, gazing out of the floor-to-ceiling windows. As I walked toward the dining area, I turned around to look back at the apartment. My knees nearly buckled.

From that spot, I knew that this was the place that America had described to me a year earlier, when she told me that she had seen my new apartment. She'd said that it was in a more modern, rather than vintage building. *Check!* She told me that she had seen a large living room. This one was 24' x 36'. She also had seen a smaller dining area and a modern kitchen. *Check!*

America seemed to have seen the living room, dining room, the den and the door leading to the master bedroom at once. From the spot where I was standing at that moment, so could I.

There was one more thing she also saw from that spot: Lake Michigan. To my amazement, there it was.

32. Movin' on Up

The move to Home #25 transported me back to the first time I felt like a grown-up, the day that Ed and I moved my things out of my mother's small apartment, the weekend before our wedding.

After living in someone else's home for nearly a year and a half, it felt very odd to have a key that fit in the lock of my own place. It was almost as if I'd never done it before. I had to reacclimate myself into the world of self-sustaining adults.

When I unpacked, almost every box unearthed a treasure. Being in the same space as my artwork, my furniture, and my books felt like a reunion with old friends. I was constantly reminded that I had taken a giant leap forward.

Inwardly, I felt like Angel, jumping up and down with glee. There was such anticipation as my eyes scanned the clutter of boxes. I could hardly wait to restock my bookshelves, sleep on my pillow top mattress again, and eat on dishes I hadn't touched for 15 months.

Not once, as I drove along Lake Shore Drive, did I spot my building in the distance without rejoicing, "I have a home again! Thank you, God!"

Neighbors *oohed* and *ahhed* over the beauty of the place. How did I get settled so fast? Did I buy furniture specifically for the apartment? Everything fit so perfectly!

As I was settling in and celebrating the return of stability, my consulting client abruptly quit her job. With her departure, the productivity demands that had been placed on her by senior management screeched to a halt. So did the long nights and hard days of work for the rest of us.

Before I could catch my breath, her successor exercised the cancellation clause in my consulting agreement. Cue the music on the roller coaster that had become my life.

Other work trickled in, generated mostly through contacts with my new neighbors. One of those projects, which started out as a two-week contract to polish a business plan written for a virtual reality golf course marketing company, turned into a research project and total rewrite. It took months to complete. Under normal circumstances, that would have been great. However, despite the client's repeated claims that investors were merely waiting for the finished document, and that there would be a high level job for me when the company launched, investors never surfaced. I received only one week's pay for all those months of work. (Can we say "karma created or completed"?)

My life was beginning to have fewer surprises. Up one day, down the next and the one after that.

A few months later, my landlady announced her decision to sell the condo. Initially, we both had assumed that I would buy the penthouse unit, but that was when I had a lucrative contract—and before she priced the unit about 20 percent over market value.

It was stupefying, on a number of levels. Why had I been sent to place that I could live in for only a year? I'd been homeless longer than that! And who in the world pays more for a property than it's worth? I didn't know what to make of any of it. It was time for me to get a clue.

At the end of the previous fall's emergency consultation with America, I'd added a semiannual appointment for the following fall. That consultation was only a few weeks away.

209

America's reaction to the asking price surprised me. Always calm and soft-spoken, this time, she was as offended as I had been.

"Don't you buy that apartment from that woman!" she said, pounding her fist on her desk.

America was preaching to the choir. I had no intention of buying anything that wasn't a bargain. In fact, the longer I stayed in it, the more eager I was to leave. Since the freight elevator, which was right outside my kitchen door, also was the closest elevator to the parking garage, I frequently heard bumping and thumping of deliveries, grocery carts, and neighbors' conversations outside my door.

Then there was the heat problem. The building had converted from rental to condo. There was a universal heating system and no thermostats in each unit. Most of the floor-to-ceiling windows in my corner unit faced south. During the winter, I either had to keep the windows open or roast. In the spring, if the temperature climbed before the air conditioning was turned on, the apartment was like a sauna.

I began to look forward to finding Home #26. I had nearly nine months to search. I visited one building after another, but I couldn't find a place with comparable spaciousness.

"I wish I could pick up this apartment and take it to a nicer building!" I complained to my high school buddy Vici, who'd become the minister of a Unity church on the west coast.

"I know what you mean," she said. She recently had stumbled upon the unopened letter to God that had been returned to her months after the annual Burning Bowl service at her church. Among the desired items she had listed in that letter was "a heavenly place to live".

Months later, she gasped when she read that part of the letter. Since writing it, she had bought a new home. It was on a road named...Heavenly Place.

"Just claim it!" she instructed me. "You are God's child! It's God's good pleasure to give you the Kingdom. Tell Him exactly what you want."

Yeah, right. If one more person told me it was God's good pleasure, I was going to gag. Don't get me wrong: I don't have a problem with the concept of "claiming" or "decreeing" stuff, per se. There are an infinite number of impromptu theaters and ensemble casts with talented, awesomely creative actors that can manifest whatever they want, whenever they want. I applaud them wildly. I'm sure I've done it myself, when I was in different bodies.

This lifetime, though, I came with a game plan, a solidly paved path. It's glaringly evident that the experiences on that path may have been painful to my body and my brain, but they totally benefited my soul and my mind. So I'm learning to go with the flow. I'm learning to allow the will of my God-Self to be in control, and to trust it more than my brain. I may never learn to enjoy roller coasters, but I'm beginning to stomach the ride without heaving.

Instead of claiming anything, I decided to say, "I now allow that which is for my Highest Good to come forth, at the most perfect time, in the most perfect way." Then I waited—and waited—to be led to my perfect place.

Before I knew it, I had deadline pressure. It was April, and my lease expired at the end of the month. I was scheduled to work for a client in Washington, DC for a week. I needed to find a home—quick, fast, and in a hurry.

"OK, God, I'm ready to be led to my perfect home!" I yelled. "I know it's already been selected. I just need to be pointed in the right direction. I need a sign. And make it unmistakable. Give me a clue, some flashing lights or something, to let me know that I've found it."

A few days before my trip, I spotted a couple of rentals listed

211

online by owners in a luxury condominium building in the city's New East Side, on the downtown lakefront. The building and amenities were awesome—a free health club, a swimming pool, a grocery store, and cleaners—but I didn't like the floor plan of the two units, which were in the same tier. I also wasn't crazy about their views.

Mary, who had lived next door to my south suburban home, had moved into the building several years earlier. When I called to tell her that we'd almost been neighbors again, she told me to check with the real estate office in the building for more rental listings. She also suggested a couple of other floor plans with better views.

When I spoke with the real estate agent the following day, he had only two rentals that were two-bedroom units. One had a floor plan that Mary had suggested. I arranged to see it that evening.

Mike, the real estate agent, led me to the end of the hall. *Hmm, it's a corner unit, just like the penthouse,* I thought.

When he unlocked the front door and we stepped into the small foyer, my heart began to pound. To my right was the kitchen, just as in the penthouse unit. Straight-ahead was the second bedroom, in the same spot as the penthouse den. Around the corner to the right, was the living room; to the left were the guest bath and the master bedroom suite.

It was as if someone had picked up the old place and put it in a better building, a *much* better building. The freight elevator was nowhere near the apartment; and the heating and air conditioning units had individual controls. *Yea!*

Then it got a bit eerie. Mike explained that the previous resident was an elderly man. He recently had made his transition. Shades of Home #19.

What adventure would await me here? I wondered.

"Would you like to see the view?" Mike asked, as he began

to open the blinds in the living room.

"Oh. My. God!" I was breathless. "You've really outdone yourself this time, Father!"

Mike looked at me quizzically, as I fought back tears. There it was, just as I had asked, and bigger than I ever had expected. My sign: flashing lights—whirling around on the Ferris wheel at Navy Pier.

33. The Golf Lesson

Home #26: There were some glaring clues that this wouldn't be an ordinary stop. Numerology breaks down 26 to an eight (two plus six). The floor I lived on was an eight, so were my apartment number and my birthday. Did it mean something or nothing? *What's in store for me here?* I wondered.

I loved opening my bedroom door each morning and seeing nothing but water and sky ahead as I walked toward the living room and into my office. I located it in the dining room, just as I had done in the penthouse.

One morning as I stood by my desk gazing out of the window, out of the corner of my eye, I saw something moving. I looked. The flap on the lid of my kitchen trash can was vigorously swinging back and forth. How could that be? I hadn't been near it.

What could be big enough to make the flap move that fast? A mouse? Oh, my God! Do they have mice in a building like this? Was there a mouse on the moving truck? What should I do? I'm scared to death of anything that crawls. As the flap continued to swing, I listened carefully for any rustling noises inside the trash bag. I heard nothing.

Deciding to whisk it to the garbage chute down the hall, I quickly ran to my bedroom to put on some shoes. When I returned to the kitchen, everything was still.

I reached under the sink and grabbed some rubber gloves, keeping my eye on the trash can lid. I quickly yanked the top off of the trash can, tied the top of the bag, and dashed down the hall. The bag was feather light, and I didn't feel anything scampering inside.

I opened the chute and tossed the bag inside, feeling awfully foolish—and puzzled. What was it? Had it jumped out of the can before I put my shoes on? The lid would have been moving when I returned to the kitchen. What was going on?

After that, I kept a close eye on the trash can, and was vigilantly on the lookout for rodent droppings. Nothing.

A week or so later, I was sitting at my desk, looking in the direction of the kitchen. Suddenly, the flap started swinging.

Someone wants me to know I'm not alone, I thought, wondering if it was the previous resident. Oddly enough, I wasn't afraid. In fact, I was a bit comforted by the presence, even grateful. I stared past my computer monitor to the wide blue yonder.

On clear days, Lake Michigan was indescribably azure, just breathtaking. Sailboats bobbed in the harbor beneath my windows. Sight-seeing boats and water taxis floated through the locks, in and out of the Chicago River. At mealtimes, ships pulled up anchor at Navy Pier and took boatloads of visitors on scenic cruises. One of them was the boat on which Louis had slipped the beautiful diamond ring on my finger.

How was I supposed to work, with all of this activity in front of my face? I wondered.

At night, Navy Pier was aglow. During the summer, I had a comfortable seat for the Pier's bi-weekly fireworks shows. And to think, I had whined when Dr. Crawford predicted that I would move downtown near the lake. Granted, the New East Side wasn't a traditional Chicago neighborhood like Hyde Park; better than that, everything I needed was within walking distance or a short cab ride. I donated my Mercedes to a nonprofit client two months after moving in, just as the bottom fell out of my life. Again.

I had been in the final stage of discussions about a long-term project when I signed the two-year condo lease. (After my one-year stay at the previous place, I wanted to make sure I wasn't packing boxes again in 12 months.) You've been watching my life long enough. By now, you should be able to predict what happened. Right! The discussion never materialized into actual work.

The only thing that kept me sane was my belief that my God would not have moved me into this beautiful place without providing everything I needed. I counted on that. I couldn't accept anything else.

For at least a decade, I had marched around, beating the drums, and affirming: "I am now paying my rent on time and paying my bills in full. I owe no one and no one owes me." I had "claimed" it, as instructed, but where was it? My ship seemed to have run out of fuel on the other side of the horizon line. With my luck, the man of my dreams probably was on it.

It was way past time to end the no-date drama, too. It had been nearly eight years. (But who was counting?) Wherever he was and whenever he arrived, I knew that he'd be worth the wait. Until then, being alone was still a helluva lot better than being trapped in some hurtful drama with a really bad actor.

As they say, you can't win if you don't play, so I went to all of the social events I could afford. I typically had a great time, but I never met him—you know, Mr. Right.

One hot summer day, a former south suburban neighbor called. James had never called me. He asked if I was dating anyone. My heart sank. Surely, he wasn't suggesting that I date his married behind, I moaned to myself. Actually, no, James had a guy he'd like me to meet.

James explained that Marcus recently had moved from Dallas and had complained that he hadn't met any interesting women. He specifically was looking for a woman who was beautiful, classy, and intelligent.

"I know just the woman you're looking for!" James said he'd boasted.

The two struck a deal. Marcus, who was a very talented golfer, promised to help James improve his golf game if he would facilitate an introduction to this woman. That was all the incentive James needed.

With so much at stake, I was almost flattered that James had bet it all on me. There was nothing flattering, however, about being bartered for golf lessons. I think James knew that, so he tried to sell the deal as a win-win-win proposition.

"He's a really classy guy," he said. "He wears this really nice, thick gold necklace with a cluster of diamonds. And he has this beautiful gold bracelet."

"Back up! He wears *what?*" I asked, incredulously. There was something about a classy man and a necklace with diamonds that didn't fit in the same sentence.

Was this James on the other end of the line? I had no idea he had an affinity for jumbo jewelry on men.

"It's beautiful!" James insisted.

"And he wears this jewelry *e-every day?*" I stammered.

"Oh, yeah. It's very classy," James assured me. "I told him that you're very picky. He said that's just the kind of woman he's looking for.

"Now, I'm not playing matchmaker, so I don't want you to think that this is a date. The three of us are just going out for drinks, OK?"

I sighed. Sipping cranberry juice in the glare of gold and diamond jewelry didn't sound like my idea of a good time. On the other hand, James and his wife, Evelyn, had been such great

217

neighbors—what the hell? I'd donate a golf lesson.

"All right," I said after an extremely pregnant pause. We arranged to meet a couple of days later.

About an hour before the non-date, James called again. *Doggone it!* He had forgotten a meeting at his church that afternoon; he wouldn't be able to meet us for drinks. Could he give Marcus my number? The two of us could go without him.

I was irritated. "All right," I sighed, clenching my teeth.

Before hanging up, James said, "Now, I want you to stay strong."

What? Where'd that come from? I thought I'd agreed to drinks, not weightlifting. "Stay strong—for what?" I asked.

"Well, I don't know Marcus very well," James explained, before hesitating. "He might be a player."

Just what I needed, little boy games. "Well, Mr. Marcus has come to the right place. I'll show him quick, fast, and in a hurry that I am not a toy."

A player, huh? I'll show his behind how to play, and who to play with, I huffed, as I hung up the phone. Moments later, it rang again. The caller ID showed a cell phone number I didn't recognize. I answered.

The voice caught me off guard. It was raspy, with a decidedly rural Southern drawl. After introducing himself, Marcus said, "James tol' me some real nass thangs abou' chu. Ah'm waitin' to meechu wit baded breath."

I cringed. "Well, don't bait your breath. It ain't that serious," I told him. In my mind's eye, I saw a lecherous old man with a potbelly and at least one gold tooth. I wanted to ring a nine-iron around James' neck!

I asked Marcus if we could postpone our drink for about an hour, so that I could complete my work (or until my heart stopped pounding with rage, whichever came first). I hung up the phone and instantly dialed my surrogate Mom, who lived in the building next door. Frances and her husband Oliver had a propensity for adopting grown folks they liked. I was the latest addition to their very large brood.

"What would make James think that this old guy was a player?" Frances wondered.

"Got me. A bona fide player who had anything on the ball wouldn't need someone else to introduce him to a woman. He'd be out on the prowl, doing his Mack Daddy thang," I said, shaking my head in disgust.

"Well, James must know something, or else he wouldn't have warned you," Frances said.

"Oh! I get it!" I screamed. "This guy's probably some good-looking, long, tall drink of water, and James *assumes* he's a player."

When Marcus unfolded himself from behind the wheel of his convertible sports car to usher me into the passenger's seat, it was clear why James had nailed him as a prospective player. He was every bit of tall, dark and handsome, with broad shoulders bulging under his pink golf shirt. A heavy gold serpentine choker with a cluster of pavé diamonds hung around his muscular neck.

My body slid into the car, but my spirit had hightailed it back into my lobby, and was halfway to my apartment, by the time Marcus' cranberry iridescent slacks slid beneath the steering wheel again.

It's just drinks, I groaned, as Marcus launched into a soliloquy about having no social life since moving to Chicago three months earlier. He complained that fraternity brothers, who had told him to call if he ever came to town, hadn't been very hospitable, either.

I was stunned. "You're in a fraternity? Which one?" I asked. This man didn't sound as if he'd finished high school.

He looked at me. "Whah you as'?"

Because I wanted to know if you even knew the names of any, I thought. "Because I'm a Delta," I said politely.

Marcus tossed his head back, laughing. "Ma firs' two wavs wuh Deltas!"

"Well, well. You're a man with exquisite taste," I smiled.

"Act'shly, ma firs' two wavs wuh da same woman. We mah'd twice, divo'ced twice. Nah, we jes bes' frins.'"

I sat up in my seat. Best friends with his ex-wife—after *two* divorces? This was an extraordinary guy. It said a lot about his character, if they were able to salvage a close friendship after their marriages failed.

Marcus talked nonstop as we headed for the restaurant and bar. There wasn't a shy bone in this guy's body. He yakked on as if we were old friends, telling me things about his life that most guys would never tell a woman within the first 15 minutes. Within that time I learned that he had lost his business and had lost his home. His wife (#3, but woman #2) had left him, and he was flat broke. In fact, he explained, the reason we were having drinks was because he didn't have enough money to take me to dinner. He'd deposited his paycheck, but it wouldn't clear until the next day.

I stared ahead. You'd have to lock most of the men I knew in a torture chamber before they'd blurt this information to a woman they'd just met. Marcus wasn't sophisticated, like most of the men I knew, but most of them weren't as refreshingly honest, either. What impressed me most was that Marcus was down, but not out. As broke as he was, he had an upbeat, resilient attitude about his life and his finances.

"Ah had lots of money befo', Ah'll have it agin!" he declared, cocking his head confidently.

Bad business decisions had led to Marcus's reversal of fortune. Like me, he'd even been homeless, living with relatives for more than a year. He got lucky when a friend who was launching a small business in Chicago offered him a job as vice president of sales.

Leaving Dallas, the scene of his financial suicide, he said, was a "vacation from worration". Marcus was determined to succeed in Chicago, because returning to Dallas as a failure was not an option.

He seemed to accept all of his losses well. Earlier that day, in fact, he'd misplaced his expensive gold bracelet. He said that he had looked high and low, before deciding he was going to look no longer. If it was gone, so what?

Wow! I marveled at his nonchalant attitude about losing one of his few remaining treasures. My admiration for this man was beginning to overshadow his big, glitzy Hollywood eyeglasses and the flashy necklace. But he was killing me with his poor diction. And have mercy, he wouldn't shut up!

Marcus's sense of humor was just as relentless. I couldn't remember the last time I'd laughed so much. Although his diction portrayed him as dull and dumb, he actually seemed quite bright. I also discovered, after we sat in my friend's beautiful but empty bar, that Marcus could possibly be an exceptional man. After surveying the stunning place and wondering why it wasn't buzzing with business, he remarked that my friend probably needed some good public relations. He suggested that I help out.

"I don't think he can afford PR," I said, noting that slow business means low income.

Marcus cocked his head and leaned across the table toward me. "Don' chu know it's nod always about money?" he asked. "Win you give, you always git it back—one way o' da udda."

Well, shut my mouth! From that moment on, I decided to focus on what Marcus was saying, rather than how poorly he was saying it.

34. Can't Judge a Book by Its Cover

Every life has a purpose. Everyone on our stages is there for a reason; each encounter is designed to teach us and to help us evolve. Of course, some of our encounters are more dramatic than others.

Once in a while, we find ourselves face to face with souls whose dramas are so intertwined with our own that we can't tell where ours stops and theirs begins. That certainly was the case with Marcus and me.

"If there's such a thing as a twin flame," I told Frances one day, "Marcus is mine. It's almost as if we've been living in parallel universes: We've both lost our homes, we both have one daughter. In fact, his daughter is four years older than Angel; and he's four years older than I am. Girl, if you saw him, you'd be stunned that he's nearly 60. He looks at least 10 years younger than he is."

"Something else you have in common," Frances snickered.

"Guess you got a point there," I said as I mentally added that similarity to my list. "Did I tell you that his most recent wife and I have the same first name?"

"You're kidding!"

"No, and he told me that if we got married, I wouldn't have to change my monogram, since our last names start with A."

"Married? Isn't it a bit soon to be talking about marriage?"

"Definitely! It's all really weird to me. Listen to this: my middle name is the same as his mother's first name. And his first wife, his best friend? Not only is she one of my sorority sisters, her company name is the same as mine."

"Oooh!" Frances gasped. "This is kinda spooky."

"Yeah, I know."

On the other hand, Marcus and I couldn't have been more different. He grew up with plenty of money in the South. My family lived hand-to-mouth in the North. He had one brother. There were six of us. His parents didn't have a blissful marriage, but they remained together. My parents were divorced when I was in first grade. His parents were entrepreneurs. Mother struggled to feed and clothe us on her small salaries as a legal stenographer, file clerk, and finally, a public aid caseworker.

We had never owned a home or a car, but negative cash flow didn't dampen Mother's dreams. She gave us the best education her money could buy. That meant paying higher rent so that we could be in a neighborhood with excellent public schools. That was tricky in the Fifties and Sixties. Blacks weren't welcome in every Chicago neighborhood.

Any extra money she had, Mother set aside for dance and piano lessons and Scouting necessities. She was both a Cub Scout den mother and Girl Scout leader. She talked so much about "when you kids go to college" that we never realized college was an option. Everyone was required to earn at least one degree—the more, the better.

Growing up, we dreaded report cards with check marks for classroom infractions such as talking, excessive tardiness, or not completing our assignments. The first thing she yanked was the TV (a huge punishment, since we were the last ones in the neighborhood to get one) and we couldn't play outside after school until the next marking period. Worst of all, we had to write: "I will not (do whatever we did)" 500 times every night. It had to be legible or we had to repeat the exercise.

"We are not second-class citizens!" Mother preached. She realized that it's possible to attend school without becoming educated, and she was determined that none of us fell into that trap because it would limit our mobility in society. She taught us that an educated person has social grace and appreciates the fine arts. She demanded good etiquette at the table and on the phone, poise, and impeccable diction.

Before the days when "equal opportunity employer" was the tagline on job ads, we had a lot of doors slammed in our faces. But whether those doors opened on purpose or by accident, Mother wanted us to be prepared to walk through them with our heads high. Once inside, we were to communicate and perform superlatively.

Marcus's parents had high hopes for him as well, and he complied. He was only 19 when he completed college. Months later, he married his college sweetheart. The following year, he was off to law school. He regretted that it was the only thing he started and didn't finish.

Growing up, Marcus—who preferred to be called by his boyhood name, Sonny—had every toy and the finest clothes money could buy. He had anything he wanted, except his parents' time. Sonny's folks were so busy that he claimed, "Ah raised ma sef!"

While Mother's eagle eye was checking to see if our knees were under the table, our napkins and one hand were in our laps, and our mouths were empty before we spoke, Sonny's parents were making sure he had enough money for a driver to bring dinner from his favorite restaurant du jour when they left for the evening. The food choices and poor table etiquette that Sonny developed while eating alone in front of the TV followed him into adulthood. He never cultivated a taste for fine dining.

In fact, he claimed that before moving to Chicago, he had never frequented restaurants that offered more than burgers, ribs and chicken.

Gifted with striking good looks, a quick wit, and plenty of money, Sonny had strutted around South Dallas like a peacock, in an eye-catching rainbow of the finest leather, linen, and gabardine suits. He had an extensive collection of expensive brightly colored shoes and reptile boots to match his fine threads. His assessment of Northerners, with our mostly dark-colored business suits and shoes, was that "y'all don' know ha da dress." He had no interest in adapting to Chicago's style; he thought Chicago should adopt his.

True to his Gemini sun, Sonny had two personalities. He was educated and mature, but didn't always act either. He wanted so badly to belong in certain social circles that he pledged his fraternity twice, until he finally was sworn in. On the other hand, he didn't engage in the typical cultural activities of educated people. He didn't visit museums, rarely attended concerts. When he accompanied me to a stage play, he said it was his first. But other aspects of professional-class social life? *Lights! Camera! Action!*

Sonny loved the glamour of black-tie affairs. Hey, if I looked that good in a tuxedo, I guess I would, too. When he stepped out, his proudest accessory was a beautiful woman hanging on his arm. *Aw, sookie, sookie now!*

Manicures and pedicures were mandatory for the lady in his life. Oddly enough, he refused to give his own hands and feet the same caring attention.

Sonny considered himself worldly, having traveled throughout America, the Caribbean and to Scotland with his golf club. Surely, he had noticed that each country, each city, and each neighborhood had its own culture, its own standards and language. Those who don't conform are considered

225

outsiders. If they don't adapt, they're considered misfits.

Sometimes we can ignore or invalidate the most obvious things, like the rhinoceros in the living room, if they don't support our personal agendas or false beliefs. Sonny's resistance to change dramatized this illogical disorder in us.

He and I were very yin/yang. This man knew no strangers; he could strike up a conversation anywhere with anyone. Put me in a crowd of unfamiliar people, and unless you've given me a chore to perform, I will try to morph into my spirit self—totally invisible.

Sonny was charming and tactful. Me? Diplomacy is my shortest suit. My strong suits? Well, Louis referred to me as a "household engineer". I can do practically anything but plumbing. Sonny, on the other hand, was the most non-mechanical man I'd ever met. He couldn't hook up a VCR or change his oil. His athleticism on the golf course, the tennis court, or the swimming pool, however, made me look absolutely inept.

We also had different reading habits. My home was full of books, including at least a dozen on English usage. The only printed material at Sonny's place was the morning paper. He worked the daily crossword puzzle to enlarge his vocabulary, but he never used a dictionary. So he only could insert words he already knew, often incorrectly. Despite that lapse in logic, Sonny was a highly strategic thinker, especially at the card table. He was an absolute whiz and loved to gamble, especially on the golf course.

Hand Sonny and me $1,000 to buy whatever we wanted, I would head directly to a designer outlet mall with my grand and return with a carload of stuff. Sonny would spend his on two sweaters, or maybe one suit. He took as much pride in spending as I did in saving. He and I were like teeth in a zipper. He zigged where I zagged. Our basic values and spiritual philosophies were a snug fit, but the little things that determined whether we'd be compatible day-to-day threatened to rip us apart.

Still, we had a haunting familiarity, a natural bond. I couldn't put my finger on it. *Who is he?* I wondered. *Why do I feel so connected to him?*

Sonny, too, was fascinated by our instant connection. He was certain that our meeting was no accident. "Ah was *sint* ta you," he kept telling me. "Ahm heah ta enhance yo' life."

That seemed to be what Sonny liked to do best, enhance the lives of others. He was as kind and helpful to strangers as he was to friends. Family was important to him. I loved hearing him end every conversation with his daughter and grandsons by saying, "Ah love ya da death." And I always laughed when he shared his father's down-home witticisms.

"Ya know what ma Daddy use da say?" Sonny frequently would ask me with a twinkle in his eye.

Each time, I would smile and play straight man, "No. What did your Daddy say?"

"Ma Daddy use da say, 'Be kefful wha' chu pray fuh, 'cuz ya jes mat giddit.'"

And he'd smile back at me, like I was an answered prayer.

35. Mr. Wonderful!

As the days passed and our friendship grew, I began to see Sonny, more and more, as a "Being of Light". He beamed proudly when I told him that.

All of my friends loved Sonny, and they loved watching us interact with each other. One friend observed that a "sweet energy" surrounded us. Another remarked that Sonny was a classic "only have eyes for you" kind of guy. When I was in a room, everyone else seemed to disappear. Angel marveled that Sonny was the first man with whom I actually had any chemistry! Doesn't say much for a girl that had been married twice, does it?

Even strangers noticed the magic. A famous retired baseball all-star, spotting the two of us in a pro shop one day, asked Sonny weeks later, "Hey, have you married that beautiful girl yet?"

"Ah tol' 'im, naw, na' chet," Sonny tossed his head backward, laughing.

We worked and played well together. We loved shopping together, doing nothing together. Sonny did the sweetest things. If it looked like rain, he'd call to announce that he was driving me to the city college, where I taught English. The school was only a few blocks away; but he didn't want me to get wet.

One morning, he called to say that he was going to cook my breakfast. As he left home, the skies opened up. By the time he reached his car, he was soaked to the bone. Then, he said, his boss called and asked him to run an errand. Sonny phoned me again to say that the breakfast date was off.

Moments later, the doorman announced that Sonny was in the lobby. I was stunned when I opened my door, and there he was, dripping wet. He wanted to give me a hug before running his errand.

No man had ever treated me like such a treasure! Sonny's playful side was entertaining, adoring, and adorable. His serious side was very wise and supportive. If he knew I was facing a particularly tough day, I'd awake to words of encouragement on my answering machine.

His was the first voice I heard every morning and the last at night. He called six or seven times a day, even though we were together most days. He often called to say that he was going to call later. Always, after talking to me for hours in my apartment, we'd talk for at least an hour more when he arrived home. On occasion, he'd even call during his less-than-10-minute drive home to the other side of the Loop.

"Ah couldn' wait," he'd whine sheepishly.

It was becoming more and more difficult to hold Sonny at arm's length. He wanted a romantic relationship; and he had warned me the night we met that he would "chase" me.

Unfortunately, as delightful as he was, Sonny wasn't coming onto my relationship stage alone. He was dragging a bunch of other drama queens with him: the star of plantation conversation, Ms. Ebonics; her flamboyant wardrobe man; and their supporting cast member, the bling-bling jeweler. There was no role in that ensemble cast for a girl who grew up in Alyce's be-your-best-self household.

I'd already been with one man who wouldn't take the necessary steps to turn his life around. I had absolutely no interest in reenacting that drama with another. Speaking as poorly as he did, Sonny was going nowhere fast in Chicago's professional circles.

Haunting me, though, was the fact that I knew plenty of professional men who were cultured, articulate, well dressed, had impeccable table manners and wore no gaudy jewelry around their necks. None of them was nearly as decent, as kind, as thoughtful, or as much fun as Sonny. Nor were they as patient. This man never complained when weeks passed and I still ended every visit with a friendly hug and sent him on his way, even the afternoon he had sat next to my desk while I was working, and massaged my feet. But how much longer could I do that without offending him?

Frances thought I was afraid of intimacy. Sonny thought I was insane, choosing to be alone for so many years.

I wasn't avoiding a romantic relationship; I simply was waiting for Mr. Right. With my relationship track record, solitude was a comfort zone. It also was the space in which I had learned more about myself, changed the things I didn't like, and decided to love myself, no matter what.

True, I could send a brother packing in a neck snap, but that's because I knew exactly what I wanted, and didn't want, in a mate. I had my list, remember? It saved his time and mine.

Sure, Sonny had solid virtues that far outweighed his liquid assets and verbal debits. If only he wanted to fit in, rather than stick out.

Call me shallow. There's no denying that we're known by the company we keep—birds of a feather, and all that. After being so visibly single for so many years, did I want to show up on the arm of a pretty boy with flashy jewelry, an expensive but brightly colored suit with matching shoes, and poor diction? Uh-uh.

Call me insecure. There would be places that I simply wouldn't take him, because I was afraid that he'd embarrass me. I didn't want the stress, and I didn't want to waste his time. I also didn't want to do or say anything that would hurt Sonny's feelings. He was so special to me. I decided to gracefully ease myself to the fringes of his life.

During Sonny's next visit, I sat in front of him and put my hand on his heart. Looking in his eyes, I told him how much I admired his warmth, his wit, and his truly beautiful heart. I told him that he was the very best kind of man.

"I have this list. And you are it," I said softly. "I appreciate you showing up to let me know that a man exists who is the kind of person that I'd want to be with for the rest of my life. But you and I have some incompatibilities."

Sonny listened intently as I explained that based on our costumes, people make assumptions about us. In Chicago, oversized gold-plated eyewear and flashy, expensive clothes topped with $30,000 diamond-and-gold necklaces were the costume of entertainers, athletes, gangsters, and pimps. Although he was entitled to wear that costume, it was not the image with which I wanted to be associated.

OK, so I wasn't totally tactful. To make sure he got my drift, I added, "I don't want to have to wear a T-shirt with a disclaimer that says, HE AIN'T MY PIMP, AND I AIN'T HIS 'HO'."

Sonny smiled and reached for my hand. He understood what I was saying. He also wanted me to understand something. He enjoyed wearing flamboyant outfits, but he had plenty of conservative clothes. He'd make sure that he wore them when he was around me. He had planned to buy new eyeglasses before we met, so that wasn't an issue, either. He also declared that he would be mindful of his diction, and asked me to help. I agreed to support him any way I could.

Sonny then explained that the expensive necklace had belonged to his late mother; so there was some significance to it hanging around his neck. He decided that he would put it in a safe deposit box. Bottom line, he was not going to let anything stand in the way of us being more than friends.

"Ah'd be *stupid* not ta wanna do beddah an' be beddah," he said, caressing my hand.

Just like that, the Being of Light in front of me began to look more and more like Mr. Wonderful, even if he wasn't Mr. Right.

36. My Date with Destiny

Have you ever captured a firefly in your cupped hands? Do you remember peeking through a little crack in your fingers to make sure its light was still shining, afraid to open your hands because your treasure might disappear into the wide-open sky and take its magic with it?

If you've had that experience, perhaps you'll understand why I debated whether to reveal any more about my dance with the man I began to call "Mr. Wonderful". This romantic comedy unfolded magically and made me grow in so many ways. Sonny taught me lessons that I needed to learn. Actually, they were lessons we all need to learn, so I've decided to open my hands and share him with you.

Take a seat. Turn off your cell phone and unwrap your candy, now. Get ready for one colossal drama!

Ta-da! As you may recall, Sonny's entrance upon my stage was dramatic. (Colorful characters know no other way to show up.) His onstage presence was magnetic; his act was positively mesmerizing; his teachings were utterly profound.

Sonny signaled a tremendous turning point for me because, in many ways, I was a firefly. I flitted about in rarefied air, in the cupped hands of the upwardly mobile. I wore the designer costumes of a social butterfly; but if you looked closely, beyond the grins and the hugs at the parties and the theater, there was no light in my eyes. I had shut down, afraid of another relationship disappointment.

Like a moat around a castle, my perfect-mate list helped me keep most men at arm's distance. It would take an extraordinary man to gather up enough nerve to approach my fortress or to inspire me to lower the bridge.

Sonny's generosity, his enthusiasm for life, and his determination to succeed provided an opportunity that I'd been denied with Louis: a real partnership, a chance to pool our diverse talents to kick some financial butt.

The more I learned about the start-up business that had brought Sonny to Chicago, the more concerned I became that his rebound would be deeply challenged. The president of the company was like an absentee landlord—so busy with other things that he wasn't tending to the infrastructure of the fledgling business. The void in leadership was evident in the lack of strategic planning and even in the company's homemade marketing materials, which wore a generic logo from the Microsoft Office clip art collection.

Mother had taught us that any job worth doing was worth doing well. I could find no passion for excellence here. There was a penny-wise, pound-foolish business philosophy that flirted with failure. Louis had demonstrated quite dramatically what havoc that philosophy could wreak.

Since Sonny insisted on visiting me practically every day, I decided that our time would be best spent discussing and developing the sales and marketing strategies that he'd need when the company officially launched. Before I knew it, I had become an unpaid consultant. It taught me a painful lesson.

"Your abundance is leaving you," America told me when I mentioned that I had been helping Sonny plan his work.

"It's leaving you. Instead of your abundance energy coming in, serving you and multiplying, it's like there's a hole somewhere. There's a leak. You're not managing well the art of generosity. Some part of you is not claiming your value."

There it was. I had dusted off my prosperity-leak script and taken that little raggedy show on the road. Again. How many people had to tell me the same thing? That's why certain situations and teachers keep reappearing in our lives. It's because we haven't learned the lessons that were previously presented to us. Until we learn those lessons, we can't graduate to the next step in our evolution. My soul wanted me to see that I still was enabling others and disabling myself.

Without expert marketing support, Sonny's success in the field was threatened, but there was no reason for me to be correcting work that the company's marketing director had been paid to do. I wasn't enjoying it; I wasn't being compensated; and I was angry and resentful that someone else was being financially rewarded for such poor job performance.

America sensed my frustration, and she was empathetic. "The generous part of you needs to be as smart as the other parts of you," she said. "If the work is exciting and interesting and matches your talents, but it's not going to pay you, then leave that space open. *Leave that space open.*"

I wanted to help Sonny succeed, but deep inside, I knew that it was not for altruistic reasons. It fulfilled an unmet need in me—unfinished business from my marriage to Louis.

We all have romantic, parental, sibling, and work relationships with unfinished business. Perhaps we lost a part of ourselves there or we didn't feel valued. After those encounters, we sometimes move through the world feeling wounded, rejected, less worthy or less lovable than we were before. Typically, we seek closure and validation from somewhere or someone else, trying to heal the hurt. We look outside of ourselves for the healing, because that is where we've been taught to look for all of our answers. At least, that's been my experience.

After feeling unloved and unvalued in my first marriage, each subsequent date was an audition for the next marriage. Wonder Woman didn't have a thing on me. I could do it all. What did he need? Someone to be his defender? A business plan? A personal shopper? A news release? A delicious home-cooked meal? A professionally produced résumé? A car wash? A birthday full of nonstop surprises? *No problem!*

Louis had not only loved my Overachieving Drama, he told me that I made him feel safe.

Earth to Pat: "Who's going to make you feel safe, Girlfriend?"

I hadn't heard that. I didn't want to. I needed to be needed. If Louis needed me, he wouldn't leave me like Dad and Ed had.

Yeah, right. At the end of my marriage to Louis, I felt more deeply unloved and more profoundly unvalued than I'd ever felt in my life. But just as deeply and profoundly, I'd been taught some important lessons about "Happily Ever After" dramas:

- Love myself first; everyone else lines up behind me.

- Choose a man who wants me, but doesn't need me.

- Shut up and really listen when a man speaks, so that I can hear who he really is.

- Control no one. It's an act of fear and desperation, and wins no awards in intimate relationship dramas.

- Others' departures from my stage should not bring down my curtain or close my theater.

- A real man acts like one; support that behavior only.

How important were these lessons? Important enough for my soul to want a guarantee that I'd learned them. Enter Sonny, center stage, to administer the advanced test!

37. Practice What You Preach

Days before I met Sonny, I had received a call from the English department chairperson at the downtown city college. She was a bit tentative when she called to follow up my résumé submission.

"Are you *sure* you want to teach in the Chicago City Colleges?" Ms. Johnson wondered.

Of course I did, I love working with young people. I didn't know why she was so puzzled until after I had gleefully accepted the part-time position. The pay was $75 a week per course—master's degree required.

It was Sonny who made me look beyond the disrespectful pay. He reminded me how desperately students needed teachers who valued excellence. Recalling my stint as a public high school teacher some 30 years earlier, I couldn't have agreed more.

Walking through the halls during my free periods, I frequently saw colleagues sitting at their desks reading newspapers or novels while their students ran amok. These so-called educators had no intention of teaching, because they had no expectation that poor black children could learn. Why bother?

Having once been a poor black child, I knew better. The teachers at my far South Side high school expected the highest level of academic performance from us, so did our parents.

For the most part, their expectations were met. My high school graduated a large number of black doctors, lawyers, school administrators, teachers, entrepreneurs, and corporate executives.

Sonny was right. Great teachers make a great difference. After his pep talk, I was energized, ready to fulfill my civic duty. To soothe the insult of having my talents valued at $75, I considered the city college stint as a reverse tithe. I was giving the Universe more than 90 percent and keeping less than ten, when I factored in the mandatory office hours to advise students and the hundreds of hours of volunteer work, grading essays and grammar exercises.

Before Sonny's persuasive pep talk, nothing less menacing than a pit bull would have forced me to walk to the college with any pep in my step. After he left that evening, I stayed up late and developed a new lesson plan. The next morning, I discovered that Sonny had called while I was sleeping and had recorded a inspiring speech on my answering machine. He was a one-man pep rally. I was fired up!

I walked into the classroom and wrote my name and this sentence on the blackboard:

"Mediocrity is self-inflicted and genius is self bestowed."

It's one of my favorite quotes. I found it in Glenn Clark's biography of philosopher Dr. Walter Russell, *The Man Who Tapped the Secrets of the Universe.*

Before the first writing exercise, I led the class in a discussion about what Dr. Russell's quote meant. Gradually, they began to understand that genius is within each of us. We are magnificent creations—mentally, physically, and spiritually.

To help them see themselves differently, I suspended the use of names. In alphabetical order, they became Genius #1 to Genius #30. For one and a half hours twice a week, each student was a genius, as far as I was concerned. And they were to consider each of their classmates as a genius, as well. My role was to support the best in them. I expected them to perform at their highest level. For the most part, they did.

While things were going quite splendidly in the classroom, the man who had inspired and supported my genius curriculum was becoming the poster child for self-inflicted mediocrity. Some days he was willing to speak intelligently, other days he was resentful of my assistance. *Is there such a thing as phonetic schizophrenia?* I wondered.

Sonny was accustomed to selling sizzle. Unfortunately, I was shopping for substance. I was willing to inspire the excellence that was within him, but I refused to support the mediocrity to which he seemed quite devoted. It wasn't as if he couldn't speak eloquently; he could. He simply refused, primarily, I think, because the suggestion had come from a woman. No woman was going to tell him what to do!

Sonny took great pride in being "street". Remarkably, as smart as he was, he didn't seem to know that he couldn't take that act everywhere. And he didn't want to learn. Or, as he confirmed, he simply didn't want to learn it from me.

One evening, Sonny's boss asked him to meet with the company's accountant, who was in town from Detroit. It was the first time Sonny had met the dapper gentleman.

Sonny had made sales calls earlier that day, so he was dressed in a beautiful suit; his necklace—which he hadn't put in a safe deposit box—was underneath his starched shirt.

During the conversation, the accountant expressed surprise that Sonny was so well dressed and articulate. He also voiced his relief that Sonny didn't wear gaudy jewelry.

What had he expected? And who told him to expect it? Sonny didn't think to ask. He was almost breathless, as he burst through the door after his meeting. "Everythang you been tellin'

239

me was rat own a money!" he shouted.

What? Did he think I had been giving him bad advice? A brother in an Armani suit said the same thing I'd been saying for weeks; and suddenly, it was gospel! I forced myself into neutral, before I said something I'd regret. I told you, I don't have much tact.

"Come 'ere," Sonny said, taking me by the hand as we sat, facing each other. I'd never seen him in such a serious mood. He briefly looked up at the ceiling, took a deep breath and stared at me intently. It was obvious that Sonny, who was never at a loss for words, was searching for the right ones to say. He was so full emotionally; he could hardly speak. His eyes were moist.

Finally, he said softly, "It's important for me to let you know how much I appreciate you. You have been behind me one thousand percent. You have supported my success. You have helped me in every way possible. And I don't ever want you to think that I don't appreciate that or that I don't appreciate you, because I do. And I want you to know that."

I was deeply touched by his sincerity and relieved that we finally could put the pesky cosmetic issues to rest. But a few days later, we were back where we started—on the "street", surrounded by Sonny's defiant army of Diction Demons.

Who is he—and what did he come to teach me? I wondered. To the best of my knowledge, it was this: What we get in life, to a great extent, depends upon how we value ourselves. Who do we think we are, anyway—humans, with the capacity for ordinariness? Or are we sparks of the everywhere present God—with the capacity for greatness and excellence? If there is excellence within us, what is the price of choosing to be ordinary, or less? In fact, what is the point?

Sonny was a textbook case study. On the inside, he was a warm, generous, beautiful, lovable, extraordinary Being of

Light. Unfortunately, he only saw the man in the mirror—a cool, prosperous, handsome, well-liked, run-of-the-mill "street" dude. It was dizzying, for a girl who likes things smooth and easy.

Ask Angel. She'll tell you about the day we rode the roller coaster in St. Paul's Como Park. Poor Angel was mortified. How does a four-year-old explain having a mother who screams bloody murder on a kiddy ride? Needless to say, that was Angel's last roller coaster ride with me. And it was my last roller coaster ride with anyone else, until Sonny.

Don't get me wrong, Sonny was a great guy. I loved him, but I wasn't in love with him. I wanted him in my life always—but stay on his roller coaster? Forget it! Maybe if we saw and spoke with each other less frequently, I'd enjoy the relationship more.

How does a girl who's brutally honest convey that without saying anything hurtful? I rushed to the computer, where I could edit myself. I wrote Sonny a letter that lovingly reiterated my initial concerns about our incompatibility. I concluded with an offer of forever friendship.

After receiving my letter, Sonny tried for hours to write a response that was as eloquent. He gave up, deciding instead to call and address each issue, line by line. I was immensely impressed by his very mature problem-solving approach. There was no defensiveness, no argument, and no avoidance. He was very adult and very direct. Bottom line: he told me I was important to him and he wanted to prove that to me.

That was an offer I couldn't refuse. But a month after his mea culpa, we were re-enacting the same ear-throbbing drama. Sonny's old excuse for his poor diction was that he had picked up poor habits from friends and customers in his South Dallas neighborhood. His new excuse was that he simply was lazy.

Wrong answer. I had spent three years with an industrious man who had morphed into a lazy lump. What I learned was that a man who neglects his own needs certainly will neglect mine. Been there, done that, dusting the furniture with the raggedy T-shirt.

On Christmas Eve, Sonny came by and we had a long talk. He confirmed what I had suspected for weeks: I had mistaken his "I wanna do beddah" bravado for "I'm determined to do better" bravery. He hadn't meant one word of his declaration. He'd said what he thought he needed to say to change my mind about our Platonic relationship.

"Ah din' necessar'ly agree dat ma speech was dat bad," he told me. That wasn't exactly breaking news. He'd even challenged me on several occasions to record our conversations to prove that he had made errors in his grammar or diction. "Ah jes' wen' alon' wit' chu. *You* said dis was what needed ta be done. 'N ah said, 'Well OK, mebbe she's rat. So ah did it—not necessar'ly because dat was what *I* wonita do, but because it was wha' *chu* wonita do. You felt dat was da image ah needed da po'tray. But, dat's da image *you* wonit me da po'tray."

Sonny looked away. He was as frustrated with our relationship as I was—and for more than one reason.

"Ahm use da bein' in control uh ma relationships," he said, looking at the floor, holding his head in his hands. "Ah made da mistake a' lettin' you git inta ma head. I been doin' wha *chu* wonit. I needa figga out what *I* wont."

Oops! The dreaded "C" word. Control was something I wasn't interested in exercising in a relationship, or having imposed on me. I didn't defend myself or chastise him for lying to me earlier. I'd been suffering with the flu for more than a week—a blatant violation of my "I don't do sick" rule—and I was pretty annoyed about it. I didn't need further aggravation.

"I believe that we were brought together for a reason," I said, calmly. "Has our mission been fulfilled? I don't know. We clearly have some outstanding issues. We can either muddle through them—or forget it, altogether. It's up to you."

Sonny decided that we should slog through the mess. I was willing to hang in there, in case our mission had not yet been accomplished, as long as he flipped off the control switch and dismantled the roller coaster.

With just a few hours left to complete my holiday shopping, I tossed on my coat, put on a smile, and Sonny and I lunged into his first cold Christmas Eve in Chicago. When we returned to my building, he playfully jumped into the same section of the revolving door. Everything seemed back to normal.

Later that afternoon before he left, Sonny gave me a warm hug, kissing me on the neck. "Ya know, you a'right, PA," he said. "You aw...right."

38. The Grinch Stole My Christmas

Christmas morning, I had an inexplicable urge to complete a book manuscript that I had begun eight years earlier. I had written hundreds of pages in the interim. Each time I resumed the project, I invariably rewrote it from page one. This time, I decided not to look at any of the previous versions; I was going to start from scratch.

I wasn't sure what was motivating me to write again, but I was sure that my decision would make my beloved angels dance like joyful Munchkins. They'd been badgering me to complete the project since my first consultation with America.

"They told me to ask you about the writing," was the message she gave me near the end of that initial visit.

Huh? What writing? I hadn't mentioned to America that I was writing anything or that I had any writing skill. Then I remembered my unfinished manuscript.

"I don't have time for that! Recreational writing is a luxury I cannot afford. My life is upside down! I need to find some stability, first."

"They want to know if you could set aside an hour each day to devote to the writing," America pressed.

I didn't know who these angels were, but they were starting to tick me off.

"Listen," I said impatiently. "Tell my angels that if they'll get rid of the no-income gnats the late-rent and negative-bank-balance gnats swarming around my head, I'd be more than happy to sit down and write whatever they want me to. Until then, *I don't have time!*"

For years, our sessions never ended without America asking the same question. Each time, I gave her the same perturbed response. What in the Universe were these spirits thinking? Couldn't they see that I was too busy putting out fires over here? *Give me a break!*

My financial life was still out on a limb that Christmas Day. The time consuming work I had performed at the city college had been emotionally rewarding, but fiscally debilitating. I loved my students, but I became a city college dropout after only one semester. I promised to return after I was independently wealthy and could afford the gig.

I stared at the computer monitor, not having the slightest idea what to write. All I knew was that I needed a concentrated period of time to focus on the new manuscript.

Sonny and I already had canceled Christmas dinner plans with my family. His car couldn't shift into reverse, but my flu symptoms certainly did. The relapse was enough of a distraction as I began the writing project; Sonny's frequent phone calls would totally disturb my concentration. I asked him if I could initiate all of our conversations for a few days.

By the third day, the last day of our pact, I began to detect some distance in Sonny's voice. We had agreed to work through our issues; everything had seemed fine when he left, but I could sense a shift in his tone. With New Year's Eve a few days away, I wondered if we'd celebrate together. It disturbed me that I had to ask.

"Ah ha'n thought about it," Sonny said. "Did you have inny plans?"

"No, I generally stay in. One year, I threw a small party at the last minute. But no, I hadn't made any plans."

"OK, Ah'll thank aboudit and call ya laduh."

Did Sonny just say he wasn't sure if he wanted to bring in the New Year with me? *Whoa!*

"No problem," I said, wondering what was going on. The next day brought some clarity.

"Ah have some decisions da make," he told me. "An' nat's wha ah bin—not negligent, but cernly, stan-offish. *You* made me stan-offish."

"What?" *Who knew I had such control over him?*

"Yeah, you made me stan-offish. It was dat ledduh."

"The *letter?*" My head snapped backwards, as Sonny's roller coaster suddenly jerked into reverse, and was now tearing full speed into the past. "You're kidding! That was last month; I thought we had resolved that."

Better hold on tight—and please, don't scream, I coached myself. This could be the wildest ride of all. "Listen, I told you that if you didn't want to proceed, it was fine with me. It was your call."

Based on the claim he'd just made, I figured that Sonny would immediately dash out of the door that I just flung open. Going, going...he screeched to a stop.

"Theh ah some thangs 'bout ma'sef dat ah hafta take a hod look et," he said pensively. "Ah cernly needa be honnis wid me, you, and ehbah'y else. I hafta decide what *I* wont, not what somebody else wonts. In so, ahmo take some tam 'n' figga id out."

That would have been a good place to end the conversation, but poor Sonny never did know when to shut up. He pompously declared that my "stannuts" were too high for "*inny*" man to meet. Before my head could bounce back from that pimp slap, he popped me again.

246

"You make me feel inadequate!" he shouted.

Why do we do that? Why do we blame other people for our reactions?

Sonny's accusation was as ludicrous as it would be for me to accuse my former newsroom bosses of *making* me hate my job. I chose to allow their negativity to impact my attitude and performance. Instead of pulling back, caring less, and not working as hard, I could have chosen to conduct myself as a consummate professional, no matter how little my efforts were appreciated. Who was I hurting by doing otherwise?

If I really wanted to irritate newsroom management, I could have dug in my heels and decided that I was going to enjoy my eight hours there, no matter what they did. Or, if I really wanted to spook them, I could calmly have said, "I assume you're treating me the way you want your boss to treat you."

The bottom line was that my reaction was my choice, and my outcomes reflected my choices—not theirs. It took me a while to accept responsibility for that, but it's a lesson I learned very well. Obviously, Sonny hadn't yet.

I suspected that he was trying to goad me into becoming angry or defensive. I'd listened very carefully when he said that he liked to be in control, so I was on guard.

"I don't have the power to make you feel inadequate," I said quietly, refusing to wear that jacket, and so disappointed that the former Being of Light had tried to put it on me. "Sonny, you always say my happiness is my responsibility: you can't *make* me happy. You're absolutely correct; no one can *make* anyone feel anything. So help me out here. I have never disrespected you, I've never been condescending, and I've *never* told you that you were inadequate.

"If I told you that your skin was green and your eyes were purple, could I *make* you feel that you had green skin and purple eyes?"

He sighed, knowing exactly where I was going. "Naw."

"I'm sure. Even if I told you, flat out, that you were inadequate, or fat, or ugly, or stupid, I couldn't *make* you feel that way," I said. "Don't get me wrong. I'm not saying that you don't feel inadequate, but let's be clear. *You* choose your feelings. I can't *make* you feel anything."

I had no idea that Sonny could play the powerless-victim role. It was so unattractive, so unmanly. He typically let his God-Light shine so powerfully, and he did it so effortlessly. Was that an act? Or was this? I was baffled.

I was also relieved. Sonny had given me an opportunity to see how much I had grown. A few years earlier, I would have been absolutely devastated by Sonny's spiteful accusation. Back then, I would have allowed his cutting words to make me feel undesirable and unlovable. I might even have believed what he wanted me to believe: that I would be one lonely sister unless I got my act together and lowered my standards.

That was then. This was now. Little did he know it, but Sonny's song-and-dance routine was merely an evolutionary field trip in my graduate level course: Unconditional Self-Love.

Don't go to the "What's wrong with me that I can't attract a man who loves me unconditionally" place, my God-Self instructed me. *Do you want to repeat this excruciatingly painful curriculum, or do you want to heal?*

I certainly wanted to heal.

Then sit your butt down!

The God of my heart was right—this was only theater, after all. If I wanted to pass this test, I needed to watch Sonny's manipulative little drama from a comfortable seat in the audience. I wouldn't resolve anything by sparring with him. I sat and waited for the curtain to rise on Sonny's next act.

Child, it was a showstopper! I've never seen a more convincing portrayal of a character who'd mistaken his limited physical body for his real self. Part of it was no act. I didn't doubt for a minute that Sonny truly felt inadequate; I simply doubted that inadequacy was true.

As someone who had felt "less than" for much of her life, I knew how real Sonny's inadequacy felt to him. I knew that he needed an "I'm OK, you're OK" minute. He wanted his flamboyant outer self and poor diction to be embraced, accepted, and valued. He needed validation.

After all, he had relinquished ownership of his self-worth. In fact, he'd put it on the auction block. If others looked at his $30,000 necklace and fur jacket and determined that he was "the man", then he was "the man". If not, he felt "inadequate".

We've all been there at some point. When others praise us, we feel good about ourselves. That's OK, unless we need praise from others to feel good about ourselves. And, too often we rarely feel good about ourselves without others' validation. We spend much of our lives reaching outside of ourselves for what we need, dressing up our bodies to elicit certain responses from others because we don't think we're good enough.

Dewey Bunnell didn't write it first, but perhaps he said it most poetically, in the rock band America's 1974 hit song: "Oz never did give nothing to the Tin Man that he didn't, didn't already have." Bunnell was right; everything our souls need is already inside us. We think it's somewhere else; that's why we're always so disappointed and so unfulfilled.

We want the spotlight to shine on us, unaware that the brightest Light is within us. I wanted to value Sonny as a Being of Light. Instead of looking at the dust collecting in his empty wallet, I tried to stare at the richness within his generous heart. Instead of making a fuss over his uncommonly good looks, I admired and praised his genuine goodness. Instead of supporting his ordinariness, I encouraged his greatness. I valued the inner part of him. He was enthralled with the outer.

Because I didn't value what he valued, he felt inadequate, which set the stage for the next scene—what turned out to be a drama of tragic proportions.

Sonny, who prided himself on keeping his word, had said that he would advise me about his New Year's Eve plans. By the afternoon of December 31, I hadn't heard from him.

I could have called, but I'd been telling him practically since we met: Be yourself. Do your thing. I don't want you to do anything you don't want to do. I simply might not want to do it with you. I can love you—from over here.

To dramatically demonstrate to Sonny that I only wanted him to do what he wanted to do, I did absolutely nothing.

39. Kicked to the Curb

A ngel called every half hour, hoping that my New Year's Eve was faring better than hers. She and her boyfriend were plowing through a breakup that evening. We both wished that she had been able to come home for the holidays so that I could mother her in person. Although we talked every day, often several times, the phone was no replacement for a real life hug. This was an emotional emergency, after all.

Angel's life had been quite unpredictable for a while. She reluctantly began modeling, after being coaxed by a keen-eyed colleague at the Upper West Side private school where she taught. Within a few months, the part-time modeling experiment had catapulted her out of her teaching job. Within a few years, Angel had become one of the most successful full-figured models under contract with one of the world's largest and most prestigious agencies.

It's not exactly what her father and I thought she'd do with her degree from an elite college, but the education wouldn't rot. Plus, the lucrative income gave Angel both time and money to pursue her first love: singing and songwriting. If she were to write a song about that particular holiday season, it would be nothing short of what Mother would have called the "rot gut" blues: low down, dirty, and wailing in pain.

A hectic schedule of modeling assignments before and immediately after the holidays had grounded Angel in New

York, forcing her to attend both the wake and funeral of her two-year relationship with a popular local musician. She bemoaned the time she'd wasted with him.

I argued that relationships are never a waste of time. Each one teaches us something valuable and prepares us for the next.

"It's a rehearsal for the Great Relationship," I tried to console her.

"Well, that was one long dress rehearsal," she said wryly. "And an even longer strike party."

We laughed. Angel was downright comical most times. Bubbly and upbeat, she had the wit and timing of a good stand-up comedian. But when Angel was unhappy, she was downright morose. As the clock hastened the arrival of her soon-to-be ex and the ceremonious memorabilia exchange planned for his visit, her anxiety grew.

Comforting her did temporarily distract me from Sonny's hurtful "I don't want to start my year with you" act, but I really needed to pay full attention to what was going on in my own relationship. I'd been progressing quite well in my Unconditional Self-Love course. I didn't want to bomb this important exam.

I had completed previous courses with really great teachers: first my father, then my boyfriends and husbands. Sonny was proving to be the most effective teacher of them all. He was exactly what I needed him to be—my greatest hope of healing my rejection and abandonment pain in this lifetime. Yes, I certainly needed to give him my full attention and take copious notes.

Boom! BOOM! It was midnight. In the first seconds of the New Year, gigantic plumes of electrifying color exploded outside my window, brightening every inch of the front of the condo. In the back, in the darkness, a ball of humanity was curled up on my bedroom floor in full meltdown.

Kicked to the curb. I had never imagined that Sonny, of all people, was even capable of being so dehumanizing. He didn't even call to say that he didn't want to bring in the New Year with me. He treated me as if I were totally insignificant, as if I didn't even exist. I had never witnessed him being so mean to anyone.

Sonny had treated me better than any man. Who knew he'd treat me worse than all of them? Had I been blind or blind-sided? I wondered, relieved that the thunderous fireworks finally had ended, and looking forward to the noisy crowd below returning to their cars and restoring the flow of traffic on Lake Shore Drive.

My world did not look the same on New Year's morning. I felt as if my heart had been surgically removed. Doctors always insist that you get up and walk as soon as possible after an invasive procedure.

That afternoon, I took my first step. Since we always reap what we sow, I knew that Sonny's meanness and disrespect would be met with meanness and disrespect. My job was to make sure that I did and said nothing that created any unwanted karma on my side of the ledger; so I decided to react the way God reacts to all bad acting: with patience and forgiveness.

As if nothing had happened, I called Sonny and casually wished him a Happy New Year. After some small talk about the progress of my writing project, I was off the phone.

He probably hung up, dumbfounded, wondering what happened to my righteous indignation, my tearful guilt-trip, and the down-home cussing out he expected? Had I delivered any of those reactions, I would have ended that conversation trembling with rage, heart pounding, sweat pouring from every gland, and a whole sack of karma to balance. Not the kid.

I walked away from the phone feeling more powerful than I'd ever felt in a woman's body—invincible, in fact. Instead of stomping around, replaying my tirade, and thinking about what spiteful words I could have said to retaliate, I put my thoughts and all of my energy where they belonged—on me.

We've learned to feel small or be angry when someone we care about is disrespectful or hurtful. We don't realize that they disrespected and hurt themselves much more.

We have no control over others' actions. We have total control over our reactions. Knowing that karma balances everything, we have to put ourselves first: Bless them, forgive them, and get out of the path of their karma-boomerang.

Was I disappointed? Yes. Did I feel betrayed? Totally. Sonny's bait and switch act was precisely why I had lived in a relationship-free, no-heartache zone for nearly eight years. But as Ellen had often warned me, "What you resist persists." I'd just learned, the hard way, not to avoid painful experiences but to grow through them.

If I focused on Sonny's mean-spiritedness, I'd probably crawl back into my shell. If I focused on how much I had enjoyed male companionship, I'd be open to take another risk. I had to admit it; I'd had big fun most of the time.

The years of solitude also had served me well. I had learned to love myself so much that I didn't want to shut down my heart and deny myself the opportunity to embrace the right man— the man who shared my values, the man I deserved. I wanted to remain receptive to that man.

I'm not going to lie; adjusting to life without Sonny's constant courtship wasn't easy. During the adjustment period there were days that I was excited to see the sun peeping over the horizon and dancing playfully on the lake. Other days I'd burst into tears at the slightest reminder that Sonny's lilting announcement, recorded into my office phone, would not beckon me across the room.

"PA! It's me! Pick up da phone, Dahlin'," his voice had sung through the phone's speaker whenever his number appeared on the caller ID.

In addition to the caller announcements, the high tech phone also recorded and played back personalized greetings to frequent callers. No one called more frequently than Sonny. He had been so proud of the salute I had recorded for him. When he knew I wasn't home, he sometimes would call and let his friends hear my greeting for "Mr. Wonderful".

I erased it.

As the days passed, I used my new manuscript as a tool for healing the wounded part of me. In it, I questioned everything: What did I believe about life? What did I believe about death? Fate? God? What did I believe about love? And of course, what on Earth did I believe about Mr. Wonderful?

I wrote a docudrama featuring a man who eerily resembled and acted like Sonny, and a woman who looked and acted like me. What a catharsis!

Sonny had resumed calling after New Year's Day—and only once a day—but he no longer visited. That worked for me.

I decided to do a little goading of my own. (*Friends tease that I'm so "evolved", but I haven't evolved to the point that I let my God Light shine 24-7. The best I can do is be consciously aware of which part of me is on stage.*)

During one evening's conversation, I raved that he'd been a great muse; he had inspired my writing, and I was very pleased with the results. Sonny instantly asked to see the manuscript. I snickered mischievously all the way to the post office.

I didn't hear from Sonny for several days after he received it, so I called to make a "pulse check". Was he OK?

No. As a matter of fact, he was highly offended.

"You made me look lack a buffoon!" he shouted.

Had I misrepresented anything he'd said or done? No. It

was simply that people and scenes can look totally different from the audience. Sonny watched a character who was his mirror image, and he characterized that the man as a buffoon. Was that buffoon my creation, or his?

Sonny concluded that I was "venting" (and I think he realized that I had earned that opportunity), so he resumed his nightly calls. Still, he made no plans to visit. That was as radical a change for my once daily suitor as the new sounds he was piping in my ear: Standard English with a regional accent.

Have mercy! I jumped to my feet and applauded. To what did I owe this pleasure? Sonny explained that he had become more articulate because he was interacting with professionals.

Hello? Wasn't that why I had suggested that he speak more intelligently in the first place?

I wish I could report that the other scenes in his new drama were as entertaining, but unfortunately, he decided to reprise the role of the hero from his last drama. You know the one—the frustrated dude who liked to control his relationships (i.e., his women). And wouldn't you know it? Our hero had brought along a script for little ol' me.

My lines? I was supposed to ask why he hadn't visited. *Was he kidding?* I hadn't the slightest interest in seeing a man who didn't want to see me. What was the joy in that? I tossed aside the pitiful little script and didn't say a word about his absence.

Sonny had called me "an enigma". What made him think I was going to act according to script?

Sonny's transparent little drama played nightly for nearly four weeks. Only my Angel, at age three, was more persistent. Each night, I hoped that the culprit who had body-snatched Mr. Wonderful would scram and stop stinking up the stage.

One night, it happened. Sonny was reflecting on my manuscript's description of my painful New Year's Eve. Lo and behold, I could see a light beginning to glow from within. Mr.

Wonderful was about to make a cameo appearance.

"You know, I never intended to hurt you," he said solemnly.

Could it be? Yes, it was the same guy who once told me that he'd hurt himself before he'd hurt me.

There was no doubt in my mind that Sonny meant those words with all his heart. Intentionally hurting another person was not part of his act.

As Gary Zukav so eloquently explained in his bestseller *The Seat of the Soul,* our intention shapes our experiences. Most of us don't realize that there's a world of difference between not intending to hurt and intending not to hurt someone. The words are the same, but when we change the order, we change everything, including the consequences that greet us later.

Not intending to hurt means passively or accidentally causing someone pain. Intending not to hurt, on the other hand, means actively choosing to do nothing that would hurt another. If we knew that there was a consequence for our every action, would we allow ourselves to hurt someone unintentionally, or would we intentionally not hurt him or her?

Every time we find ourselves saying, "I didn't mean to—" we've opened the door to be hurt unintentionally, because we've unintentionally hurt someone.

How many of these dramas do we create unnecessarily, simply by not paying attention, by not vigilantly choosing to cause no harm? If we want some control over what we reap, it might be worthwhile to monitor what we sow. We can ask ourselves, "What consequence do I want to receive? How would I want to be treated if the shoe were on the other foot?"

Phrased another way: Whatever we do the least of our brothers, we also do to ourselves. On an intellectual level, Sonny thoroughly understood reaping and sowing. As he often said, "Win ya treat people bad, you won' ha' no good luck." It was his credo.

Sometimes, even those of us who understand the laws of the Universe simply forget. No problem. Life has an unlimited supply of powerful reminders—and an eternity to deliver them.

40. Fear of Loss

It's almost impossible to be both drama critic and performer, but that doesn't stop anyone from trying—at least it doesn't stop me. By the time I arrived at America's office for my next semiannual visit, I already had written my review of Sonny's manipulative drama. I generously had given him a half star for plot, direction, staging, and performance. Oddly enough, America saw a totally different act.

"Sonny has major *loss* issues," she said definitively, yet almost whispering. "Those are contributing more than the control issues. *Major* loss issues."

I hadn't thought about the impact loss might have on his behavior. "You mean the loss of his home and his money?" I asked.

"No," she said. "The loss of a *life*."

"Ohhhh." This was a lot more serious than I'd thought.

"It's the loss of a life," she repeated. "It's the loss of a past. And it's also the loss of a future that could have been."

My perspective was beginning to broaden, beyond Sonny's stubborn resistance to speaking Standard English and dressing less flamboyantly, to the losses so many of us experience through workplace restructuring, the physical death of a loved one, business or romantic relationships. We cherish happier times. We're not always ready to invest or energy into the future. Out of insecurity or sheer defiance, we may tighten our grip on the past.

"Sonny did what human beings do," America explained. "We retract, go within, build a cocoon, and say, 'No investing, for now'. And we think that no investing means no losses."

I could totally relate. "I did that for nearly eight years!" I laughed. Of course! Why hadn't I thought of that? As French philosopher and essayist Michel de Montaigne, once wrote: "He who fears he shall suffer, already suffers what he fears."

Life has taught me that the best way to overcome anything, including loss, is by repeated practice. Unless we've experienced enough loss to know that it's not the end of the world, and have the confidence to move through it, we may fight it, or be paralyzed by it, afraid to move.

I suspected that the soul currently known as Sonny called me onto his stage because he had wounds to heal. I eagerly agreed to come because my soul had its own healing that he could facilitate.

On a spiritual level, we design our scripts to be mutually beneficial, a win/win drama. Sonny's and my pact was to regain power over pain.

Our most vital lessons are not learned in a vacuum; they're learned through others. Our relationships are much more powerful and empowering than we've ever dreamed; they're designed that way. A fair God wouldn't intentionally make life so complicated that we'd be lost in our own ignorance. We've been given a huge supporting cast.

We see our own souls in the mirrors held by those with whom we have closest contact. They are our teachers, our healers. Some of them are specialists; they know exactly how to get our attention, and how to get the best results. Typically the specialists—like a good bone-cracking chiropractor—make us want to scream and cuss. But when we feel the results later on, we have to admit: "It hurt so good"!

Sonny came into my world as my teacher. As such, he wore

a mirror around his neck. I couldn't come close to him without seeing myself. What reflected back to me were abandonment and rejection wounds that were deeply painful for me to look at. These wounds had shown up in every mirror I'd stood in front of, since I was a little girl.

I had a choice: avoid them or confront them. I decided not to turn away, not this time. Instead, I declared that these wounds no longer had control over me; I wanted back all of the power they'd held over me, power that had made me hide from relationships. I haltingly, then fearlessly, stared into that mirror until the wounds evaporated into nothingness. I felt so good about my accomplishment that I almost forgot I'd agreed to help Sonny deal with some of his demons. There were many.

One of them stemmed from one of his many extra-marital affairs. That time, he fell in love with a woman who betrayed him; she was dating two married men. When the other man forced her to choose, she kicked Sonny to the curb.

It hurt him so deeply that he compared his despair with the death of his mother. I found it odd that he saw no connection between his betrayal of his marriage vows and his mistress's deception. Instead of learning that betrayal invites betrayal, the lesson he took away from that experience was that he would never again let another woman "into his head". He would always maintain control of his relationships by not making an emotional investment.

Remember, what we resist persists. Sonny's body and brain had decided to protect him from heartache, but his soul wanted to grow through it; so it called me onto the stage. In my mirror, Sonny could see a reflection of his old heartbreak and losses. He moved closer, thinking he was ready to deal with them, and let them go. Turned out, he wasn't.

As we faced each other, our mirrors reflected a series of pain-filled images that stretched into infinity. Framing the mirror that Sonny peered into: hurtful rejections by some of his friends and family members after he lost hundreds of thousands of dollars, his wife, and his home. Loved ones to whom he'd been extremely generous turned him down or shut him out of their homes.

He quickly looked away. Sonny's mirror was so wracked with pain that many of my attempts to help him "do better and be better" were distorted. On days when he recalled that he had asked for my help, I sounded supportive and constructive. Other days, those same words sounded critical and judgmental.

It's difficult to be with folks who look at the world through a filter of painful memories. They're difficult to appease, difficult to please, and it's always your fault. So I kept bailing on him, writing loving "Dear Johns", but "Dear Johns" nonetheless, which only fueled Sonny's insecurities.

When he pulled his disappearing act and I didn't respond the way he expected, his frustration reached a fever pitch. One evening he told me bitterly, "You jes *ran* me away. Dat's wha chu did—you jes *ran* me away!"

The sharpest blade in the world could not have made a more precise incision. Sonny opened another old wound; this one was on a deeper level than the others—my unworthy, undesirable wound. I had to make a choice, and quickly: hurt him or heal me.

Believing that God constantly works on my behalf, and does nothing and sends no one to harm me, my response was a no-brainer. I perceived Sonny's bitter rejection as yet another chance to acknowledge my pain, grow through it, and stop re-creating and attracting Unworthy, Undesirable Dramas into my experience.

How can I fix them, if I don't feel them? When the brain rings the pain alarm, our natural reaction is to focus our attention on the site of the wound or the cause of the pain.

I wasn't going to waste such a valuable opportunity to heal. I didn't defend myself, and I certainly didn't want to create any new karma by responding in anger. So I quietly apologized, and told him I hadn't intended to "run him away". Was that the response he expected? Probably not. But verbally knocking him into the next zip code was going to hurt me, so I silently sent Sonny Unconditional Love and Forgiveness, and I thanked him for masterfully helping me to heal my wounds.

Was I angry at any time during this process? I have to admit, I had my moments. But Life is always fair; when you hurt someone, you hurt yourself, too. Who can stay mad, knowing that?

I don't know if I taught Sonny anything, but he taught me plenty. Among those lessons: I could feel valued, as I did by him, and really not be; and I could be valued, as I was by my father, and really not feel it. More important, Sonny taught me that I was lovable enough to attract an attentive, thoughtful, adoring man. By helping me heal so profoundly, he also enabled me to attract a man who is healed—or at least, is willing to be.

It's interesting that painful encounters typically cause us to do everything but heal ourselves. We instantly focus on the other person. We assign blame, become bitter, judgmental, or even plot revenge. Perhaps it's the way we think we're supposed to react. After all, we were introduced at an early age to stories of a vengeful God who drowns, smites, and kills those who offend Him. That is our model.

There was a time when we blamed God's wrath for all natural disasters. It made sense; the hurricanes, typhoons and tornadoes came from the sky, the place we thought God lived. Not knowing any better, we interpreted these disasters as evidence that God was angry, because He became violent and killed multitudes when He was angry.

Times have changed, almost. When three killer hurricanes hit rural Polk County, Florida in 2004, not one weather forecaster characterized it as punishment for the region's epidemic sinfulness. On the other hand, several questioned God's intentions when a tsunami hit Southeast Asia, killing nearly 50,000 children and more than 100,000 others.

The waves were a third the size of the largest tsunami in history, and the death toll from the earthquake that spawned it didn't approach the record high, either. Still, many God-fearing folk voiced concern that the "End Times" and Judgement Day were closing in on us—albeit, 2,000 years later than the Bible writers' predicted the world would end.

Since our perceptions about life stem from our perception of God, what would we do if we thought God was Unconditional Love, that Unconditional Love would never hurt us, and that It could only create a world that was always fair?

If we began with the premise that God is good all of the time, rather than unforgiving, judgmental and violently destructive, is it possible that we would view all hurtful encounters differently, perhaps stop blaming God for causing or not stopping *natural* disasters?

I don't believe that we entered this theater called Earth to be hurt, or entertained for that matter. What I believe is that our evolution—our spiraling to Godliness—requires us to heal, grow, and overcome our identity crisis. We can't approach Godliness until we believe with every fiber of our being that we are not simply human, we are made in the image of God.

The good news is that we don't have to heal, or grow, or overcome any false impressions of God or ourselves today. We have all eternity. Sure, we can postpone our evolution by making unnecessary stops along the route to create karma; but like it or not, we cannot stop evolving any more than the Earth can stop revolving. So we can heal ourselves now, or hurt ourselves so badly that we'll wish we had.

I don't believe our life goal is be on Earth, or to keep coming here. If the Earth Theater were the destination, rather than an important stop on our evolutionary journey, at least one soul would have remained here permanently, don't you think?

Our goal is to evolve here, learn to transcend the drama. Our goal is to meet God in every soul, see God in every heart, and know, without a doubt, that God is everywhere, as Love.

As America reminded me that day, our goal is to love unconditionally and resist the urge to be a critic—no matter how little entertainment value we get from someone's act. He is merely performing at his level of consciousness, acting his heart out, within a very small, pain-filled box.

So how do we respond to this bad acting? The same way we respond to anyone with a disability—with compassion and with prayer. We understand that the disability is an experience they're having; it's not who they are.

I realize that it's difficult to be "big", to be forgiving and compassionate when we think someone has intentionally hurt us. It's especially difficult when we're looking at their behavior through the "one human lifetime" lens, a lens through which we don't always see justice served. But if life is eternal, and we're eternal, and this is just one of many experiences, there's plenty of time for everything to balance out, plenty of time for every soul to learn to act in loving ways that serve all.

That was my theory, emerging from Sonny's theater, but I wondered if I could prove it. I decided to search for more evidence, to preclude any unconscious bitterness over the experience from ambushing me later.

41. Same Soul, Different Body

*B*etter hurry! My reading at the Midwest Psychic Institute was scheduled to start in five minutes. It was my fault that I was running late. I thought I had more time to spare when I got off the "L". *Not.* I'd spent way too much time peeping into the windows of the eclectic Wrigleyville shops along the way.

As I moseyed toward the school for clairvoyants, I was solidly in research mode. Sonny's profound impact, the synergy, the matching wounds, and a few other clues had aroused my suspicion that this was not the first time I had encountered the soul wearing his body.

Did we share a spiritual history? Was there anything in it that would be helpful to know? It was run-of-the-mill wonderment for a spiritual sleuth. I decided to let the students look behind the curtain to see if there was any historical context for the most recent encounter.

Ever evolving, the instructors had just revamped the clairvoyant curriculum, and they had changed the name of the Institute again. It was now appropriately called...InVision.

Three students already were seated in the reading room when I entered. As I looked at each of the women, I tried to resist the urge that grips me every time I enter a clairvoyant session. I'm not sure why I do it, or how. But I've been told that I "read" the readers.

I was caught in the act, the first time I had a reading. I distinctly recall looking closely at each of the seven or eight students seated in front of me. I wasn't trying to read anyone's energy because I didn't know I had that capability. I merely was trying to figure out if this energy reading process had any validity, in the real world or on planet Earth. I also was trying to discern if the students sincerely believed in it, had any clairvoyant skills, or were merely going through the motions.

The instructor, for sure, was clairvoyant. From the back of my head, Ken saw exactly what I was doing.

"Did you see what she did?" he asked the class, when my reading ended. He told them precisely how I had scoped each of them immediately after sitting in the chair. He was excited that I was able to read his students, even though I had no formal training. He expressed the hope that they would soon be able to read others so effortlessly.

I was floored, and a bit embarrassed, that he had "seen" me do it. I also was quite fascinated when the reading revealed that I had accurately determined which of the students knew what they were doing, and which were flying by the seats of their pants.

During the next 20 years, I had at least two-dozen clairvoyant student readings at the Institute. Every time, I scrutinized the students and tested the validity of clairvoyance. I made them prove to me, again and again, that the physical world is but a fragment of what we believe is Life.

Over the years, the student reading process also has evolved. Instead of seven or eight students in a reading, there typically are three, no more than four. It's a richer experience for all of us.

The latest improvement, I discovered that day, was something called the "Center Chair." The student designated as the Center Chair was the most senior or the most naturally gifted. By the time we reached the question-and-answer portion of that reading, I had concluded that all three of the students were either naturally gifted or had learned their lessons extremely well.

As usual, I was intentionally vague when the Center Chair invited my questions.

"I'm real curious about the dynamics of a relationship," I told her. "I'm wondering if I have a history with this guy, so that I can understand better why we're interacting the way we are."

Before I tell you how she responded, let me remind you how clairvoyance works: Your soul—the real you, not your body—is like a massive DVD recorder that stores data about everything you've ever done, said, and thought. It carries the memories of every character you've ever played in your endless dramas, from one physical experience to another.

When I ask a question in a clairvoyant reading, it's like pushing the REWIND button. My soul searches the archives and plays back the pertinent scene revealing my answer. A trained clairvoyant can see the pictures my soul is projecting. A highly experienced clairvoyant also can interpret these pictures. Got it? OK, let's go back to the reading:

"Tell me your names, at birth," the Center Chair said.

The first step in this fact-finding mission is to ascertain the names of the persons involved in the drama. Everyone's name has a unique energy vibration, particularly in relationship to another soul.

I told them my birth name and Sonny's, repeating our names twice. The three readers waited, eyes closed, for my soul to retrieve my answer and play it on their "screens". As is the case with all of the readings I've previously shared with you, the following quotes are directly from the audiotape of that session.

"I'm not getting a clear picture," the Center Chair said, frowning. "Mary Ann, are you getting anything?"

"I'm flashing between two pictures," said the woman to her left. "I have this tall, very distinguished looking gentleman. And there's this picture of this portly man right behind him."

The image confused her for a bit before she was able to interpret it. "The picture means that the world is seeing this very distinguished, very put-together man, but the image he's projecting is different than what he believes about himself. There's a lot of rhetoric; but it may not be a true representation of himself."

She was absolutely on the mark. She picked up on Sonny's essence. Looking at him in one of his expensive business suits (one of the more conservative suits, that is), you'd never guess that he wasn't financially successful or that he felt insecure or inadequate in any way.

I chuckled at the picture of the portly man. It was the same image I'd had of Sonny after our first phone conversation! Wait a minute. The center chair reader just saw something:

"Yeah, I immediately see him." She sighed, "Ahhh, he turns toward you and he adores you, almost. There's a sense that he admires you. He really admires you and really appreciates you."

Fascinating. I stared down at my notebook, so that I would not signal that she was onto something. Her words reminded me of Sonny's emotional speech of appreciation.

"He really does have a pleasant, polished appearance. It seems like he's a successful man at whatever he does, and he's intelligent. There's also this ability for him to be really real. He's just got a down-to-Earth quality about him. He kind of connects to you in a down-to-Earth way."

A bit too down-to-Earth for my taste, I chuckled to myself. I didn't doubt that she was "seeing" Sonny.

"Mary Ann, what are you seeing?" she asked.

"I've got a past-life picture that popped up. It looks like you are a woman in a very fine gown, and he looks to be a manservant or a butler. He's opening the door for you in a very formal black and gray suit with a white shirt. It's in the era when you had a big bustle on the butt, the parasol, the hat, and the proper gloves. You're very, very proper."

I almost laughed out loud that time. Sonny once told me how he had described me to his golf buddies back home: "I told them, 'she's very, very proper'," he'd beamed.

"His role in your relationship was very formal," Mary Ann continued. "He was there to wait on you and take care of you, and make sure all your needs were met. Everything you desired, even before you thought of it, was taken care of."

That wiped the smile right off of my face. Sonny had been very much like that during our current encounter! Whatever I wanted or needed, he wanted me to have. In fact, he would be annoyed if I wanted to do something for myself, instead of allowing him to do it for me. He complained that I was much too independent.

Mary Ann seemed to tap into my thoughts. "I got a present-life picture; it's the same kind of thing. He's down, sort of at your feet, laying down a carpet—or a coat—over a puddle. His job, his role with you is to make sure that whatever you need, whatever you desire, he's going to take care of for you. It's that kind of relationship."

I instantly recalled the mornings that Sonny awoke, saw clouds in the sky, and called to say he was going to drive me wherever I needed to go. He didn't want me to get wet.

"You got a chauffeur," he declared one afternoon. "Where evah you wanna go, whatevah you wanna do, Ah'll take yuh." He was intent upon catering to my every need.

What I hadn't realized was that, on a spiritual level, Sonny's soul also catered to me. I needed to grow. I needed to re-open wounds so that I could heal them properly—and permanently. His soul made sure that need was fulfilled.

I needed to make sure my "unlovable" button was disconnected. He tested it for me, pushing and pushing. Nothing happened. I needed to make sure my "abandonment" button was really inoperative. He leaned on it with all his weight. Nothing happened; I had no reaction.

The years I had spent alone, working on myself, had served me well—and apparently, so had the few months I spent with him. Thank you, God. What a blessing!

42. The Spoiled Brat

Prior to every question-and-answer period, the students conduct a variety of diagnostic readings; the first is a "rose" reading. During this reading, one student envisions a rose that symbolizes my soul, the immortal part of me. The length of the stem reveals how long I have been taking bodies on this planet. In every reading, I've been told that my stem is very long.

In the rose reading, clairvoyants may also see gold rings around the stem. These rings are said to represent past lives that are pertinent to experiences I'm currently encountering. This time, they saw several rings.

The scene surrounding the first ring placed me in a location that looked like Fiji, or somewhere in that part of the world. I was in a male body, preparing for an arranged marriage to a woman I didn't know. I loved someone else, but was marrying this woman out of duty to my tribe. I couldn't imagine what the pertinence of that picture was, or what duty I could be fulfilling in this lifetime, but whatever.

The second picture my soul revealed was of a female in an attic, sorting through memorabilia.

"You're at a point where you're trying to make some changes," Mary Ann explained. "And you're collecting the information you need to go forward to make those changes, to make those decisions."

I certainly could see the correlation. I'd been poring through dozens of books, tapes, and transcripts—memorabilia—in the process of writing my manuscript, deciding what was relevant and what was not.

They also saw a current life picture. I was sitting on the edge of a bathtub, crying. Then I stood and refreshed my makeup, scolding myself to get my act together and figure out what to do.

I was stunned. That's exactly what I had done that fateful moving day, moments before I called Abdul and Badriyyah, and asked if I could spend the night.

The final picture stumped all of us. I was a pilot during a war, heading off to a dangerous mission.

"I'm not sure why you're showing me this," Mary Ann said. She explained that it appeared to be my last day in that body. I knew that I wasn't coming back from that mission, she said, but I wasn't afraid. I was proud to do my duty for my country.

Another "duty" picture, I thought. What's that about?

I would soon find out. That wartime picture reappeared during the question-and-answer phase of my reading.

"I keep seeing that life that Mary Ann mentioned, when you were the pilot," the Center Chair said. "You knew Marcus in that lifetime."

Both of the women flanking her nodded, in agreement.

She said, "You took a bullet or something for him. You took the hit in your plane. I see your plane going down."

"That's what I saw, too,' Mary Ann piped in. "You were comrades. You were pilots together. Do you want more on that, or do you have another question?"

"Yeah. I'm not sure that explains the current dynamic between us," I said.

Sonny had become uncharacteristically cold, rude, and mean-spirited. Whenever we spoke, he seemed furious with me. I didn't understand what I'd done, and I was tired of guessing. All I said to the women was, "There's some tension. I'm not sure where it's coming from."

"The picture is that in some ways, you're putting out an energy that says 'you owe me.' And the picture I'm getting back from him is: 'I didn't ask you to do that for me.' So there's a resistance there," Mary Ann told me. "In the other picture, when he was your servant, the energy looks like he was angry or annoyed that he waited on you hand and foot. That was his responsibility, but there was never any gratitude. He was treated much like a second-class citizen."

Interesting, I thought. This time, I'd urged him to be top-drawer, but he preferred to act second class.

She continued. "At the end of that life, he felt that he worked hard to be your equal. He came into that next life being your equal, your buddy. Then the whole heroics thing kind of happened; on a spirit level, he doesn't want the pendulum to swing back."

Things were beginning to clear up. Sonny liked to keep the scales balanced. He didn't want to be indebted to anyone. As compensation for my professional consulting services, home cooked meals, and the mounting parking fees in my garage that he seemed unable to reimburse, he'd given me a beautiful, but gently worn leather bomber jacket. I wondered whether he rejected my attempts to help him fit into Chicago's professional circles because he didn't want to owe his success to me, either.

"Ah don' neeju, da be successful!" he'd shouted the night he told me that I had run him away. "Ah kin be successful all bah mahsef!"

"Hmmm..." Mary Ann moaned, jolting my attention back into the room. "He is one furious dude!" She shook her left hand vigorously, as if casting off his angry energy.

Now, we were getting somewhere. "Can you figure out what he's angry about?" I asked.

Mary Ann nodded. "The energy of the picture I'm seeing is that your interactions light up pictures of him and his relationship with his mother," she said. "His anger is directed at you, although what's really setting him off are his interactions with his mother. The way he reacts to you is like a little boy not getting his way with his mother, and throwing a tantrum. That's the picture."

And what a vivid picture! On Christmas Eve, Sonny had accused me of trying to control him. To avoid an ugly scene, I apologized, telling him that I had never intended to do anything controlling. Sonny jumped up and down, arms flailing like a spoiled brat, throwing a tantrum that could rival one of his young grandsons'.

"You not sorry!" he screamed. "You not sorry! You. Not. Sorry!"

It was the most childish, stupefying act in his repertoire.

Mary Ann continued, "I see this big, grown man pounding his feet on the floor and stomping. He's angry, yelling and screaming, and you're just looking at him, saying, '*What* are you doing?'"

I burst into laughter. *Bingo!*

"He's throwing this complete fit, being completely irrational. You're not even quite sure what you did. It looks like maybe the way you say a sentence. Maybe it's your tone in response to a question from him. It's not even so much what you say, it's more how he perceives it that sets him off."

For people who didn't know us or anything about our interactions, these students were phenomenal. And the hits just kept on coming.

"What I'm getting is that it's a male control issue," said the woman in the center chair. "It's like he has all these pictures lined up in his space from past generations: The man is the powerful one. The man is in control of the situation. He's a

275

modern man, but he's got this outdated idea of how a man should be perceived."

Yeah, like "Me Tarzan, you Jane." Had she been in my living room when Sonny said, "I'm used to being in control of my relationships" or when he excused his infidelities with "That's jes the way it was done"?

"You're looking at the two of you as equals who can just talk about this and that," she continued. "And on a very deep level, it just sets off this male control energy. It sets off something in him that maybe he doesn't even like in himself, but it's deeply ingrained: This is what he has and this is what success looks like. This is how a successful man looks and behaves and blah, blah, blah."

That certainly summed it up.

"He's very invested in keeping up this image," the Center Chair continued. "Then you do or you say something that challenges his perception of himself. You don't even know you're doing it, but it hits him in the wrong way and sets him off as a challenge to his maleness. Yeah, it's about male control. He feels more powerful if he can take away your female power and put you under his control."

That explained the verbal pimp slaps. Once again, not only had I confirmed that my life as spiritual energy is eternal; I had seen some fascinating details of my soul's history, and had gotten some insightful analysis of current events.

I had a gut feeling there was more, but unfortunately, time had run out.

43. Write NOW!

For years, you may recall, America had reported that my angels were begging me to "begin the writing". Each time, I had the same cryptic response: They could blow it out of their ears. Were they asking me to fiddle while Rome was burning? Anyone could see that my life was in turmoil.

What on Earth did they want me to write about, anyway? And why were they so persistent? The nagging questions demanded answers because, in the back of my mind lurked an incredulous prediction I'd been told 20 years earlier, when I launched my Ruth Montgomery-style investigation into the spiritual realm.

I'd found Beverly under "Psychics" in my neighborhood Yellow Pages. She said that I was going to write a book that would change a lot of people's lives.

Yeah, right. What did I possibly have to say that would have that kind of impact? I wondered. Louis, who was convinced that we were soul mates, was certain that the book would trace our fairy tale trip to the altar. I did write about our relationship.

Years later, when our marriage was imploding and I was tired of biting my tongue, I began a cathartic tome entitled *He Ain't Heavy, He's My Husband.* Leaving it around the house in plain view, and watching Louis's facial expression was enough reward. I tossed the manuscript.

Months later, when the bank was seizing my home, I

whined to my friend Sandra, "I've allowed people I barely know to live in my home for months. It doesn't make sense that someone would be trying to make me homeless. I don't understand why this is happening. "

Sandra raised her eyebrow and flashed her PR smile, "Maybe it's so that you'll have a story to tell."

Sandra seemed to be onto something, especially during a long stretch when it appeared that I was winning the battle. I began writing a book to inspire ordinary people to fight corporate injustice: *How to Fight a Lion and Win*. But after I'd been evicted from my home, I dumped that manuscript, too.

A year later, after a stupefying break-up with the Nutty Professor, I launched another cathartic writing exercise that began by seriously questioning the fairness of life and its encounters. I set out on several spiritual sleuthing expeditions to find answers. What I learned transformed the manuscript. Initially a cynical look at Life, it embraced the possibility that everything in it was a miracle. For the next few years, I revised and re-wrote the manuscript many times, but I was too busy swatting "lack gnats" to devote any serious time to it.

Then came the Christmas morning when I was compelled to do nothing else. I wasn't sure whether it was "the writing" America and my guides had been urging me to do, the book the psychic had said I would write, or the story Sandra thought I was supposed to tell, but I gave it my full attention. I questioned, researched, and listened for guidance from the Divine. Perhaps the first to weigh in was the Angel of Humor.

I had written more than 200 pages under a different title the day I heard someone say, *"Earth Is the Mother of All Drama Queens*—that is your title." I laughed out loud! The whimsical title gave me new direction and set a new tone for the work. I started again from page one.

I sifted through two decades of spiritual research: dozens of books, boxes of articles, transcripts and audiotapes from consultations, and chapters from previous drafts of the manuscript.

I wasn't quite sure how to piece it together. I wondered if I'd get some clues by taking an additional look behind the curtain. I returned to InVision. Instructors were surprised to see me again. I'd had more student readings in a few short months than in the previous ten years.

During my rose reading, my soul showed one of the students a picture of a previous lifetime spent in the body of an African American woman. It appeared to be the early 20th century. This woman had worked as a nanny, and had studied the law books in her employer's library. With legal knowledge under her belt, she was ready to pursue another career. There was a little blond boy pulling on her jacket, begging her to stay.

"It appears that you had tamed this really incorrigible child," the clairvoyant student said.

Two things about that picture struck me. A decade earlier, in the reading with Dr. Peebles, he'd told me that I'd had a fascination with man-made law during a number of incarnations. It was a "fragrance and a flower", he'd said. The not-so-fragrant part was that I used the law to control large numbers of people. Was it any wonder that I later attracted someone who wanted to control me—which brings me to the second intriguing aspect of the scene: the brat.

When the students moved on to the aura reading, the Center Chair saw someone at my door, but I refused to answer. I glanced at my purse, where my phone was nestled in a pocket. Sonny had called that afternoon. As she said, I hadn't responded. I had no intention of jumping on that roller coaster.

The next picture she saw was a current-day scene. I was standing in front of my television, which was off. She said I was telling her that I had chosen not to look at it because I didn't want to be controlled by it or by what was going on in the world. She was dead-on. I had stopped watching TV. I didn't want to be taken hostage by the fear that had fueled America's response to terrorism—a response that didn't consider the natural consequences of violence, destruction, and civilian deaths. I refused to allow that energy in my home.

I switched to online newspapers for my news, and even that had become a bit of a challenge. One day, the New York Times "Quote of the Day" was from a U.S. lieutenant colonel in Iraq who reportedly said, "With a heavy dose of fear and violence, and a lot of money for projects, I think we can convince people that we are here to help them."

What? I'm a "whatever you do to the least of my brothers, you also do unto me" girl. Those who shared "heavy dose of fear and violence" values could share the karma that accompanied it. I didn't want that blood on my hands or my soul. The clairvoyant student could see it clearly. The next picture my soul showed her was of a list—no, not my perfect mate list.

"It's a list of things to do in this life, on this planet," the student explained. I'd crossed off a few things, she said. There were a few others that I was looking at and setting goals for.

Inadvertently, the student was confirming previous readings. America had told me my path was solidly paved. Dr. Peebles said I was nearing the end of my cycles of reincarnation, and that I was "cleaning up the residue" (karma) from previous sojourns.

It made sense that I had come into this body with a to-do list. It also explained why, no matter how hard I tried, I couldn't change some of the predicaments in which I found myself. As Dr. Peebles had told me, my "soul would not let me" escape certain unpleasant experiences. It needed to restore balance to a number of situations and relationships.

44. Believing Is Seeing

I could hear my phone vibrating in my purse. Sure enough, it was Sonny again. I turned it off. I wasn't mad. As far as I could tell—but stick a fork in me to be sure—I simply was done. Just as in the past-life picture the students had read moments earlier, I was ready to move on.

Sonny had called several times that day. He'd discovered my connection to some powerful people who could place large orders and spin his sales commissions and his friend's fledgling business into another stratosphere. Why call me? He did say he could be successful without my help, right?

I was done, for sure, but I had to ask the students whether we'd accomplished the mission of our present encounter. I didn't reveal whether our relationship was business or personal. Cynthia was the first to see an image: a boxing ring.

"The bell has rung, and both of your hands are being held up by the referee," she said. "You're both winners. You could walk away and call it a match, at this time."

Sounded like "mission accomplished", to me.

"I saw Marcus Aurelius," said Ruth Ann, surprising me by mentioning Sonny's birth name. This time, I had intentionally given the students his nickname because one of the students had been in the previous reading. "There seems to be some need or agreement that the two of you could take the energy of aggression, and use it for some greater cause."

Matt nodded, in agreement. "Whether it's complete or not, I see you walking away from it. You're in an airport, going somewhere cold to have fun. You look back at him, way in the distance. He's under a palm tree, nursing his wounds. He's rubbing his knees and his feet. He looks old and thin; and he's really preoccupied with his wounds."

That picture pained me. It was much too close to reality. Sonny frequently complained about aches in his knees, his back and his feet. I often teased that he was the oldest middle-aged man I knew.

What troubled me most was the vision of him under a palm tree. I hoped that a future picture hadn't slipped onto my soul's reel. Did it mean that Sonny would return to the South unsuccessful, wounded by the mistakes he'd made in Chicago? Would that be his natural consequence?

"I see a picture of a broken dream," said Mari, confirming my unspoken suspicions. "And there's another picture of two red straws stuck together, spiraling and intertwined. Part of him is in your space. He's putting himself in your space."

I'm not going to let that happen, I thought, but he certainly had been trying. Sonny's repeated calls that day weren't his only attempt to put himself in my space. In previous months, I could physically feel his energy in my heart chakra. It was the energy of a pouting child who was demanding attention. Within a few days, he would invariably phone Frances or me.

He won Frances' heart the day they met, when she asked him, "So, how do you like my girl?"

Sonny sighed. "If it wudden so soon," he said, "ah'd say ah love uh da death."

Suddenly, she had one more adopted child. Frances loved the way Sonny revered me. It reminded her of how Oliver doted on her.

After more than 40 years of marriage, Oliver still did special little things to keep their love alive. My favorite was his alarm clock, which he set to ring each evening, just before 7:30.

For the past four decades, when the alarm rings, he and Frances have to kiss, even if they're arguing. They wanted that kind of love for me. Frances felt that Sonny had that potential. She was crazy about her new child.

Maybe he just emitted "son" energy. After his first visit to my apartment, I told Frances that I'd had the eeriest feeling that I had been Sonny's mother. I'd never experienced such a specific memory before. I hoped to get more clarity by sleuthing our spiritual history.

"How many lifetimes have we shared?" I asked the clairvoyant students. They disagreed on a precise number. One said we'd been together in 76 different bodies. Another said I had been his mother on at least three occasions, confirming my unspoken suspicion. Whatever the number, we were deeply connected. Given the dynamics of our relationship, I wasn't surprised. I suspected that Sonny came to inspire me to do what I always do after a significant relationship ends painfully: I self-medicate through cathartic writing.

"Why did we agree to reunite at this time?" I asked, wondering if their assessment would match mine.

The Center Chair, Ruth Ann, spoke up. "You're showing me a picture of you as a young girl. It's a *Little House on the Prairie* type setting. He came into your life when you were a teenager. He came from the city. He encouraged you to write."

Bingo! Of course, none of the students knew that I was a journalist or that I had a manuscript in progress. I had suspected that my angels, fed up with my adamant refusal to start "the writing", had called in the one soul in the Universe who could get me to do the pivotal work that was on my list when I stepped into this body.

"Now, the picture is advancing, and you're older," Ruth Ann

continued. "He's encouraging you to have bigger vistas, and get out of your limited environment."

Talk about flipping a script! How many times had I told Sonny that his poor diction limited his mobility, his power, and his profitability? If these students only knew.

"Is there any unresolved karma between the two of us?" I asked.

Suddenly, the boxing-ring picture reappeared. "This round is finished," Cynthia said. "You have the option of calling it a standoff or going back into the ring."

And run the risk of either of us creating some new karma? No, thank you very much.

"I'm seeing a picture of stuck energy," Matt piped in. "It has something to do with duty and obligation."

This was the second team of students to see a picture that related to some duty or obligation. *What was that about?*

"You're a Catholic priest at a pub, taking care of him," Matt continued. "He's a drunk, and he's passed out. You've talked with him again and again, but it doesn't seem to penetrate. He keeps doing the same old thing, continues the same destructive behavior. You think that he's hopeless."

Pour the liquor down the drain, and you've got a current life re-run, I chuckled to myself.

"You have your Bible open, asking, 'What do I do, Lord? I want to walk away.' But you feel an obligation coming from God and society to perform this duty."

What's with all the "duty" pictures? I wondered. This one was intriguing because I'd been told years earlier that I'd had a number of "religious" lifetimes. In fact, nearly 20 years earlier, a past-life regression therapist hypnotized me and instructed me to transport myself to the lifetime that was most pertinent to this one. When I was deeply enough into trance, Greg told me to open my spiritual eyes and look down.

Eek! I was startled. I saw two fat, dry, calloused feet in sandals with thick leather straps. They were peeking from under a very full burgundy-brown floor-length vestment. Not cute. Not cute, at all.

I was a monk standing on a cobblestone street, talking. It definitely was a European setting, perhaps in the 14th century. I had the feeling that I had some kind of authority, because the others were listening to me very intently.

Greg instructed me to go to the last day in that lifetime. Looking down from the ceiling, I saw my body lying below on my deathbed in a very small, drab, candlelit room. Two others were keeping vigil, heads bowed.

Next, Greg instructed me to tell him what happened at the moment of my death. Suddenly, I felt myself floating backwards, through the outer wall of the monastery. I could see the gardens outside the building; then everything became distant before I was enveloped in a gentle white light.

The final step, Greg said, was to go to the moment that I was reviewing that lifetime, evaluating my performance. I saw myself sitting alone in a garden that looked very much like the one I had seen outside the monastery. But the review? It was a strain. For some reason, I wasn't eager to look at it, so I didn't.

I never discovered that lifetime's connection to this one, because I never tried past life regression therapy again. It was like being two places at one time, and much too eerie for this spineless spiritual sleuth.

Cynthia interrupted my regression memory with the reading's final scene. "This picture is bathed in gold (the color of healing). You're being dropped a rope ladder, and you can step onto it, free yourself, and rise above."

Healing is a good thing, rising above, even better. But the only steps I climbed were onto the Belmont "L" station platform. I had a lot to think about, as I headed downtown.

Shortly after I arrived home, the phone rang. Sonny, again. I listened as my answering machine's generic greeting responded to the former Mr. Wonderful. After the beep, I heard a deep sigh. Then he hung up.

Later that night, I once again marveled at the clairvoyants' accuracy and insights. Not once in 20 years had they failed to tell me something I already knew, things they had no way of knowing. Who told them I no longer watch TV—and why? How did they know I was a writer, or that I had sat on my bathtub and cried, or that I had consciously released someone's karma? These weren't generic predictions that many accuse clairvoyants of making; they were verifiable details of moments I had lived in this body. In many cases, these details were plausibly linked to eerily pertinent "past life" scenes.

This evidence again revealed for me the awesome power of our eternal souls—a power we don't tap into, because we think we're "only human" and nothing exists outside of our physical world. So we don't receive the benefit of the pictures from our spiritual movie projectors that unmask the prequels of our current dramas and give us the context to understand our experiences and the people in them.

Having this critical information enables us to react with more power and less fear. Fear creates panic. We don't think clearly when we're afraid; we're easily manipulated by others and less able to make decisions that serve our best interests.

If we believed we were eternal, indestructible energy, what would frighten us? What threat would throw us into a panic if we knew that our bodies are merely costumes; in reality, we are indestructible, and fully accountable for our actions?

The discovery that I am immortal energy turned everything I thought I knew about myself upside down. It set me free. It not only gave me new insight into the dramas that I create, it gave me a compelling reason to consciously create dramas in which

I intentionally do not hurt anyone. That's the only way I can be sure that I won't be hurt in a sequel during the days, years, or even centuries to come.

Dramas are exclusive to the physical domain, this planet in particular. They are purely man-made, created from the part of us that feels fearful, inadequate, powerless, unworthy and unloved—not from the part of us that knows that we are divine and inseparable from the Source of All Things, known as God. Most of us have been taught that we're here, and God is way over there somewhere, judging our every move.

The Bible tells us that all things work together for good to those who love God. But we've all seen things working horribly for those who do love God, and working splendidly for those who don't appear to give God a moment's thought.

Feeling that there's really no magic bullet that will make things "work together for good" can make us feel powerless, insecure, and fearful—the perfect recipe for drama. But how many of us really believe in a petty, insecure, quid pro quo, "I'll love you and give you goodies, if you love me" God? Then, why can't we entertain the notion that our limited idea of "good" might not be the same as God's?

To the all-knowing, all-powerful, everywhere present God, things may always be working together for good, no matter what it looks like or feels like to us. What God sees is that everything in Life is in sync, working together with perfect precision.

If you're honoring and serving others, and creating good karma, great! If life is a bit stressful because you're balancing some bad karma, wonderful! If we understood the Divine Plan, the simple synchronicity of life, we'd never feel like victims, and we'd never blame God for any kind of adversity or tragedy.

45. Some Things Ain't That Deep

I had spent weeks on my spiritual sleuthing expedition, trying to unearth the origins of this eerily familiar soul who had leaped onto my stage, catered to me adoringly, then treated me as if I had called him vile names and spit in his face. Even his friends treated me like a leper. What was that about?

The suspense had intrigued me so much that I wandered behind the curtain and looked deeply into Sonny's soul for any hidden plots or subplots. For weeks, I tried to unravel the mystery surrounding our encounter.

As it turned out, my answer wasn't behind the curtain; it was right there on the stage, in plain view. All I needed, after all, was ordinary sight and good old common sense.

The not-so-mysterious answer had been dropped into my hands months earlier; now was in my grip, once again, jammed into my mailbox with the overdue bills and advertising flyers. Not one of the clairvoyant students had seen it; America hadn't even mentioned it.

I ripped open the envelope, and was devouring the letter inside before I reached the elevator. It was the Texas Bureau of Vital Statistics' response to my public-record inquiry. It confirmed my suspicions—the only reason Sonny would make such a dramatic about-face: he was still married.

Sonny had said that his wife left him. They hadn't lived together for at least a year before he relocated, and she certainly hadn't come to Chicago with him. We had laughed that, among our similarities, both of us had drafted our own divorce petitions because we couldn't afford lawyers.

One hot afternoon, a few weeks after we'd met, I inadvertently spotted the fruits of his labor. While moving a pile of papers from the window well of his convertible, to his trunk, I realized that I was holding his signed divorce petitions. On the first page was a note with court filing instructions.

We were just friends. It was none of my business. I totally dismissed what I had seen, and never mentioned it.

During the subsequent weeks of his intense courtship, Sonny introduced me to his friends here and, by phone, to family in Texas. He told anyone who would listen—including his godmother and best friend ex-wife—about this incredible woman he'd met in Chicago. No one acted as if Sonny was a married man.

I don't even think he considered himself married, until that fateful Christmas Eve. Irritated that I had brought another linguistic faux pas to his attention (per his standing request), Sonny asked me why I always said what was on my mind. In other words, why did I mention the flaws in his diction?

Information is power, I told him. I believe in empowering folks so that they can make informed decisions, and take whatever action they feel is appropriate.

Then, Spirit moved me to add: "Full disclosure is important. For example, some men don't wear wedding rings. They'll flirt with a woman, or even start a full-blown affair, and the woman hasn't the slightest idea that she's involved with a married man. By withholding this information, he violates her right to make an informed decision about being in a relationship with a married man."

At the time, I wasn't sure why that analogy came to my mind. It had absolutely nothing to do with speaking intelligently. I'm also not sure why I didn't pay attention to Sonny's reaction. He looked as if he'd seen a ghost! He was about to sit down, and almost fell on the floor.

Months later, I realized that Spirit had provided me more than words; I was given plenty of physical clues. If I had paid attention to them, I would have expected Sonny to be noncommittal about New Year's Eve, and I would have understood what he meant when he said that there were some things about himself that he "had to take a hard look at."

"To than own sef, be true," he'd said. Apparently, he was the only person with whom he planned to share that truth. And the truth was that those divorce papers had been signed by his wife and himself, but they had never been filed. Ergo, he was married the minute he met me, and married every minute he spent with me. It certainly was time to be true to himself, in fact, past time.

Often we get so caught up in our dramas that we fear the human consequences of our bad acting, totally forgetting the more serious, spiritual consequences of our actions. In this case, Sonny feared that full disclosure so late in the game would anger me and cause me to judge him. He probably envisioned me calling him dishonest and manipulative, and pulling up the drawbridge so he couldn't return.

No matter what my reaction, it should have been of no concern to Sonny. After all, he wasn't responsible for any karma I'd create for myself by reacting angrily or judgmentally. It would have been in his best interest to focus on the karma he was creating.

In all fairness, I have to admit that integrity was vitally important to Sonny. It ranked way up there with treating others well. He prided himself on keeping his promises. He had no patience for those who behaved disrespectfully or dismissively toward others.

Stuff happens in life. Being human as well as divine, we will make mistakes. It's how we recoup that makes the difference. We get caught up and forget things like—"Oops, I'm still married. Maybe I should take care of that little detail before I chase this woman like she's the last female on Earth." Ignoring the facts doesn't change the facts.

Failing to admit our errors and make amends, because we want to avoid a confrontational scene or compensatory damages, only creates brand new dramas our souls have to suffer through later.

We invent excuses. Lawyers even muddy our outcomes by advising us not to admit liability or wrongdoing. Then we have two invoices to pay—the attorneys' and our souls'. Ignoring the consequences won't make them go away. It's an eternal debt that must be settled; the integrity ledger must be balanced.

Ironically, integrity was one of the reasons Sonny loved golf. To him, golf was a microcosm of the perfect world: A golf course is tranquil. Those on it respect its natural environment and the other souls traversing through it. Courtesy, encouragement, and patience abound in golf. Each soul's greatest competition comes from within, an inner drive to be his or her personal best. The only way to control someone else's outcome on a golf course is to cheat.

"Innybody who cheats own a goff cose will cheat in laff," Sonny insisted, with righteous indignation.

Sonny had principles. He was a Being of Light, which is why I had hoped we would always be friends. He was so honest that he had the naïve candor of a child. Unsolicited, he'd blurt unflattering things about himself, his parents, and his marital infidelities to people he barely knew, like the little folks on Art Linkletter's vintage *Kids Say the Darnedest Things*. Revealing that he was separated, but not divorced, absolutely paled by comparison.

On the other hand, I had to be realistic. When was there a good time for him to drop the "I'm still married" bomb on me? He certainly couldn't have done it when he was in hot pursuit, especially when I had resisted his advances, on the grounds that we were incompatible.

Come on, now. No salesman worth his salt would have volunteered much stronger grounds for rejection. He probably knew my response: "You're still married? That, my brother, is a bigger incompatibility than that bodacious necklace hangin' 'round your neck."

Nope, telling me right away would not have been a good move. Instead, Sonny wooed me every day for weeks. He was relentlessly charming, irresistibly attentive, and adoring. Not even the flowers he brought me could rival his sweetness.

He certainly couldn't fully disclose his marital status that Christmas Eve, either, especially after he'd decided that we should push through the crap that was clogging the relationship. That also was the day I declared that lies of omission violated a woman's right to make an informed decision. Definitely not a good time. By then, he'd stopped me from walking out of the relationship four times in four months.

If you were Sonny, what would you have done? Clearly, it would depend upon whether you believed that life was fair, and there was a natural and appropriate consequence to your every action.

If you understood how life worked, then your next step would be to design the consequence that you wanted. If you didn't understand how life worked, if you thought that admitting error diminished you in some way, that apologizing when you caused another harm would give that person control over you, you'd probably do the same thing Sonny did: create one grand and glorious drama, with a predictable sequel of natural consequences.

Manipulating the end of relationships was one of Sonny's favorite dramatic devices. Remember, I told you he talked too much? Before we'd gotten three blocks away from my building, on that first non-date, Sonny bragged that he was still friendly with every woman he'd ever dated, and he explained why. He always "wucked it so dat da woman would ind it." That way, he said, smugly, he could drop back into her life later, since he wasn't the injured party.

I wish I had paid attention. Now, his New Year's Eve insult and subsequent weeks of voice-only visits made total sense. I was supposed to complain about his negligence and end the relationship. He'd be off the hook, would never have to admit his lack of integrity, and he would never look like the bad guy.

There was just one hitch. I didn't fall for the plot. I didn't make an issue of his absence. In fact, I didn't even mention he'd been absent. It was his frustration that made him so furious and mean when we spoke. For the first time, he couldn't control the outcome—and for the first time, he had torpedoed the bridge back to a woman's door.

Sonny's drama (what he probably would call "buffoonery") re-ignited my quest to understand life—the synchronicity of it, in general, and this raggedy little hard-knock incarnation, in particular. Years of research had revealed that everything and everyone is in our lives for a reason. As souls, we invite them onto our stages for our mutual benefit. We serve each other's divine purpose in a very unique way. Hadn't Sonny told me, again and again, "I was *sint* to enhance yo' laff"?

From the stage, I wondered *how* he was going to enhance my life. And, have mercy, when in the world was he going to start? After he'd breezed through it, my life certainly didn't look or feel enhanced, unless disillusionment counts.

Feeling like the butt end of a cosmic joke, I screamed at God, "I waited eight years and you sent a *married* man onto my stage—a man who knew all the Universal principle buzzwords, but didn't really practice them? A man who insulted my intelligence and played sophomoric games? What was the point? Why would you do something like that to me?"

As I sat on my living room sofa, glaring angrily at the lake, something said, "Who are you talking to? You act as if God is outside of you!"

Ah, yes. I was yelling at the Bogeyman God, the one with the frightening countenance, who highly favors some and not others, who punishes with violent rage, and breaks little girls' hearts. I forgot. I didn't believe in that God any longer. I believed that God was within me, and would not hurt me.

In that case, no one had done anything *to* me; if anything, something had been done *for* me. So changed my question to, "Why did I invite Sonny onto my stage? How did the encounter serve me? Please reveal it to me."

Like God, our answers are never far, but they're often beyond what we normally view as physical evidence, the residual damage: broken hearts and tear-stained pillows, upheaval from downsizing, intimate betrayals, catastrophic illnesses, or crime scenes. We have to look behind the action, beyond the drama, to reality.

My soul, not the human personality known as Pat, had invited Sonny into my life for several critical reasons: to heal past hurts, to be the catalyst for fulfilling my writing assignment, and to delight me so much that I would never again hesitate to take the risk of being in another relationship. If I had merely looked at the physical evidence, the action on the stage, I probably would have shut down emotionally, and denied myself the possibility of unconditional love.

My soul needed the experience with Sonny to be exactly what it was. I didn't need it to last a minute longer than it took to learn my lessons. America had said that he was exactly what

I needed for "right now"; he was "the Mr. Right of many days". I didn't realize that I should take her literally. When she says days, the girl means *days!*

I certainly don't want to demonize Sonny. He's no different than the rest of us. No one can act at a level higher than his awareness of who he is. To a large extent, that awareness is based on our beliefs about what or who God is, and our relationship to the Divine.

I've heard devoutly religious people angrily assert that God did not create everyone, and is not within everybody. Of course, they're referring to those souls who are considered "bad" or "evil". What they're saying is that they believe there is more than one Creator, and that God is not omnipresent.

When things go awry, these souls are quick to say, "That's nothing but the devil." I'm no mathematician, but if the devil has even a tiny fraction of power, then God doesn't have all of it. So they also believe in a kinda-mighty, mostly or partially potent God, rather than an almighty, omnipotent God. I make no judgment about that; whatever floats their boats.

It might be enlightening, however, if we ventured into our belief closets on a regular basis and tried on new clothes— perhaps tried on the belief that God is truly omnipotent, omniscient and omnipresent, and stuck an arm in a garment that revealed that nothing and no one is outside of God's kingdom. That does not mean that God controls everything.

Control stems from fear and operates as force. God, on the other hand is fearless enough to grant us free. That's power. As David R. Hawkins, M.D., Ph.D., so eloquently explained in his epic, *Power vs. Force,* our inability to distinguish between power and force is one of the greatest tragedies of human life.

I'm always fascinated that those who believe in a controlling God who violently punishes sin can't explain why God didn't paralyze the Nazis in their tracks before they fired up the first oven, or why the inhumane institution of slavery was allowed to thrive for hundreds of years, or why terrorists were allowed on planes with box cutters. Wouldn't a controlling God who responds so violently to sin have stepped in to stop them before someone was hurt?

Then, there are those who believe that God gave Satan control over the Earth and earthlings—essentially mandated all of us to slavery—but they can't explain why anything "good" happens on the planet. And it's even more difficult for them to explain their love for a God who would subject them to the control of an evil spirit, and then punish them eternally if they don't free themselves from Satan's diabolical grip.

On the other side of the scale sits an All-Powerful God. True power directs, supports, empowers, and leaves room for growth. This God realizes that spirits in bodies often make growth spurts through lessons that stem from human error, and allows plenty of room for them to grow by encouraging them, through a simple process of natural consequences, to make choices that serve everyone's Highest Good.

When looking at God through the fearless All-Powerful lens, rather than the fearful All-Controlling lens, we realize that there's not only a reason everything happens, there's a very good reason.

Instead of judging others or even incidents, we begin to look at everything and everyone in a different context: How does this incident or this person serve my Highest Good? And perhaps more important—how will this enlighten me, so that I can see the world as the Omnipotent God sees it?

46. Lost and Found

Nearly a year after I'd last seen Sonny, hardly anything in my life had changed. My perfect mate hadn't wandered anywhere near my zip code, and I barely had enough income to meet my living expenses. *Jiminy Christmas!* It seemed as though I couldn't attract a profitable project if I'd used an electromagnet the size of the Sears Tower. But I was not discouraged. God was near, and all was well, no matter how it looked. I refused to believe anything else.

One day, I received an e-mail message from a friend, inviting me to participate in a 40-day, online abundance program. For five weeks, a group of us meditated on abundance prayers, maintained thoughts of prosperity, and journaled powerful affirmations asserting that God was the sole source of everything.

As the end of the 40 days neared, my bank called about two suspicious debit card authorizations. Someone who obviously didn't believe in natural consequences had charged two purchases totaling $1,843. I was absolutely livid! My rent was due in two days, and it would take much longer than that for the bank to restore the funds to my account.

When was curtain going to fall on the "Late Rent" Drama? I vented my frustration in an angry e-mail to the online workshop leader and others who were enrolled in the program.

I received empathetic responses from friends. Several ministers reached out to me, too. A couple of them speculated that the theft stemmed from some random, negative thought that I had allowed to slip into my consciousness.

A fleeting negative thought was more powerful than hours and weeks of positive thinking? Really?

Everything happens for a reason, but that doesn't mean we can explain it. A classic case: one morning I walked into my kitchen and there were small wet puddles of red wine on the counter below my wine rack. I wet a paper towel and wiped every bottle. Not one was wet; not one had leaked. It happened for a reason, but hell if I know why.

In the case of the nearly $2,000 my bank had authorized to be withdrawn from my account, one minister offered this thought-provoking explanation: *Thefts are always difficult because we often don't remember what we have stolen. I also believe that a theft is not only what you take; it is also what you don't give.*

I immediately bristled. Who was this stranger, accusing me of theft? She didn't know a thing about me! I hadn't stolen anything!

Then I calmed down. Of course, she didn't know Pat. She wasn't even referring to Pat. She was referring to a basic law of the Universe, the reaping and sowing of my soul. Her words echoed those of Kahlil Gibran's *The Prophet*: "Do not forget that the robbed is not blameless in being robbed."

Indeed, I had forgotten. This body was born in the mid-twentieth century, but my soul has been alive *forever*. Most of that time, I saw so many people not getting what they deserved and others not deserving what they got, I was convinced that this reaping and sowing thing was a lark, not a law. Its justice hopped and skipped; it didn't touch everyone. If I was lucky— or if no one was looking—it would skip me, too.

So I did hurtful things. I refused to forgive debt or error. I controlled other people's lives. I broke a heart (or two or three). I stole others' land.

With that in mind, I knew exactly how to react to the debit card drama: Forgive myself for my human failings, and thank God for the opportunity to balance any harm I'd inflicted.

An odd thing happened. The merchant who had requested the $1,843 authorization never attempted to transfer my money into his account, and the bank restored the money to my account faster than they'd originally forecasted. Had forgiveness done that? I can't say, for sure.

About six months later, I stood in front of a machine in a downtown subway station to insert my transit card. I reached into my purse. Where was my wallet? It was in my hand when I left home. I'd obviously dropped it along the way. *Bummer.*

The sidewalks were packed when I emerged from the station. Swarms of holiday shoppers were taking advantage of the gorgeous, unseasonably warm December afternoon. I walked back home, scanning every inch of the sidewalk, muttering, "OK, why did I create this experience?"

I wasn't thrilled about the predicament, but I was notably calm. Once I was home and had called the bank to cancel my new debit card, the doorman called. Someone was downstairs with my wallet, a nice guy who lived in the next building. He refused a reward. What a blessing!

A few weeks later, just days before Christmas, I returned home from scooping up a few bargains at a last-minute sale at Marshall Field's, and discovered that I had misplaced my wallet. Not *again!*

By that time, it felt like winter in Chicago. It was a brutally cold and windy Saturday night. I grabbed my mink jacket and retraced my steps to the "L" station outside Field's, where I had stopped to recharge my transit card.

I recalled putting my wallet in my purse as I walked down the stairs. With all of the bags in my hand, I obviously had missed the opening, and the wallet had fallen to the ground. I sighed, disgusted.

"If the intent was for me to lose the darn thing, why didn't you just keep it a few weeks ago?" I fussed at my angels, as my eyes scoured the sidewalk. "How does this serve my Highest Good?" I fussed. "I want an answer. And it had better be good! This doesn't make any sense at all!"

Just before I reached the station, I looked up and there was a gorgeous guy I hadn't seen since college. I had attended parties at his fraternity house. He always seemed very shy; I rarely saw him dance with anyone. In fact, I didn't recall ever knowing his name.

Is he the reason I was dragged outside on this bitterly cold night? I wondered.

Seconds later, the hunk's eyes met mine. He raised his eyebrows flirtatiously and moaned an approving, "Wow!" Then he walked right by.

Okeydoke, so that wasn't it. As I reached the landing at the top of the stairs inside the station, I saw a man curiously huddled near a window, rifling through something with a lot of white paper sticking out of it. I had a bad habit of stuffing receipts in my wallet after each purchase. The man looked up, startled to see me standing there. He quickly looked away.

Spotting the station agent, I called out, "Did anyone turn in a wallet?"

She looked at me as if I didn't have a brain cell. "Are you kidding? It's almost Christmas! Ain't nobody gonna turn in a wallet!"

"I guess you're right," I sighed. Then, loud enough for the gentleman in the corner to hear me, I said, "Everybody doesn't believe that you reap what you sow."

Even louder, the station agent screamed, "Aw, yeah. It'll bounce back on 'em, all right. They'll get what's comin' to 'em!"

I turned around and walked slowly down the stairs.

What was that about? I wondered, as the first blast of icy-air hit me. "How does this serve me?" I pulled my collar over my ears. Not wanting to mess up my new hairdo, I hadn't worn a hat. *Duh.* No wonder the agent thought I was clueless. I was suffering from brain freeze.

I returned home and immediately canceled my Field's charge. Moments later, the phone rang. When I saw Elaine's name on the caller ID, I didn't recognize it, but I knew exactly who she was. Just as I thought, she had found my wallet on the steps of the station. Someone had rummaged through it and removed the money before she found it, but as before, all of my identification, receipts, debit and credit cards were there.

My friends and I couldn't stop marveling that I had lost my wallet not once, but twice in downtown Chicago; and it was returned both times.

Then, believe it or not, it happened again! Three times in less than six weeks! This time, I dropped my wallet as I got out of a cab in the West Loop. I didn't make the discovery until an hour later, as I prepared to pay for snacks in a nearby store.

What is going on? Why do I keep creating this? I wondered. When I reached for my mobile phone to cancel my debit card, I noticed that I had a voicemail message. I had forwarded my home and office lines to my mobile phone so I wouldn't miss any calls while I was out. Somehow, I'd missed three.

As I began to dial the bank's number, something said, "Check your messages first."

Someone has been walking around with my debit card for more than an hour, I argued. *I don't even recognize this number. I'd better call the bank first.*

"Check your messages," it insisted.

Could it be...? I thought.

It certainly could. Her name was Jan. She'd spotted my wallet on the sidewalk, about a mile away from where I'd dropped it. I met her in the lobby of the office building where she worked.

When I tried to give her a reward for returning it, Jan smiled, shook her head and said, "I'm paying it forward!'

And there it was: the reason I kept creating the same scenario. I needed a demonstration of how this shift in consciousness was impacting my life and affecting my results. Each time I discovered that my wallet was missing, I knew there was a possibility it would not be returned. I also knew that the Universe balances everything. I acknowledged that I might be responsible for others' losses. If I was repaying a karmic debt, I was glad to get it off the ledger. That completely alleviated any distress.

One theme ran through all of the incidents: Even in the instances in which I lost a little money, I suffered no real loss. In the Big Picture, everything real exists only in the realm of the invisible, anyway. Everything else is merely a prop on an imaginary stage.

47. The Prodigal Son

J ust when I thought I was coasting, had figured out how life
works on planet Earth, the Universe gave me a pop quiz—a
scriptwriting exam. I had to tie up the loose ends of the "Mr.
Wonderful" drama.

Was anybody still sitting in that audience, after nearly two
years? Who cared? I certainly didn't. (Sigh) I guess I should
have expected the assignment since it was so inextricably
linked to this manuscript; still, I was surprised.

Frances was the first to return to the stage. With mixed
excitement and caution, she phoned me with the news.

"I heard from Sonny today."

I gasped. "Are you kidding?"

"No, he said that he has a job for you, and it pays a lot of
money—a *lot* of money. He said the people are ready to go, and
he told them that you were perfect for the job. He wanted to
know if it would be OK for him to call you."

Sonny was no dummy. He knew he had to ask permission
to contact me, since he had burned the bridge leading to my
door. Frances couldn't have been more thrilled. Ditto for Oliver.
It appeared that their prodigal son was ready to return home,
and he was toting a good paying job for me on his back.

"Absolutely, I'll take his call." Maybe Mr. What-Was-That
had decided to make restitution for his dishonesty, I thought.

After checking back with Frances to get the green light, Sonny called me the next afternoon, damn near breathless. He was "in rare form", he said. Then he laid it on me: the "job". He proposed that the two of us start a business. Together.

I cheered. This was merely a re-run of Sonny's bait-and-switch drama. The Universe wasn't really delivering him back into my life. *Thank you, God!*

True to form, Sonny still didn't mention that he was married or that his wife had moved to Chicago. He probably had no intention of explaining his future business partner to her; he clearly had no intention of explaining her to me.

Things obviously were not going well for him on the job, as I'd predicted—and, in light of his proposal, they didn't appear to be going well at home, either. Cue the violins.

Sonny's business venture was as delusional as the thought that I would partner with someone who had violated my trust, but I was impressed that he had the guts to call. I also felt vindicated. This was the guy who spitefully said that he could be successful without my help. But where did he turn when he needed rescue from failure?

Sonny's desperation had blocked his memory and blurred his vision. Maybe the blood had drained from his head when I "ran him away". There had to be a logical explanation somewhere in this mess.

As he babbled, a wall hanging near my fridge caught my eye: "Oh Lord, help my words to be gracious and tender today, for tomorrow I may have to eat them." I shook my head. Sonny had walked by it dozens of times without reading it. Attention is a terrible thing to waste. I should know.

I listened to his threadbare idea to launch a community newspaper. He'd sell the advertising; I'd take care of the editorial duties. I calmly explained that not only was there no need for another paper in the neighborhood he wanted to serve, his plan simply was not viable. He ended the conversation, pledging that he'd make it viable. *Not a chance*, I snickered, as I hung up the phone.

A few months later, while shopping in a South Loop grocery store with his wife, Sonny walked up to a woman who looked familiar. As it turned out, they'd never met, but Lady Luck was on his side. The woman owned a staffing firm.

By this time, Sonny had abandoned his entrepreneurial fantasy. He probably would have sacrificed a few of his beloved Calloway golf clubs for any job with a decent salary.

"What kind of position are you looking for?" the staffing firm owner wanted to know.

Something in sales, of course. Could she help?

The woman quickly assessed that Sonny's poor diction would lock him out of a number of high-end sales positions. After spotting his big gold and diamond necklace, she felt that he didn't have the polish of a professional man. She wondered how she could possibly help him.

This well-spoken entrepreneur had grown up with none of Sonny's advantages. In fact, Norma was reared in a single parent home near a tough Chicago public housing development, had dropped out of high school, attended college much later in life, and had launched a multimillion dollar business while standing in an unemployment line. She couldn't quite relate to the man in front of her.

Not wanting to dash his hopes, she offered to look at his résumé. That's when Lady Luck checked out of the express line. Sonny didn't have a résumé.

Norma raised an eyebrow. "How can you look for a job with no résumé?" she asked.

Sonny boldly asked if she would help him create one.

Norma gasped. No, but she would refer him to her

communications consultant, who was an excellent writer. She warned him that her consultant was expensive. Sonny was willing to pay whatever was required. Norma agreed to make the referral.

A few days later, while riding in a taxi, her cell phone rang. After exchanging pleasantries, she took the phone away from her ear.

"There's a young man who needs help with a résumé," she said, extending the phone toward me. "Can you help him?"

Much to everyone's surprise, Sonny's soul had sent him back for another helping from the "Ah kin be successful own ma own" banquet table.

This was no coincidence. There are no coincidences in the Universe. In a city the size of Chicago, what were the odds that Sonny would wander through a jam-packed grocery store and walk right up to one of my new best friends?

I was fascinated by this dramatic demonstration of how our souls support our growth. Sonny had been running toward success for nearly two years, and had gotten nowhere. It appeared that his soul was going to make him stay on that treadmill until he took care of some unfinished business.

OK, spank me—I couldn't resist gloating. That evening, I called Sonny. Without a hello, I said, "A very wise man once told me, 'Win ya treat people bad, you won' ha' no good luck.'"

He pretended that he didn't have the slightest idea what I was talking about. Maybe it was no act. After all, this was a man who didn't see any connection between his numerous marital infidelities and his fatal attraction to a mistress who was unfaithful to him.

Sonny begged me to help him; he even claimed to be on bended knee. Liar. He had bad knees—and that was almost all he had left to stand on after he insisted that he owed me no apology for failing to disclose that he was married.

He and his wife had intended to divorce when we met, so he'd done nothing wrong, he'd insisted. I shook my head, thinking about the karma he was creating through this stunning act of cowardice.

I shifted my attention to my incomplete scriptwriting assignment. How was I going to end this drama? There was only one desirable ending: I had to leave the stage karma-free.

I agreed to help him with his résumé. It was the most powerful seed I could sow, if I wanted a fruitful harvest. Sonny had provided me an opportunity to make a hefty deposit into my karmic bank account, "pay it forward", as Jan had said. I didn't want to continue suffering consequences for treating people "bad". Been there, done that.

What my 20-year investigation had dramatically revealed was that I constantly create my future experiences with every thought, word, and deed. I can choose my consequences now, rather than let them ambush me later. I do that by simply trying to treat others the way I'd want to be treated: I will always want to be treated empathetically, as an evolving soul who is not yet aware of the Perfection within. If I need help from those to whom I've been unkind, disrespectful, or deceitful, I will want them to be merciful. So I was.

That holiday season nearly two years earlier, when Sonny ducked into that phone booth to slip out of his Mr. Wonderful costume, he called and told me he needed to be true to himself. Obviously he hadn't gotten around to that yet. If he had, he might have considered this: It takes a lot more than a great résumé to get a good job. We have to be willing to grow, act responsibly, be authentic—and, by all means, willing to leave the drama behind. Otherwise, we'll be stuck on life's treadmill, or worse, we could fall off and skin our bad knees.

Sonny was a better teacher than student. He wasn't stubborn, immature, manipulative, deceitful, or unwilling to shed his limiting behaviors; he merely acted that way. There's a difference. We too often confuse the actor with the act, and reality with drama.

What this soul has so generously portrayed for us, through the personality known as Sonny, is that few of us are truly authentic. We don't consciously project our divine selves into the world, and we don't trust that the Divine within us always serves our best interests. If we did, we wouldn't be so afraid, and we wouldn't do the self-destructive things that fearful people do.

Others don't revere us as divine beings because we don't revere ourselves. So we keep hurting each other and hurting ourselves. If we only knew that each soul standing in front of us—whether in the unemployment line, the rock concert, or the mirror—carries the Light of God in her spiritual DNA. The Light might be undercover, concealed under a really bad personality, but it's impossible to extinguish it.

Our God Light is eternal and indivisible. It is our true essence, supporting our return, and illuminating the path Home. It cannot and will not forsake us.

Not one soul came here to stay. We came to learn how to unveil our God Light. Our souls are not going to let our stubborn, childish personalities block our evolution, or unnecessarily delay our return to our true Home. When they tire of entering the Earth Theater again and again, performing poorly and getting bad reviews, our souls will do whatever is necessary to break the cycle, even if it means forcing our personalities into submission, as I have learned so painfully.

I now realize that I have sole (and soul) responsibility for what I sow and harvest. What others do is their spiritual business. In the case of Po' Sonny, as he sometimes referred to himself, I forgave him for his bad acting, and released any karma that could later re-cast us in a similar drama. Just in case his act was payback for a betrayal I had perpetrated on him in a different body, I forgave myself, too—can't be too careful. Then I took my final bow and let the curtain gently fall.

I guess someone forgot to turn on the house lights because Sonny didn't notice that the show had ended, and I had left the stage.

Were we friends again? he asked, prompting my return to the stage. It was important to him that we were friends, he insisted.

That wasn't in my script. When did our friendship become important? Was this poor soul unaware that it's damn near impossible to retrieve your credibility, once you've trampled on it?

"We can be friendly," I said, as kindly as I could, "but I don't trust you enough to call you my friend."

House lights, please! That was definitely my final curtain call. This assignment was done—splendidly, I might add.

Forgiving others doesn't require us to hold onto them. Forgiving actually is the act of releasing, letting go of the hurt, the anger, the resentment—and the bad actor. What we really want to hold onto is our sacredness. It is our responsibility to filter what and who comes into our space. We can choose to admit everyone, or only those who honor our sacredness. Each choice comes with a consequence.

In Sonny's case, his choices landed him back in the South, as the clairvoyant student had unwittingly predicted. Whether he'll be nursing his wounds there is yet to be seen, as is the forecasted fate of his marriage. Whatever happens is none of my spiritual business; I can only send him Light and support his soul's desire to resolve everything for his Highest Good.

I love the God part—the *real* part—of Sonny, without reservation, even though I don't care at all for his human self.

If we must share another life experience, I certainly hope it's under more honorable circumstances. That is not to say that I didn't prosper greatly from the lessons he taught me. They have positively and joyfully changed my life, and I sincerely appreciate him.

But when I leaped to my feet at the end of that drama, it was not to give him a standing ovation; it was to make a mad dash out of his theater.

'Scuse me, please; there is nothing more to learn here.

epilogue "Happily Ever After"

There is no death, there is only change.
There is no failure, there is only growth.

Dr. James Martin Peebles

One morning, as I opened my eyes and began to clear my head, I distinctly heard someone say, "Drama queen workshops—empowering women to heal the Earth." What? Another assignment? *Aw, man!*

Inviting total strangers behind the curtain of my hard-knock life was one thing, but workshops? How in the world could I empower women to heal the Earth? I wondered.

Almost instantly, my question was answered: Women shape the lives of their children and influence the lives of their men. Teach them how to consciously create consequences so that dramas end "happily ever after" for everyone.

Happily ever after? I'm not qualified to teach something that I haven't experienced myself! I argued. Then it occurred to me that everything on this planet is constantly changing. I'm not going to be broke forever. I'm not going to be alone forever. At the most perfect time, in the most perfect way, I'll arrive at "happily ever after." I set the manuscript aside, and waited.

A couple of months passed. During one of my daily chats with Angel, I mentioned that I was waiting on God, waiting for my life to change so that I could write the "happily ever after" ending that would qualify me to lead Drama Queen Workshops.

She was stunned.

"Have you read your own book?" Angel wondered. "Mom, the magic in it is that you demonstrate that appearances aren't real. You teach us that happiness doesn't come from being in control, having your perfect mate, having money in your pocket, or even having a home to call your own. It's none of the outer stuff. It's the inner peace.

"*Look at you!*" she shouted. "You're happier and more peaceful than I've seen you in years!"

Out of the mouths of babes. She was right: nothing in my outer life had changed, but I had never been richer, more peaceful, more fulfilled, or had more fun in Pat's body. I'd had multiple epiphanies since I'd started this manuscript. (For a girl who hasn't had a date in a minute, I can tell you epiphanies are exquisitely and profoundly superior!)

Based on everything I've learned about the synchronicity of my life—and the synchronicity of Life, in general—I don't doubt that my soul probably cleared Pat's social calendar and work schedule to provide the time to chronicle this 20-year journey of discovery. Most of that time, I was not even aware that I was traveling, let alone where I was going.

What a glorious process it has been, looking behind the scenes of my dramas to find the plots and the underlying, invisible Truths that were driving the action. It gave me the opportunity to seriously consider, for the first time, that what's real is permanent. It lasts forever. It doesn't change. The Absolute Truth doesn't change. It's timeless. Universal Law doesn't change. It applies to everyone, always.

I can't say that about anything or anyone on Earth. Absolutely nothing on Earth lasts forever. That would be a clue that this planet is not reality, the realm of Absolute Truth. That's one of my most profound take-aways from my pilgrimage, along with the comforting discoveries that Life is *always* fair, God is *never* far, death is not *(ta da!) The End,* and absolutely *nothing* is unforgivable.

As souls, we cycle on and off of Earth's many stages. We return again and again, until we effortlessly and with unconscious competence create win/win dramas that end happily ever after for everyone in our circles of influence. We struggle feverishly in our body costumes until we metamorphose into our most beautiful selves, our spirit-filled God-Selves.

"Happily ever after" is subjective. Your body's idea of it may not be the same as your soul's. So I invite you to bring your limited physical body into agreement with your unlimited divine soul. Allow the will of your Divine Mind to be done, rather than that of your limited brain.

Most of us are strangers to the All-Knowing part of ourselves because we've been told that we're not divine. They've told us that we're so shameful that God wouldn't want to be in our presence. If we think God doesn't love us, or like us, we're more likely to move through the world as unlovable, and behave as unlovable children do: frightened, defensive, judgmental, and unable to love those who are not like us.

We choose what we believe. We can choose to believe that Unconditional Love doesn't judge, condemn or hurt. If we choose to look at our challenges through the "Why is this happening to me?" lens instead of the "How is God supporting my growth?" lens, we won't see our answers.

On Earth, we're taught to look with our eyes, and not with our hearts. We're encouraged to make decisions with our brains, and not through our souls.

My body's concept of happiness, for example, is joyful work with lucrative pay, and a luxuriously furnished home (or two) that I can easily afford. My body also wants total financial freedom, plenty of food in the fridge, luxury cars in the garages, beautiful clothes in the closets, and bills that are paid on time and in full. After all, I have the résumé, talent, and work ethic to warrant these things, and much more. So for dessert, my body will take a healthy helping of genuine, unconditional love and the affectionate companionship of a man that I deeply respect, admire, and completely adore.

Boring, my soul yawned. It had absolutely no interest in that kind of experience—at least, not now. That lifestyle would not have served its purpose for being in this body at this time.

My life may look hard-knock, but it is perfect, in every way. I do believe that. This was a perfect opportunity to catch up with some souls and give each the opportunity to settle some karmic debts. Of course, some of them created more karma, but that's their problem, not mine.

I've learned to disregard what everybody else does, is, or has. Their souls came here with customized agendas that were perfect for them—and not such a good fit for me.

If I had veered from my soul's script, I would have had no dramas to share with you. I would have missed this blessing, this wonderful opportunity for our souls to touch each other.

If my body were running the show, trust me, I never would have hosted this theater party and unveiled my embarrassingly hard-knock life. But following the lead of my soul, learning that life isn't as fearful or as final as I'd been led to believe, I opened a curtain that led to miraculous healing.

As I said before you entered my theater, you don't have to believe that any of my dramas is true. Even if the entire book were fiction, its purpose is not to encourage you to run to your nearest psychic or scare you into joining a religion. It doesn't matter to me if you believe in reincarnation or in a benevolent, forgiving God who does not play favorites and who would not leave anybody behind, even if it were spiritually possible. Whatever your beliefs, I honor them. As Jesus of Nazareth instructed, "Judge not, and you will not be judged; condemn not, and you will not be condemned..." (Luke 6:37)

I humbly respect the writers who believed that God is not spirit, and whose stories have portrayed a supreme being who embodies the worst in human nature: jealousy, rigidity, control, violence, judgment, sadism, homophobia, racism, terrorism, and vengefulness, to name a few. These legends have been piously embraced for many centuries, and have had an enduring impact on humans and human relationships.

This is merely my story, a collection of personal dramas depicting what I believe and how I came to believe it. I'm not suggesting that you change your beliefs. If they work for you, if they bring you peace, cling to them. I do, however, want to suggest that whatever you believe about God directly impacts what you believe about yourself and the other souls who share this planet with you. It also impacts how you treat yourself and others, which determines the consequences that greet you.

If you believe that life is unfair, or that physical life is all there is, and all you are, only what you can see, touch, taste, hear, or smell is real. Right now, there are millions of microscopic bugs crawling on every inch of your skin. Can you see them or feel them? No. Are they real? You betcha.

If your soul chose this time and this place to be in that body surrounded by those special people, you can choose to trust that it knew what it was doing, and always has known. It's a matter of deciding whether your soul has the Big-Picture view, or your eyes do. Most of us fret because our lives don't look like we'd hoped, but I believe that they look exactly as they should, based on the decisions we've made during our eternal life, including our current physical experiences. It can change. The decisions we make today impact the quality of our tomorrows.

Our behavior barometer is typically based on whether something is "right" or "wrong". To avoid being "wrong", we justify all manner of painful behavior, from adultery to genocide. When we flip the script, as Life does, and base our actions on the consequences we want to reap, we make different choices. Do we want our loved ones to betray their commitments to fidelity? Do we want to be victims of violence, theft, deception, ridicule, vote stealing, or a computer virus?

The question isn't: "Am I right or wrong?" It's: "What consequence do I choose?" There's always a consequence. Either you can choose it, or it can choose you. As my friend and teacher Reverend Virginia once said, we're not punished for our sins; we're punished *by* our sins.

Hey, if we're creating nonstop drama anyway, why not write scenes that cause us no pain or suffering, instead of the "I Win/You Lose", "Inadequacy" and "Unlovable" dramas; the "Illness", "Addiction", "Fearful", "Look What You Did to Me" and "I Can't Apologize" tragedies; and the judgmental "My Religion's Better than Yours", "I'll Never Forgive You" and diabolical "I Won't Get Caught" thrillers. These are all masochistic scenes, created by uninformed play writing.

As you know, I didn't want this book writing assignment. However, I discovered that honoring the will of my soul by going through this process has helped me to become a better writer. I've picked up some simple scriptwriting tips that now enable me to consciously create empowering scenes for everyone who shares my dramas:

- Love and respect myself deeply and unconditionally.

- Love and respect everyone else's God-Self, even if I don't like their personalities or their dramas.

- Take total responsibility for my actions and feelings.

- Admit my errors, forgive myself, and make amends as quickly as possible, even though there's no statute of limitations on righting a wrong.

- Forgive others, to avoid sharing the consequences of their bad acting.

- Act with power, rather than force.

- Before acting or reacting, ask myself: *Would I want someone to do that to me?*

- Give others loving allowance to believe whatever they want.

- Judge nothing: It's all good.

- Judge no one: Every soul is inherently good.

As I neared the end of this chapter, I received a call from my friend George, a Los Angeles physician. He's been reading the manuscript-in-progress, and has delighted me with his feedback. A man of few words, that morning George got right to the point.

"This book is going to change a lot of lives," he announced.

I was speechless. George's words were almost the same as Beverly's 20-year-old prediction. I hadn't yet sent George the chapter in which I mentioned her prophecy.

I'm a spiritual sleuth, not a psychic. I can't predict my future beyond the inevitable reaping of what I have sown, but I do know that this is the book I was born to write. I've been told that I was a scribe in an ancient time. Perhaps, as some other personality, I authored a book that was not as empowering or healing as many have found this to be. I forgive myself for that, and I thank God for this dramatic opportunity to balance my error.

I am convinced that this is just one of many theaters in which I have performed, and just one of many roles I have played. I've been the rich kid and the poor one; the black one, the brown one, the yellow, and the white one; the queen, the knight, the scholar, and the village idiot. I've been male, and I've been female. I've been heterosexual and homosexual. I've been

317

the monk, the murderer, and the thief. I've lived in mansions, palaces, huts, lakefront high-rises, and cardboard boxes. I've spoken many languages.

I have been killed countless times, succumbed to a variety of diseases, and peacefully slipped out of many bodies while they slept. But my soul has never died. It is—I am— indestructible and eternal.

In some of my roles, I manipulated and controlled the lives of others to fulfill my whims. In this one, I didn't even have control over my own life, which was laced with financial debt I couldn't pay when due, the result of karmic debts that were paid right on time. How's that for the fairness of Life?

Each of my human experiences and personalities was unique, although many members of my ensemble cast— including soul mates Ellen, Angel, and Sonny—have shared the stage with me on countless occasions. Our dramas are part of a long-running series, each one impacting the casting and scripting of its sequels.

Throughout many of the current scenes, I was stressed and frazzled, trying to keep a roof over my head. All the while, my God-Self was holding me together, supporting me in the most important ways.

I know that I could not have learned to trust—would have had no *need* to trust my inner self, my Divine-Self, my *real* self— if my soul had directed my life any other way.

I'm delighted that it chose this theater. I'm ecstatic that it ushered me onto this particular stage, and reserved a seat in this very special audience so that I could get a wide shot of my dramatic creations.

No matter what hardship or heartache I've experienced, I am grateful for every minute of it. I love it. I embrace it. I consider it all drama, and count it all joy.

I pray that you enjoyed your visit to my theater. As you walk back into the glare of your own life, go with the knowledge that

I support your every effort to consciously love yourself deeply enough to create healthy, nonjudgmental, peace-filled, oh so forgiving dramas that always end "happily ever after" for everyone in your theater.

I love you dearly. I applaud you wildly. You are indisputably the Light of the world!

curtain call Life is Always Fair

I t has been difficult for most of my friends to wrap their arms around my claim that Life is always fair. A world-renowned theologian and author even challenged me on it. I stood my ground: Life is fair, I insisted, because God is fair.

The day after the 2004 U. S. Presidential election, however, my declaration was really on shaky ground. My fellow Blue-Staters were out of their minds with grief. They thought I was out of my mind, period.

"How in the world can you claim that life is fair?" one friend cried. "More than a thousand American soldiers have died in Iraq—sent to protect us from weapons of mass destruction that didn't even exist! Is that fair? Our soldiers have killed thousands of Iraqi civilians—women and children. Is that fair?"

"We've probably killed more Iraqis than Saddam Hussein during a comparable period of time, and we've virtually destroyed an ancient land!" moaned another. "Our hard-earned tax dollars will be repairing our damage over there for generations to come, instead of funding our own needs over here. Where's the fairness in that? And can we talk about the widespread reports of vote fraud in a nation that's ramming democracy down the throats of countries abroad?"

What could I say? These intellectuals were accurately reporting what they saw, from where they stood: on the stage.

I had to admit that I was fascinated by some of the plot twists of the campaign drama, the miraculous religious conversion of Jesus of Nazareth, in particular. The new millennium Prince of Peace not only supported violent revenge, he instigated pre-emptive attack, allegedly whispering into the ear of a devout follower: *Attack them before they attack you.* Of all people, you'd think He'd know they didn't have anything to attack us with.

The Jesus who directed a stone-throwing tribunal to mind their own spiritual business and punish another's sexual sin if, and only if, they were without sin, was now purportedly leading the attack on others' sexuality. The 2004 Jesus yanked a page out of Leviticus' book of homophobia and inhumane punishment, and pasted it into his own script.

Most stunningly, the same Jesus who touched lepers no longer valued life—unless it was unborn. He could not have cared less about the thousands of women and children killed by American troops in the streets near his native land. They were mere war casualties.

To those in the Blue States who revere Christ-like behavior, it was a horror flick. For them, the Anti-Christ had emerged, mesmerizing millions of terrified citizens into rabid support of behavior that was the polar opposite of Jesus's values.

Religion is not my beat; I'm not a political analyst, either. However, as a bona fide spiritual sleuth, I felt that I could make some sense of this drama, and defend my unwavering belief that Life is always fair.

I invited my friends to extricate themselves from the energy of fear that permeated the entire scene. On stage, reality is often distorted. From the audience, they could see things from a much broader, deeper perspective. It's from this objective perspective that political experts and theological scholars have examined this historical (or hysterical) election.

Among them is Episcopalian Bishop John Shelby Spong, a world renowned Biblical scholar and prolific author of books about Bible history that lay people can easily comprehend. I have never met the Right Reverend Spong, but I am an avid fan of his works. His bestseller, *Rescuing the Bible from Fundamentalism,* is one of the most engaging books I have read.

Bishop Spong publishes weekly essays online, and in his series of post-election essays, "An Analysis of the Evangelical Vote in the 2004 Election", he looked behind the curtain of the curious campaign and its results. To see it up close required a bit of time travel. We had to journey to a scene that was set thousands of years before the birth of Jesus of Nazareth,

Arriving there, we meet pagans who lived in constant fear of angering their god(s). For centuries, they'd heard and repeated stories about natural disasters—phenomena that can now be explained by meteorology, climatology and other sciences— that descended upon entire tribes as punishment for errant behavior. In their ignorance, they believed that they could avoid this punishment and mollify the gods' wrath by offering substantial gifts, including human sacrifices.

Theological history tells us that after it was determined that there was only one God, these ancient beliefs about cantankerous pagan gods seeded the basic plots for books that were later written and compiled in an anthology of diverse and sometimes conflicting works portraying the life and culture of people in what's now called the Middle East, at that stage of human development. These books were comprised of poems, allegories, letters, prophesy, memoirs, history, and religious laws. The theme of many of these books reflected the pagan belief that humans are punished severely, even eternally, if they disobey their God.

Fast forward to September 11, 2001. The safety, sanctuary and security bubble surrounding the United States burst, big time. In an instant, the energy in millions of American homes was charged with fear. Many prayed for peace; others plotted or supported bloody revenge.

With such a threat at our doorsteps, many who've repeatedly read those ancient books concluded that we desperately needed the God who "trains hands for war" to come down and help us fight this terrorist attack on freedom and the American Way. Because they still held the ancient belief in a *quid pro quo* God who must receive something before He gives, they concluded that they must do something dramatic to win His favor.

They banded together to regulate the values and behavior of everyone in the tribe to align with the mandates of their punitive, judgmental God. They were in dire need; so, like the pagans of old, they decided to make human sacrifices, starting with the basic human rights to life, liberty, the pursuit of happiness, and in some cases, the vote.

Those who hailed from states with the nation's highest divorce rates proclaimed themselves models of family values. In lock-step with their perceptions of a controlling God, they decided to exert control over which American citizens could make a lifelong commitment to the ones they loved. They made every effort to force pregnant women to give birth, even though it violated these women's free will.

With such precious sacrifices, they were confident that God would see that they were on the side of Right. Surely, He would join them on the battlefield, so that Americans no longer would have to fear for their lives.

Oddly enough, Paul of Tarsus, the man most responsible for the spread of Christianity, asserts in a letter to Timothy that God did not give us a spirit of fear. Yet, not one of these fearful people stopped to ask, "From where did I get it, then?"

They would not have had to look far for their answer. Even the most near-sighted could read the huge convention banners with the subliminal message: "Don't forget the day you were scared out of your minds. *Be afraid. Be very afraid.*"

Again and again, they were fed the story about the 2,792 innocent lives lost in the Twin Towers. These memories fanned their fears and eclipsed the memory that their country had won "world power" status by killing 200,000 civilians in Hiroshima with a nuclear bomb. So blinded by fright, they could no longer relate to the books in the ancient anthology that claimed that we reap what we sow and commanded that we"shalt not kill". For the fearful, this commandment was crafted exclusively for expectant mothers and doctors in abortion clinics.

To these fearful, values-based voters, there was no wisdom in Jesus's admonition: "Whatever you do to the least of my brothers, you also do unto me." They did not value the lives of thousands of civilians killed in Viet Nam, Iraq, and American-sponsored coups in Central and South America. They easily dismissed the millions of slaves who lost their lives while being transported to America under brutal and inhumane conditions.

There was no connecting the dots, just fanning the fears. They confused *power* with *force,* like many confuse *fame* with *notoriety.* These words are not synonymous, and neither are the consequences.

Ironically, while their leaders were scaring folks at home, they were inadvertently terrifying smaller countries throughout the world with vivid images that they, too, could be violently invaded. The seeds of these fears blossomed into the development of a real cache of weapons of mass destruction, and accelerated the cycle of fear and violence worldwide, germinating the Armeggedon the fearful had long anticipated and hoped for. Through their violence and control, they would be rewarded with rapture.

Watching this drama unfold from the safety, sanctuary, and security of the audience, my friends could clearly see that on a spiritual level, where everything is real and unchanging, these souls had taught us some important Life lessons: Fear truly is the opposite of faith. Violence really does breed more violence. And, Life is fair because whatever you do comes back to you.

These are powerful lessons, critical lessons—taught through an evolutionary partnership of souls who are learning to trust something greater than the might of man. The victors in this election may call their actions righteous, holy, or even Christian; but they can't accurately define them as Christlike.

Despite what it looks like on the stage, this has been an invaluable opportunity for all of us to see what fear does, and learn not to be imprisoned by it. Everyone—those acting in this fear and violence drama, and those observing from the audience—obviously desired a lesson so demonstrative that we'll never again forget that Life is synchronous; it works with great precision. Otherwise, we wouldn't have chosen to be citizens of this country, at this time in its bloody history.

We're all in the process of evolving. If we had completed the process, we wouldn't be here; so we must give loving allowance for every soul to grow to enlightenment at its desired speed. Others' fearful behavior might destroy our bodies and decimate our nation's budget, but thank God, it cannot destroy our souls.

In the election of 2004, people of faith voted for peace. They've learned to be less fearful and more Christlike in their response to danger or terror: "Forgive them, for they know not what they do (to themselves)." They've also learned to be more Godlike in their allowance of individual freedoms. They know that, contrary to the Edenic myth, each soul is accountable for its own choices, and its own errors, not someone else's. That is the unalterable Law of the Universe.

If you voted for peace and balance (yes, even in the national treasury), your soul will reap peace and balance. If you voted for the free will of each soul to make its own decisions and reap its own consequences, you have freed your soul from another's control in the future. If you voted for fair treatment of all humans, you will experience true justice—not man-made.

We reap what we sow. This is the essence of Life and the simplicity of its synchronicity. A fair and loving God would not have set us up to fail or to fall. Our God would not have designed the world any other way.

Fear not, my loved ones, God is with you. Always.

Applause, Applause!

My deepest gratitude to my eternal best friend and sister, the late Ellen Ina Samuels; my wizard, the late Marjorie Goodson; and my minister, the Reverend Dr. Johnnie Colemon. These souls taught me that God is wherever I am. Thanks also to the Rev. Dr. Evelyn Boyd-Castillo, the Rev. Virginia Fullman, and the late Dr. James Martin Peebles, who helped me understand my soul. To the Rt. Rev. John Shelby Spong and other learned scholars, who have inspired and empowered me through their quests for the Truth, I admire and appreciate you.

To Michael, Gabriel, Raphael, my muses and master teachers, and all of my ethereal guides who have been so patient, loving, instructive and supportive: I am deeply humbled to have earned your loving attention. You inspire me with every breath.

Special thanks to my parents, the late Alyce and William Arnold; my brothers and sisters: Gerald Walton, Joyce Townsend; Helen and Rodney Massey. Dear to my heart are Dr. Frances & Oliver Holliday and Badriyyah & Abdul Waheed, who have adopted me as their own; my valued friends Raymond Barbosa, Ben Bradley, Denise Blackwell, Rosemary Campbell Bookstein, Ann-Rita and Eldridge Brown, Catherine Chiesa, Craig Clark, Gloria Cooke, the Reverend Vici Derrick, Rosalind Green, Dr. Barbara Henley, Dr. George Jackson, Phil Jett, Dr. Ronald C. Jones, Dr. Ali Mafee, America Martinez, Judith Walker Miles, Jerry R. Mitchell, Gail Morse, Dr. Jewell Oates, Anita Omitowoju, Bernice and Cordell Reed, Deborah Starr Seibel, Jewel Simpson, Pat Travis, Lauren Verdich, Gail Walker, Norma J. Williams, and Lu Ann Wing, who challenged, encouraged, supported, and celebrated with me throughout this writing process. The depths of my love for each of you is indescribable.

To my dear friends, whose awareness extends beyond the five senses: the phenomenal Ken Jones, Garrett Walters, and the clairvoyant teachers and students at InVision, who facilitated the energetic conversation between my body and my soul. I could not have yanked the curtain on so many dramatic plots without you. Thanks so much!

Sandra Finley, you were utterly prophetic! Ditto, Beverly Bonner, Dr. Robert Crawford, Barbara Cromartie, Carrie Martin, and Alzina Mayo.

Group hug to my creative partners: the mega-talented graphic artist and web designer extraordinaire David Handschuh; Rema Smith, my proofreading wizard who reminded me of punctuation rules I'd long forgotten; my childhood friend Eric Werner, who developed into a masterful photographer and astute metaphysician; and artist Bhairavi Shah. All of you were such blessings to me!

To my evolutionary partners who played such pivotal roles in helping me complete my karmic housecleaning at various stages of my life, "Bill", "Ed", "Louis", "Rick", and "Sonny": Wow! I couldn't have done it without all of you.

Loving thanks to my midwives who helped me deliver this book to the world: my baby girl and best friend, Maiysha—who blossomed into a beautiful person, as well as a gorgeous woman—and Beverly Bianco Kennedy, my former executive producer in the newsroom and forever friend in Life.

Most enthusiastically, I appreciate my Mother-Father-Everything God, the only true presence in the Universe, who lovingly gives me all I need to learn and to grow, through one evolutionary drama after another.

Thank you, thank you, thank you, all-powerful God, for being so fair, so loving, and so forgiving!

Printed in the United States
42436LVS00005B/133-147